# minority group adolescents
## in the united states

# minority group adolescents in the united states

## EUGENE B. BRODY, M.D.

professor and chairman
department of psychiatry and director,
the psychiatric institute,
university of maryland school of medicine
baltimore, maryland

THE WILLIAMS & WILKINS COMPANY
Baltimore 1968

*Made in the United States of America*

Library of Congress Catalogue Card Number—68–11215

Printed at
The Waverly Press
Mt. Royal & Guilford Aves.
Baltimore, Md. 21202 U. S. A.

# Foreword

"If there ever should be a time for mere catch arguments, that time is surely not now. In times like the present, no man should utter anything for which he would not willingly be responsible through time and in eternity."

Those words, so applicable to modern social problems, were spoken by Abraham Lincoln. To them, we can add only that there never was a better time than the present for Americans to take a good look at ourselves; we cannot offer meaningful solutions unless we make a real attempt to understand modern problems. This book can help us do that.

Little wonder, as we look about us at the chaos in our cities and in our world, that so many of us become afflicted with a homesickness for the past, or hide our fears in simplistic solutions, or burst forth in irrational behavior, or escape to non-involvement.

Most of us barely grasp and little comprehend the changes which have occurred in our country.

We still idealize America as a place where the real American lives the peaceful, uncomplicated life of the farm and small town with room to grow and breathe, knowing and known by his neighbors and secure in a sense of community, of belonging.

But that is not an accurate picture. This is an America where seventy per cent of our people live in impersonal urban areas, where decision is far removed, where neighbors are faceless, where smoke and smog and concrete and steel crowd us in and threaten to choke us down.

This is a country where elevators run themselves, and ditches are dug by machines, and a workman has no product to call his own—nothing of which he can say at the end of the day, "This is mine; this is what I've done." It is an America where a physician is more and more required to specialize in a narrow field and think of "patients" instead of people, where a teacher in a crowded class-room deals only with "pupils," and a harried social worker with numbered "cases."

We idealize the family as a close-knit group constantly together, seated around the dinner table, presided over by an understanding but governing father, with each member a contributing, valuable participant, each essential to the family's susccess and well-being.

But this is a country where young people reach physical adult-hood at the average age of twelve, not seventeen as it was a century ago, where there is no real work for children, none needed and none required. This is an America where knowledge has exploded louder than the Hiroshima bomb, where modern communications have made it impossible for any young person to live in isolation, insulated from the dominant society and unaware of the outside world, and where every father has a harder time trying to communicate with his child. This is an America which requires ever higher standards of training and education, over longer periods, for those who can participate.

If Erich Fromm is right, as seems likely to me, that the deepest need of man is to overcome his separateness, "the prison of his aloneness," that need, surely, has always been most deeply felt by adolescents, no longer children and not yet a part of the adult community.

And today's young people must feel even more alienated in a time when the young mature earlier, physically and intellectually, are held out of society longer and longer, and in the meantime have less to do, and when the adult world with which they seek a sense of community is, itself, increasingly bewildered by modern life as it sees its culture heroes, gods and myths losing some of their potency and the values of its society increasingly challenged.

If today's young person is a Negro, a Kiowa-Apache Indian, or a Mexican American, or if his parents or grandparents came from Puerto Rico or Japan or China, adolescence can be even more excruciatingly painful and the communications gap between generations, the chasm between childhood and adult membership in the total American community, even wider.

Today, two great forces are at work upon us all—and most of all upon the young. First, there is a mounting desire to have more control over our own destinies, each individual's yearning to have some real part in the rather impersonal decisions which govern his life. There is no force, no power, no restless spirit so potentially destructive as this, unless we accept it and build upon it and use it for good in our society. This is the shout heard around the world. It is the voice of young and old alike, but most of all the young.

The other force is one which points the way: the anxious searching for meaning, for relevance in our lives, for the value and worth in what we do.

This book can help us better understand America as it is today, as it is for adolescents and as it is for minorities. It can help each of us better govern his acts and his life, make better decisions, so as to rebuild a sense of community in this country for all Americans and throw open the channels of communication and meaningful interaction, working together toward mutually worthwhile goals, between members of minority groups and the total community, but still encouraging pride of heritage and group which can be a powerful force for human development. We can construct un-dreamed-of avenues whereby all of us, especially the young, can move with greater ease toward widened opportunities for service to others. We can create mechanisms which will permit all of us, especially the young, enlarged power over our own lives and a real stake in the American system.

This book should remind us, once again, that each of us is a part of mankind, each with the same basic hopes and dreams and needs, particularly the need to belong, and that we must work with a renewed sense of urgency to make social, political and economic justice real for all Americans.

*Washington, D. C.*                     FRED R. HARRIS
                                        U. S. Senator from Oklahoma
                                        Chairman, Senate Subcommittee
                                        on Government Research

# Contributors

EUGENE B. BRODY, M.D., Professor and Chairman, Department of Psychiatry, and Director, The Psychiatric Institute, University of Maryland School of Medicine, Baltimore, Maryland.

ROBERT L. DERBYSHIRE, Ph.D., Associate Professor of Sociology in Psychiatry, The Psychiatric Institute, University of Maryland School of Medicine, Baltimore, Maryland.

STANLEY L. M. FONG, M.A., Research Assistant, Department of Psychology, State University of New York at Buffalo, Buffalo, New York.

DANIEL FREEMAN, M.D., Fellow in Psychiatry at The Hospital of the University of Pennsylvania and at the Philadelphia Child Guidance Clinic, Philadelphia, Pennsylvania.

CHESTER M. PIERCE, M.D., Associate Professor of Psychiatry, University of Oklahoma, Oklahoma City, Oklahoma.

EDWARD PREBLE, M.A., Associate Professor of Anthropology, New York School of Psychiatry, New York, New York.

WALTER WEINTRAUB, M.D., Associate Professor of Psychiatry, The Psychiatric Institute, University of Maryland School of Medicine, Baltimore, Maryland.

JOE YAMAMOTO, M.D., Associate Professor, Department of Psychiatry, University of Southern California, Los Angeles, California.

# Contents

# Adolescents as a United States Minority Group in an Era of Social Change

EUGENE B. BRODY, M.D.

THIS ESSAY is introductory to a series of research-based papers. These papers deal with the crises encountered by people, no longer children and not yet adults, who belong to important minority groups in the United States: Negro, Mexican, Puerto Rican, Oriental, and American Indian. In addition to surmounting the universal hurdles of adolescence—the transitions from one series of roles, from one social identity to another—these young people must struggle with the stresses of biculturality. They are not only in transition from one age-defined social status to another. Each is also in transition from the social world of his parental culture of origin—an ethnically determined minority world—to that of the surrounding, dominant United States society. This is a complicated matter, for the status of the adolescent himself has much in common with that of a minority group member. His relations with the power-holders of the society and his ways of coping with outer pressure and inner tension all suggest the position and behavior of a minority group member. It is with these considerations in mind that this introductory chapter presents an essentially speculative formulation of the adolescent as a minority group member. The hypothetical person who emerges from this formulation is not the introspective, isolated, self-conscious but searching individual known to us through published diaries and occasional intimate contact. He is an abstraction limited by the boundaries of the minority group concept. He is a psychological construct: an expression of a culture, a unit of a social system, or an element of a collectivity. We are concerned with his intrapsychic state only as it is reflected in his interpersonal behavior

1

and with his private feelings only as they influence his public actions. Finally, he is in this essay a creature of an historical era characterized by rapid social change.

## MINORITY GROUPS AND PREJUDICE

First, how may a minority group be defined for purposes of social and psychiatric research? A minority ". . . is a set of people who, capable of being distinguished on the basis of some physical or cultural characteristic, are treated collectively as inferior" (9). A member of a minority group is, thus, socially visible, i.e. his appearance or behavior permits an observer to categorize him from a distance. He is, furthermore, to the degree that he is perceived as representative of a category, deprived of his status as an individual: the attitude of the onlooker toward the minority group man is apt to be determined less by the latter's personal characteristics than by the former's stereotyped feelings and beliefs about the social category into which he can be placed. In other words, minority group status carries with it the probability of becoming a target for the prejudices of the majority.

What is a prejudice? Allport has described it as ". . . an antipathy based upon a faulty and inflexible generalization. It may be felt or expressed. It may be directed toward a group as a whole or toward an individual because he is a member of a group . . . . The net effect of prejudice . . . is to place the object . . . at some disadvantage not merited by his own conduct" (1).

A prejudice held by majority group members usually influences the behavior of its targets; individual behavior is in part a function of the attitudes and expectations of others, or, as Mead has put it, of the "generalized other" (2). If others expect a person to behave in a hostile or irresponsible or contemptible manner, they tend to evoke this kind of behavior through the cues, verbal and non-verbal, emotional and symbolic, which they transmit to him. This impact of expectations, which may not be fully conscious to the transmitter, has been described as the "self-fulfilling prophesy" (11). The stereotyped attitudes and feelings of the prejudiced onlooker become part of the climate of expectations in which the minority group member responds.

Minority status usually includes a history of more recent arrival on the scene (i.e. a shorter period of territorial dominance) than the majority. In some instances, e.g. the American Indian, prior territoriality has no prestigeful significance. The superior force of arms or the more complex and effective culture of a conqueror are important, and in the evolution of a culture high prestige goes to the man of the dominant society whose ancestors arrived first. In other instances, e.g. the Negro in America, the time of arrival is less significant than status upon arrival. An arrival in the status of slave or chattel carries with it the added factor of obliteration of one's cultural history as it had existed before the onset of slavery. The slave is not an adequate culture bearer. Thus, a society emerging from a group of freed slaves is peculiarly vulnerable to the incorporation of fragmented or distorted aspects of the dominant society which surrounds it. Such a society also exemplifies the reality factors which tend to perpetuate minority status: relative distance from sources of community power, incomplete access to social, educational, and economic opportunities, incomplete participation in the dominant culture, and certain other types of restricted behavior including segregation imposed by the larger society.

These features of the minority combined with low socio-economic status contribute to the maintenance of a significant social distance between members of the minority and of the majority. Without sustained emotionally reciprocal relationships, they have only partial and sometimes distorted information about each other. Such a relative information deficit reinforces the tendency on the part of one group to think in stereotyped terms about the other (4). The minority, which tends to use the majority as an emulative reference group, may, because of its limited knowledge of majority standards and values, adopt such partial or misunderstood variants of these that their behavior when dealing with emulative reference (majority) group members will be a caricature of what the latter regard as desirable (12). In this way the prejudiced feelings, attitudes, or beliefs of the majority are reinforced.

## The Adolescent as a Minority Group Member

How does the adolescent fit into this scheme? His primary identifying characteristics are those of age. The body and face of pubescence, arbitrarily defined as between ages 13 and 18, are easily recognized. He is also a recent arrival on the territory dominated by his elders. He is relatively powerless from the social and economic standpoint. By virtue of age he is excluded from places in which alcohol is served; he is not franchised; he cannot marry without the consent of his parents; he is, after all, legally defined as a "minor."

These features are present in pre-adolescent children as well. Why are they not, then, similar targets for the restrictive practices of their elders? In fact, they are. Young children are much more restricted in their range of activities than their adolescent older siblings. They do not, however, have the will, the strength, or the social capacity to challenge these restrictions. Their continuing dependency needs reinforce their tendency to maintain in an unchanged fashion a security-receiving relationship with a more powerful, sheltering, nurturing figure. The child's physical and psychological weakness, his lack of mastery of the techniques for independent survival, his absolute need for close contact with a source of security—all contribute to the maintenance of a single social world inhabited both by him and by his parents.

In contrast to the child who requires preservation of a social *status quo* the adolescent is upwardly mobile. He is moving from the role of conforming, dependent child to that of independent, initiating, coping adult. He and his parents are no longer comfortable sharers of the same social world. In a certain sense he may be compared with the "marginal man" who has one foot in the majority world and one in his own but does not feel completely accepted by or comfortable in either. As Kurt Lewin has put it, the marginal man by virtue of his transitory condition and ambiguous status suffers from "uncertainty of belongingness" (8).

This lack of certainty about belonging, and the precarious self-esteem associated with it, appear to account in part for the adolescent's strong need to find others of his own kind. This is a narcissistic object choice to the degree that the people in whom he is interested mirror his own lack of certainty and his own concern with his changing bodily, emotional, and social status. Overwhelmed by the consciousness of his own changing state, and of his difference from comfortably dependent younger humans as well as from more stable older ones already fixed into their social niches, the adolescent looks for reassurance and support to those who resemble him. Together they form a community of individuals with shared anxieties, preoccupations, and, to some degree, feelings of alienation from the age grades which precede and follow them. This alienation is reflected in the emergence of their own folk-heroes. It is also reflected in the compensatory attempt (seen in a variety of minority situations) to form one's own group as a basis for social anchorage and identity formation. This requires the loyalty to group customs and intense conformity which is so prominent in the adolescent culture.

The threat of loneliness in the face of the mass of those who do not understand because they are too young, or because they are too old and have forgotten, gives rise to an intense need for communication. In the privileged classes of United States society this need is met in part by the telephone which provides an immediate network through which an aggregate of adolescents may be transformed into a social system. This is a means by which, though geographically separated, they may transmit and receive the information which tells them that they are not alone and validates their perceptions of reality.

In the less privileged classes this need is met in part by the formation of gangs or street-corner groups. Communication is also facilitated by the development of distinctive signals which permit recognition of a person not only of like age status but with similar values. Extreme styles in hair and clothing, the faddish embrace of vigorous dances, and familiarity with current songs are examples of the communicative cues through which mutual recognition is possible. In the lower socio-economic groups lack of a stable home base and dependence upon shifting loci for congregation may interfere with the formation of a true community. Under such circumstances, the place in which face to face contact is possible becomes invested with particular significance, and the home becomes proportionately devalued. The other forms of non-verbal communication and identifying displays may also assume added importance.

To the degree to which shared values reflected in shared behavior and the use of shared symbols unify the group of adolescents in the pursuit of common aims; to the degree to which these elements provide a set of guidelines for behavior in a variety of situations; to the degree to which they are socially transmitted from one generation of adolescents to another; and to the degree that they constitute a set of standards, symbols, and values acting in opposition to those of the dominant or adult culture; to that degree the group of adolescents in United States society may be said to be a collectivity with a culture, whch is in some ways a contra-culture, of its own.

Adolescence viewed in this manner is not identical with puberty. It is possible, in fact, to conceive of puberty as a physiologically defined period which may be traversed under certain circumstances without the emergence of much characteristic adolescent behavior. The pubescent child, for example, who is part of a large, well-integrated, and extended family, in a society with stable institutionalized age roles and which permits little individual choice in regard to marriage or occupation, would not be expected to experience the throes of upward mobility and marginality. In such a situation he would always "belong" and there would be no threat of status ambiguity or of loneliness. Under such circumstances, one would not expect the emergence of defensive manoeuvers, reflected in a contra-culture, of a type which would elicit particular attitudes in the adult power-holding society.

## Evocative Adult Behavior in a Context of Social Change

The foregoing discussion has focused upon the "uncertainty of belongingness," individually and as a group, of people in the age period between childhood and adulthood. Uncertainty of status, however, is not confined to members of this group. It is present, as well, in adults who historically have had the responsibility of assigning role-patterns and functions to less mature members of society. But in the contemporary Western world the adults, who constitute the economic basis of the social system and who manage the agencies of social control, are unsure about how to exercise their own prerogatives. Rapidly increasing population pressures, new technology, vastly improved world-wide communications, and increased social and geographical mobility have destroyed the base of consistently reinforcing experience necessary for the maintenance of value and symbol systems. The jostling of values and behavioral modes, previously nurtured under conditions of relative cultural isolation, has fostered a condition of relative ambiguity and a diminished sense of group-distinctiveness; it has also made it increasingly difficult for individuals to arrive at consensual validation of their beliefs about what is really worthwhile. Societies in the process of accelerating change, especially ". . . if the change is not guided by a set of sharply defined master symbols that tell what the change is about," (14) may be, thus, assumed to be less effective than stable groups in the socialization of their young. In these latter, "Cultural prescriptions of a powerful nature define the usual sequence of statuses and roles that individuals are to assume during their life span . . . . Advances . . . occur according to certain schedules which integrate his capabilities with age-graded requirements of the society . . ." (4). However, in complex and changing societies, geographical and social mobility, the heterogeneity of sub-cultures, and the rapid social changes which render inadequate much childhood learning place unpredictable role-demands upon the individual. "Discontinuities between what is expected in successive roles is greater . . . subgroups with deviant values emerge which do not prepare the child for performance of the roles expected of him by the larger society . . ." (4).

Thus, the quality of adolescence as a socio-cultural condition is determined by the changing nature of society and mediated by shifts in adult values and acts. This is superimposed upon an inherently unstable youth-parent figure equilibrium which depends upon a system of mutually transmitted, often inconsistent, signals between pubescents and adults. The adults signal their expectations which encourage increasing independence, but at the same time, they emit contradictory messages which discourage changes in the *status quo*. The adolescents signal their own needs for recognition and self-esteem and, simultaneously, continue to express, although in disguised fashion, their anxieties and persisting needs for support. Even if the desired support is forthcoming, it is often perceived as unacceptable and triggers hostile or rebellious behavior directed against its source. Any locus of support in the dominant society can be regarded as potentially stifling, inhibiting the movement toward increased freedom. The inferred threat of suppressed mobility and of deprivation of the anticipated freedoms of adult status, as well as the anxiety of identity confusion, motivate a range of security operations including those manifested in cultural terms.

Adults as a group respond to the defensively motivated contraculture with fear and anger and the development of a series of false premises and generalizations. These last are couched in terms of the lack of responsibility of the adolescent, his impulsiveness and untrustworthiness, and his laziness and disregard for moral values. In turn these attitudes have their own evocative impact on the adolescent group, which now in the position of a collective minority engages in a series of adaptive manoeuvers which, temporarily successful in dealing with the majority, may actually impede the ultimate capacity of its members to become full participants in the majority culture. Adaptation to the stress of adult pressures may result in the establishment of a time-limited reciprocal relationship in which the adolescent attempts to disprove the prejudicial hypotheses; the unstable equilibrium may be maintained by the adolescent threat to run away or to behave in a still more unacceptable manner (including an outbreak of acute mental illness viewed as a protest, a cry for help, a panic, or a temporary substitution of fantasies for unbearable reality); it may involve a pseudo-passivity, reminiscent of the "Uncle Tomism" of the conforming Negro which hid a deep reservoir of resentment; or it may be achieved through a variety of complementary behaviors which fit the prejudiced beliefs of the adult world. It may happen, then, that adults who have participated in such pseudo-mutual compromise formations are jolted by non-complementary behavior and respond with emotional disturbance, even though the non-complementary move is palpably in the direction of greater social usefulness and competence, e.g. a social protest movement. In this instance, the disturbance of the adult may be compared to the anxiety of a majority group member when confronted with irrefutable evidence of the irrationality of his prejudices.

In the last case, it is assumed that prejudices are retained because they have certain psychological functions for the individual. Can it also be assumed that anti-adolescent prejudice has such functions? Adults embracing unmodifiable prejudices against such minority groups as Negroes or Jews, for example, have been shown to suffer from inadequate reality testing reflected in the active selection, modification, or scotomization of incoming information which threatens their prejudiced beliefs or attitudes. They also regard incompatible realities which they cannot deny as exceptions to the rule. In other words, their inadequate reality testing, because it has a prejudice-protecting function, suggests a strong psychological need for the prejudice (6). Much early work suggests that such prejudices are necessary because they provide a readily available target for the displacement or projection of unacceptable wishes. The target, which is selected on the basis of social circumstances, may determine the quality of the prejudiced beliefs. Thus, the Negro slowly rising from the status of uncultured slave, who was permitted neither individual initiative nor a stable marital union, has been considered as lazy, dirty, and sexually amoral. The Jew, on the other hand, with a different background, has been regarded in terms of a different set of stereotypes.

The presence of prejudice is further complicated by a protective societal response which has been termed "cultural exclusion" (5). This refers to the active denial to minority group members of the right of full participation in all aspects of the dominant majority group culture. The consequence of this exclusion is in the minority man's failure to share the values and symbols of the larger society. Cultural exclusion appears to become most intense when, with increasing knowledge and rising expectations, the minority begins to press for more privileges and more participation, and it becomes both a social and an economic threat.

Is it possible that the adolescent group is an especially suitable target in a culture such as that of the contemporary United States? Why should yet another target be necessary in the presence of the generally serviceable ones already present? Is the adolescent group used as a target only by those in search of a scapegoat? Or is there something about contemporary adolescence that evokes prejudiced behavior?

First of all, the adolescent group which is not educated beyond high school poses, yearly, a recurrent strain on a labor market increasingly glutted with non-usables because of the automation of industry and the demands for more adequate basic education even at the lowest occupational echelons. The adolescent also symbolizes the threat of youth to displace the aged in the seats of power and influence. More than the child, he symbolizes the threat of the son to overthrow the father. Certainly, with his new interest in exploring his own body and those of others and his new consciousness of physical strength and attractiveness, he becomes a suitable target for the displaced wishes and fears of those concerned with their own conflictful aggression and sexuality. And his heterogeneity as a group, his constantly shifting status as an individual, may make him an ambiguous figure vulnerable to the distorted perceptions of the problem-ridden adult. In a society in flux, then, the adolescent may be particularly useful as a figure around which emotion-laden problem-solving fantasies may be woven.

Clearly, this state of affairs is maximized in a highly developed society which contains large pockets of culturally disadvantaged people whose birthrate exceeds that of the majority and whose adolescent children, inadequately socialized, present themselves in increasing numbers at the gates of welfare agencies. It is maximized in a society in which the middle-aged and elderly have no cultural guarantees of dignity and economic security, so that they are vulnerable to the economic and narcissistic threats of those who are younger and ambitious. It is maximized in a society in which institutional behavior patterns are decreasingly significant as guides and in which, therefore, people of all ages are increasingly forced to make decisions which in the past were automatically accomplished on a cultural basis.

A number of other consequences may logically be expected to flow from this type of social order. It might be expected to produce in its adults a high degree of anxiety about status, security, and the acceptable expression of needs and wishes. Such status-centered anxiety is often dealt with by the development of security-giving systems of prejudiced feelings and beliefs. Under such circumstances there is a constant search for targets, and, for adults, the collectivity of adolescents provides a uniquely suitable target.

## SOCIALIZATION DURING ADOLESCENCE

For pre-adults, impaired role-implementation at the hands of mature members of the society could interfere with the role-cognitions which should be developing in anticipation of future statuses. It also forces greater dependence upon peers for the joint formulation of systems of values and behavioral codes. Value construction for this group does not proceed *via* the formulation of verbal abstractions but follows from action, success at which defines status. As adult society becomes less dependable as a source of status and values, the adolescent is under increasing pressure to act and to create a social position for himself in his group of peers. The type of action may be delinquent. More typically, however, it involves sports, dancing, and other socializing activities, and the search for a partner of the opposite sex (7). The need for status achievement through action becomes especially important since the youth is now ". . . a member of a group which both transcends the family and in which he is not in the strongly institutionalized position of being a member of the inferior generation class. It is the first major step toward defining himself as clearly independent of the authority and help of the parental generation." In addition to forming an identification with the sub-society of his age peers, the adolescent normally does the same with three other types of collectivity:

". . . (1) the school which is the prototype of the organization dedicated to the achievement of a specified goal through disciplined performance; (2) the peer-association, the prototype of collective organization to satisfy and adjust mutual interests; and (3) the newly emerging cross-sex dyad, the prototype of the sole adult relation in which erotic factors are allowed an overt part. . . . These identifications form the main basis in personality structure on which adult role-participations are built. Through at least one further major step of generalization of value-level, participation in the youth culture leads to participation in the values of the society as a whole. Participation in the school leads to the adult occupational role, with its responsibility for independent choice of vocation, a productive contribution and self-support. The peer-association identification leads to roles of cooperative memberships in a variety of associations of which the role of citizen in a democratic society is perhaps the most important. Finally, the dating pattern of adolescence leads to marriage and to the assumption of parental responsibilities" (17).

This quotation from Talcott Parsons emphasizes the continuity from the objects of identification in childhood to the role and collectivity structure of the adult society. This underlying, though partial and fragmented continuity, despite the surface evidence of a separate, discontinuous youth-culture, suggests the place of minority group status in social evolution. The process of growth and upward mobility seems to require a stage of separation from the original group and a period of development of special capacities before assimilation into the new and dominant group.

The significance of social change as a factor determining the problems of adults and the message transmitted by them to adolescents was discussed earlier. In terms of the youth themselves, "ties to class and family, to local community and region become more flexible and hence often 'expendable' as more choices become available." The process by which the erotic component of sex relations, for example, ". . . has become differentiated, allowing much greater freedom in this area, is closely related to the differentiation of function and the structural isolation of the nuclear family . . . . Since much of the newer freedom outpaces the changes in norms and general values it is very difficult to draw lines between the areas of new freedom in process of being legitimated and the types which are sufficiently dysfunctional . . . so that the probability is they will be controlled  or even supressed. The adolescent in our society is faced with difficult problems of choice and evaluation in areas such as this, because an adequate codification of the norms governing many of these newly emancipated areas has not yet been developed." In complex societies ". . . the impact on youth of the general process of social differentiation makes for greater differences between their position and that of children, on the one hand, and that of adults on the other than is true in less differentiated societies. Compared to our own past or to most other societies there is a more pronounced . . . and increasingly long segregation of the younger groups centered above all on the system of formal education" (15).

The increasingly prolonged dependency and segregation for educational purposes required by progressive societal differentiation create conditions similar to those experienced by minority group adults expressing new goals and aspirations. Effective information transmission implants new wishes for status, autonomy, and consumer goods in individuals who possess neither the social techniques, the money, nor the power to obtain them. The impossibility of desired achievement may have varied results: hyper-ambitiousness occasionally coupled with a degree of deviousness in attaining particular sub-goals; impulsive aggressiveness; hopelessness and resignation associated with an overwhelming awareness of social and economic powerlessness, resulting in abandonment of the leading social value of achievement; self-narcotization through the use of drugs or alcohol as a means of simultaneously denying the unacceptable aspects of adult (majority) society and facilitating the emergence of substitute fantasy gratifications; the embrace of "radical" political or social beliefs associated with membership in a group of like-minded people, etc.

These alternatives present a spectrum of more or less pathological efforts at problem solving. They omit the more adaptive and less symptomatic course which involves the acceptance of adult values and goals and requires long-term effort toward their achievement with the attainment of a series of symbolic sub-goals, e.g. graduation from high school or college, on the way. A universally reported characteristic of adolescents which has classically been attributed to problems stemming from newly active sexual and aggressive drives is a concern with meaningfulness, an attempt to find coherence in a disorderly universe. It seems more plausible to attribute this concern to the inevitable inability of the younger generation to utilize the standards of the older to cover all exigencies. In an era of rapid change, such concern would be expected to be intense.

Dependency and segregation are not confined to those adolescents who continue in the societally required channel of socialization through high school. They may be even more onerous for those whose capacities have been outpaced by the accelerating demands for competence and responsibility. This group of high school "dropouts," or those, primarily of lower class, who continue as nominal students while learning little in the anonymity of huge urban schools, are subject to progressive alienation from the sources of dominant society power. For them, the pathological solutions are often the most available, especially when they offer an added increment of pleasure in a world promising little aside from the immediate and from bodily-linked gratification. Within the context of the age-segregated social group the utilization of asocial or anti-social techniques of anxiety-reduction or need-gratification tends to be mutually reinforced, and the influence of restraining parents or other agencies of social control is diminished.

A comparable set of consequences within the middle-class group may flow from parental uncertainty about standards and the use of discipline. This forces the adolescents to look to each other in order to develop their own social codes and values, i.e. ideas about what is worthwhile, what is condemned, and what is rewarded. As Parsons (16) has stated, the "continual reorganization of the normative system" characteristic of an era of change results in "important elements of indeterminacy in the structure of expectations." Under these circumstances the adolescent must deal both with an outright lack of guidance where it is needed and with conflicting adult expectations which cannot simultaneously be fulfilled. The conflicting expectations generated by a society in change are added to the conflicting expectations and messages inherent in the usual parent-adolescent structure. The resultant paralysis, panic, or maladaptive solution exhibited by the vulnerable adolescent is reminiscent of the behavioral consequences of the conflicting parental messages which have been labelled as the "double-bind" (2).

One little discussed aspect of modern society permitting the development of an adolescent culture is its affluence. The minority aspects of adolescent life would not be so prominent if people in this age range were needed as part of the labor force, i.e. if they were immediately integrated into the adult work system. Those pubescent youths who are in the labor force, are married, or are in the armed forces are chronologically but, in Bernard's words (3), not ". . . culturally, teen-agers. They are neophytes in the adult culture. . . . Teen-age culture is essentially the culture of leisure class." Bernard made the point that since adolescents of the lower socio-economic classes are more apt to take jobs, enter the military services, or get married early, they disappear into the adult world, so that those who remain are disproportionately from the higher socio-economic background. It is these latter who constitute the teen-age market for clothes, cars, record players, and cosmetics. In a manner akin in some respects to that of the minority group person striving for recognition, acceptance, and personal status they engage in the cult of conspicuous consumption. Again, like the minority group person this consumption may result in appearance or behavior almost like a caricature of those with high status in the adult world. Similarly, a major preoccupation is how to be attractive in order to be popular. This, of course, is not confined to middle-class youth and Bernard's statement did not take into account the teen-age culture of the less affluent with similar wishes but without the financial means to readily gratify them. For these adolescents, hard-won wages may also be rapidly spent to acquire the current symbols of status.

The inferred underlying fantasy that one is unlovable or inferior is the same as that which appears to motivate much striving behavior and concern with the opinions of peers in adult members of certain minority groups. Feelings of unlovability or of diminished self-esteem are reinforced by contact with members of the majority. They seem, however, to be displaced onto the peer or normative reference group, and it is in relation to each other that adolescents or adult minority group members strive for popularity and status.

## REFERENCES

1. Allport, G. W.: *The Nature of Prejudice.* Addison-Wessley Publishing Company, Inc., Reading, Mass., 1954.
2. Bateson, G., Jackson, D., Haley, T., and Weakland, T.: Toward a theory of schizophrenia. Behavioral Science, *1:* 251–264, 1956.
3. Bernard, V.: Teen-age culture: An overview. Annals of the American Academy of Political and Social Science, *338:* 2, 1961.
4. Brim, O. G.: Socialization through the life cycle. In *Socialization after Childhood,* edited by O. G. Brim and S. Wheeler, pp. 18–30. John Wiley & Sons, Inc., New York, 1966.

5. Brody, E. B.: Cultural exclusion, character and illness. American Journal of Psychiatry, *122:* 852—858, 1966.
6. Brody, E. B.: Psychiatry and prejudice. In *American Handbook of Psychiatry*, Vol. III, edited by S. Arieti, pp. 629—642. Basic Books, Inc., Publishers, New York, 1966.
7. Helanko, R.: Sports and socialization. In *Personality and Social Systems*, edited by N. J. Smelser and W. T. Smelser, pp. 238—254. John Wiley & Sons, Inc., New York, 1963.
8. Lewin, K.: *Resolving Social Conflicts.* Harper & Brothers, New York, 1948.
9. Mack, R. W.: *Race, Class and Power*, p. 2. American Book Company, New York, 1963.
10. Mead, B.: *Mind, Self and Society.* University of Chicago Press, Chicago, 1934.
11. Merton, R.: The self-fulfilling prophecy. The Antioch Review, *8:* 193—210, 1948.
12. Merton, R.: *Social Theory and Social Structure.* The Free Press of Glencoe, Inc., Glencoe, Ill., 1957.
13. Parsons, T.: The incest taboo in relation to social structure and the socialization of the child. In *Social Structure and Personality*, p. 75. The Free Press of Glencoe, Inc., Glencoe, Ill. (Originally published in British Journal of Sociology, *5:* no. 2, June 1954.)
14. Parsons, T.: Youth in the context of American society. In *Social Structure and Personality*, p. 158. The Free Press of Glencoe, Inc., Glencoe, Ill., 1964. (Originally published in Daedalus, *91:* no. 1, 1962.)
15. Parsons, T.: Youth in the context of American society. In *Social Structure and Personality*, pp. 170—172. The Free Press of Glencoe, Inc., Glencoe, Ill., 1964.
16. Parsons, T.: Youth in the context of American society. In *Social Structure and Personality*, p. 174. The Free Press of Glencoe, Inc., Glencoe, Ill., 1964.
17. Parsons, T.: Social structure and the development of personality: Freud's contribution to the integration of psychology and sociology, *In Social Structure and Personality*, pp. 105—106. The Free Press of Glencoe, Inc., Glencoe, Ill., 1964. (Originally published in Psychiatry, *21:* no. 4, 1958.)

# Problems of the Negro Adolescent in the Next Decade

CHESTER M. PIERCE, M.D.

## THE NEW REALITY: HARSH IS TRUTH

I BEGIN this chapter with an apologia in the service of truth. Significantly, like many interracial communications it is made to enlighten the white and to amuse the Negro. I apologize too for the personal reference to my own youth, but it seems germane to a discussion of Negro adolescence. When I was a teen-ager, a white boy seeking to have an experimental dialogue asked me what it was like to be a Negro. I answered, "It's like being a beautiful woman." He was confounded. I went on to point out that like the beautiful woman the Negro could always expect special treatment—only instead of being ingratiating, the treatment took the form of hostility, veiled or unveiled. Like the beautiful woman, the Negro could always expect people to act in a certain way—but this predicted attitude was negative and disdaining instead of positive and admiring. Like the beautiful woman, the Negro never knew if he was accepted for himself or for what was merely skin-deep. So Negroes, like beautiful woman, have extreme confusion evaluating their own worth or estimating their true impact on associates or events.

But that was 25 years ago. Today the Negro teen-ager still knows about beautiful women in the same way that I knew about them. In addition, however, he is faced with a paradox I did not suffer. Today he knows there is much, much more opportunity and goodwill. Co-temporaneously, there are many problems to be resolved before he can be a functioning, happy, and efficient contributor to the society. He knows that it is much more difficult to be bereft of

17

crippling emotions of fear, anger, hate, and envy. He divines, somehow, that the road to effective love and work relationships is both more arduous to achieve and more probable of completion. This paradox is the harsh truth of a new reality, merciless and bountiful, which has appeared in the United States in only the past decade.

For the adolescent 25 years ago there seemed little likelihood, for instance, that he could aspire to the highest political offices. It would have been rash to aim for certain occupations, especially in selected parts of our country. Not many (or any) in his acquaintanceship would have considered it possible that Negroes would be *solicited* and *implored* to be guests at exclusive social functions conducted by the majority. A quarter of a century ago Negro youth could believe and, in fact, would have to believe that all men were not equal before the law. Furthermore, the law, that coherent interpretation and enlightened revision of custom, seemed made for the majority and only for the majority.

All this is changing. It seems almost as amazing as it is fortunate. Already it is an alien world that I recall to my teen-ager when I mention the black curtains I was obliged to eat behind when I travelled on a train. Yet my earliest memories of race struggle involving the issue of where Long Island Negroes could sit at a movie theatre will seem tame to the youngster who becomes an adolescent during the next decade, for in his early memories that youth will recall issues of calls to violence and denunciations of gradualism. He will recall the emotional genre as one of the anxiety and dissatisfaction. Today's teen-ager is correctly dissatisfied and anxious even though he has been told that a Negro could be President of the United States during his lifetime; even though he realizes that a Negro ceramic physicist is as welcomed in a laboratory in Alabama as he is in California; even though he knows about the strenuous and genuine efforts whites are making to include Negroes in all sorts of social activities; even though he reads that Negroes are much more likely to obtain justice from the courts.

Hence the twins anxiety and dissatisfaction take residence in a harsh social reality which is at the same time merciless and bountiful. These are the basic ingredients which are grafted into the usual problems of American adolescent conflicts which the Negro teen-ager must resolve. The resolution is compounded by the catalyst of extreme confusion of self-image that the Negro teen-ager shares with the beautiful woman. Most of this chapter will be devoted to a consideration of the specific and personal problems that the Negro teen-ager will have to overcome during the period of his resolution of adolescent conflicts. The new reality, though harsh, is exciting, and the world community should reap abundant harvest from the successful resolution of adolescent conflicts by American Negroes over the next couple of decades.

Before discussing the specific and personal problems of the Negro teen-ager in this new and exciting social reality, I wish to indicate some general and impersonal issues which may have a bearing on the formation and perpetuation of the attitudes of dissatisfaction and anxiousness. These issues are: 1) the existence of thermonuclear weaponry; 2) the rapid expansion and dissemination of knowledge; and 3) the world war on poverty. These are the roots of the new and exciting social reality which at that same instance is bountiful and merciless, exhilarating and frightening. From these roots spring, for the Negro youth, the twins dissatisfaction and anxiety, residents of the social reality and friends of terror and violence.

## THERMONUCLEAR WEAPONRY

Unlike any creatures who have ever inhabited the earth, any youth born in the last 20-odd years has been molded under an exquisite and concerned anxiety born out of incessant stimuli of an awesome knowledge. This uneasy knowledge is that men now have weapons capable of annihilating civilization in a matter of minutes. Even more gruesome is the grisly knowledge that whatever weapons men have fashioned in the past they have *always* used.

On a pre-conscious and conscious level the Negro adolescent must reckon with the fact that most of the awful things in his world are the result of the doings of white men. Now the ultimate in awful things can happen even before he has had an opportunity to taste life, because of the decision of white men. Thus the youth may feel an urgency to live fully each moment of his life and he

becomes involved in a host of activities which promote his definition of living urgently. Here the mature ideal is the quest to
partake in decision making for events which affect his life as well
as his white brother's. This is the absolute in social opportunity.

## KNOWLEDGE EXPLOSION

An exquisite and concerned dissatisfaction results from the
awareness of the gap between how most whites live and how most
Negroes live. To an extent which would have been unimaginable
25 years ago, Everyman is aware of this gap which is characterized
by the wonders of technology, information dispersal, and communication. The maturing Negro realizes that in order to close the
gap it will be necessary to pursue the quest for open enrollment
in all our institutions of learning. This is the absolute in educational opportunity.

## THE WAR ON POVERTY

An adolescent today is living on a planet at the brink of a very
hot war. Yet, he is also living in a situation where, for a variety
of reasons, studied effort is being made to reduce strife by means
of a world-wide war on poverty. Because of the ease with which
the battles of this war provide opportunities to help resolve conflicts of dependency, hostility, sexuality, and prestige, few teen-
agers can escape serious contemplation about enlisting in the fight.
Furthermore, warriors are needed everywhere and are loved for
whatever modicum of success they institute or achieve. Best of
all, one can enlist and engage the enemy at home or abroad in
many different ways.

The historian of the future may well emphasize that this war
had many far-reaching overtones beyond feeding the world's increasing population. Feeding, after all, is a technical problem.
Its solution might even be carried out with a generosity propelled
by a patronizing condescension necessitated by crass and selfish
considerations.

In this war the true fight has an immediate and universal appeal.
The desired end result of the war is to provide literacy and dignity to each man so that each man can live with more self-respect.
The ideal will be for everyone to contribute rather than to be
contributed to. The maturing young adult may feel heavy obli-

gations to join this quest to eliminate poverty and guarantee self-respect. This is the absolute in economic opportunity.

By definition no absolute can be attained. During the next 10 years we can anticipate all manner of troubles in securing social, educational, and economic opportunity. For example, we will see more youth who define living urgently in terms of drug addiction and criminal activity. We will watch the pitiable and angry bumbling of school dropouts who, though increasingly aware of what they do not have, will be progressively less able to achieve. We will increase the welfare lists by those who have been rendered suspicious and apathetic about their chances to extricate themselves from economic nothingness. These are the ones who will never gain enough self-respect to be able to help others and thus reduce friction in our society.

Regrettably, as things now stand, the large mass of Negro adolescents will be unable to adopt attitudes to those problems of social, educational, and economic opportunity. Hence we can expect an aggravation of dissatisfaction and anxieties. These deadly twins will entertain violence and terror with increasing frequency and grandeur unless drastic curatives are applied with celerity.

Fortunately, an increasingly large number (but by no means a significantly large number) of Negro adolescents will meet the challenges of the new reality and benefit from its magnificence. Let us now trace some of the specific and personal problems they will solve. For the youth who does not solve these problems in the new reality of the next decade and a half, we can expect only more wretchedness, unhappiness, and hopelessness, the miserable assistants of dissatisfaction and anxiety.

### New Problems: Awareness of the Gap and Awareness of the Opportunities

Unlike the Japanese-American youth or the American Indian teen-ager, the Afro-American young adult has no burden occasioned by loyalties to a dual culture. The Negro knows without equivocation or remorse that his wants in the American society are congruent with those of the large majority. In the past the acquisition of even gross and commonplace benefits of American society was beyond the grasp of the most wealthy or the best known

Negroes. The developing psychic structure for all Negroes, if it was to be in tune with reality, had to reflect this overwhelming aspect of life in the United States. By age 15 every Negro would have to know that it would be virtually impossible for him to join certan unions or to gain admission to certain restaurants or to be able to attend certain amusement parks. This held true even if one had countless riches or if one was a celebrity whose face and name might be recognized over the entire world.

To a large degree today's teen-ager must understand the same things but it is becoming less of a problem, for instance, to know if he can get service in a hotel or a store. Yet it remains true that, along with the confusion of image, the Negro must contend with a confusion of cues as to whether or not he is welcomed or to what degree he is welcomed, no matter where he goes.

The big difference today, however, is that the colored teen-ager knows that it is increasingly possible to get the most coveted benefits of our society. It means too that he must be aware that to secure such benefits he must pay the price. Herein lies another change in the psychic development of the youth of today compared to the youth of 25 years ago.

In previous times the Negro had a defense system which was an all-inclusive umbrella against any onslaught which might serve to humiliate, shame, degrade, or provoke anxiety or wrath. This defense system was expressed as "What else could I do—that's all the white man let me accomplish." Thus if one was successful, one could invoke this formula to make oneself even more lovable and competent. On the other hand, if one failed, the same formula was useful and could be applied both for one's own benefit and as a public expression to either the white or Negro communities.

With the rapid burgeoning of opportunities for Negroes, this formula will no longer suffice. It may be that the decay of the usefulness of this defense system will spell at worst horror and at best chagrin for the American people. For when the Negro teen-ager can no longer "cry race," then the twins of dissatisfaction and anxiety, along with their entourage, may mobilize to a degree heretofore unknown.

There are many corollaries to this issue of being aware of the gap and suddenly being permitted to close it. Much has been written on the problems it will entail because most Negroes, understandably, are not technically prepared to accept job opportunities or educational advantages etc. Much has been said of how defensive whites become when Negroes are given extra privileges, particularly if the Negro is unable to function at a consistently high level (or even average level).

Relatively little, however, has been said of still other issues which relate to the obliteration of one of the major defense reactions of our race. For instance, the Negro will now find it difficult to become "great." In the past, other than athletes and entertainers, the role-model for the great Negro might be, say, an Executive Secretary of the National Association for the Advancement of Colored People (NAACP). This was admirable and realistic. Now, however, the teen-age dreamer (and all teen-agers do dream) must aspire to such lofty levels as a "captain of industry" or an extremely high political rank or a famous scientist, etc. In short, it will be more difficult to be great and easier to feel dwarfed into insignificance and personal anonymity. A modest success will no longer bring the same ego satisfactions for the Negro.

Other problems will help increase potential dissatisfaction and anxiety. With education being made "free," many youths will not be able to take advantage of it nor be able to fall back on the old umbrella defense. In order to go to high school, for instance, one needs (especially if one is a teen-ager) money for the accoutrements that his peers would have. Thus a free high school or community college or on the job training institute has hidden but definite costs such as for clothes, towel fees, activity cards, etc.

Still more elements can be stirred into the cauldron. With the dissolution of the umbrella defense the Negro youth will find it necessary to learn to evaluate whites as individuals. He may also feel it necessary to be somewhat rebellious over what he sees as white *noblesse oblige* (when in actuality he diagnoses that much of the opportunity being made available is granted quite grudgingly and only because of precious advantages to the whites such as the need to fill manpower shortages or the need to stabilize the economy by not losing prestige in the eyes of the world). The youth will have to learn how to adjust to being accepted and not just tolerated.

Hopefully, some Negroes will even have to learn how to adjust to being integrated and not just desegregated. In terms of my own operational definition of integration such a goal is far remote. I believe our society will be integrated when no one has to think anytime during a day about his color. Every day of my existence in the United States I have been reminded, usually dozens of times, of my racial persuasion. A white cannot possibly comprehend the amount of psychic energy that is required to be a Negro. The teen-ager of the next decade and a half, I think, will find ample reasons each day to consider his skin color. He will burn up energy, which could be put to better use in the society, merely because he is Negro. His resentment, however, may be far greater than mine was when I was his age.

These new types of problems are inevitable in the structurinig of the new reality. Although there is potential for dissatisfaction and anxiety to a degree not yet known, the chance to compete and to be accepted (if not integrated) doubtlessly will be achieved by many Negro adolescents. Our world will profit by this achievement. What will be required to make the achievement, without the comforting solace of an umbrella defense, will be a capacity for flexibility. As more opportunities are provided (even in the face of increasing white backlash) there will be many who do override possible dissatisfaction and anxiety and do attempt to move away from the helpless and hopeless state which describes the ghetto. We should now turn to the types of flexibility that will be required of more and more as they move up to accept and to exploit opportunity.

### MOVING UP: A CHANCE FOR SOME

Over the last decade a number of Negroes have been able to procure positions in areas where Negroes were unwelcomed in the not too distant past. The clinical observations of these Negroes may provide a basis for projecting what many young Negroes will face in the next decade and a half. Public and private sectors of the economy no longer demand Negroes merely on a token basis as happened to many of the avant-garde of the last decade. Today opportunities exist if the person is qualified for the position. Even so, like their avant-garde big brothers and sisters, a not inconsiderable number of Negroes who move up into these positions will have to overcome transitional barriers and perhaps live still with an unpleasant fact of life in a society which will still be discriminatory. The man who moves up may be "under-employed" and he will still be most likely to be eliminated in times of economic duress. Naturally, the chances for such an unhappy plight are reduced in the direct proportion that the Negro will have exploitable and tangible skills. This is synonymous with saying the best educated Negro will suffer less—as has always been the case, of course. The point to be made here, however, is that there will be many more carpenters than astrophysicists who are moving up. For the many there will be once more irritations concomitant with dissatisfaction and anxiety. In this instance the twins will delight and sparkle as they operate on the Everyman who is moving up yet facing large transitional barriers and being unemployed. The best remedy for this plight is to be certain that the teen-ager is informed and knowledgeable about the struggles involved in order to gain the benefits of leaving the ghetto.

From my experience with patients who are upwardly mobile there are several broad areas to be transcended. One must appreciate that, since over 90% of American children are educated in segregated schools, the Negro (especially the one at the carpenter instead of the astrophysicist level) who moves up goes into a totally different world. In this situation the incessant burden is on him to prove himself to the satisfaction of the majority. The converse does not hold. The drain on the psychic economy can be of a quality and quantity that the person has never experienced in a lifetime in a segregated school and segregated community. Thus the Negro adolescent who has the possibility of moving up must be prepared for a "culture shock."

My patients frequently express concern about their verbal and reading skills. Many are sensitive also about the expression of niceties and graces even to those whites for whom they have respect and trust. Problems arise concerning identification with white fashions or entertainment. There is an awkwardness related to being marginal in a group where you are uncertain as to the basic cues, assumptions, and beliefs. My patients seem over-eager to return, at the end of a work day, to the security of a group which they know and which brings up no issues of acceptance. Curiously, for many there are disenchantments in the closer contact with the white world. So successfully has the Negro been brainwashed concerning his image and the image of whites that he is sometimes shocked to find rampant and flagrant human fraility among whites, even though the Negro may have expended considerable time and effort berating whites for their assumption of superiority. Patients have told me how unsettling it was to discover how widespread petty office thievery or promiscuity or hostile interpersonal relations were among the whites with whom they worked.

This chagrin tells only part of the problem, however. For the deficiencies of the whites are observed in a setting where the Negro is striving for acceptance. Yet, often he feels he has been thrust into positions where he can fail or at least mark time. He feels the constant fear of being retaliated against for the presumption of arriving in the better life situation. At the same time he is aware of possible criticism from the Negro group which he interprets as an angry envy at his alleviated condition.

Under these conditions of ever present doubt and fear of biracial criticism it is not surprising that the individual focuses on thoughts of whether or not he is different. The consequences of being different on the one hand might loosen the ties to what is known and secure (the Negro world) and yet might gain only tolerance, not acceptance or "integration", in what is unknown and insecure (the white world).

In the past there were two common psychological manoeuvers that aided solution of this dilemma for the upwardly mobile Negro. First, one could appear to be good, but not too good, to the Negro world. One avoided being "too hinckty." Secondly, one settled for a job for which he was over-qualified and/or was the best worker in that position. This makes him appear not too good to the white world.

Now, under the terms of the new reality and under the worldwide pressure for individual self-respect, these manoeuvers may dissolve along with the ego mechanism of "What else could I do—it's all the white man allowed me." Thus the adolescent of the future will be resolving his conflicts along lines that demand that he get the best available job and that he function well in it. Further, he will have considerably less concern about peer relations since there will be more vicarious positive feeling about any individual's achievement by the black community. That is, as the Negro self-image modifies, each person will recognize that achievement by man A helps man B get to a place where he might be able to achieve. At the same time this modification of self-image will lead more and more toward the expectation (and desire) for man A to try to be more directly helpful to man B. One result of such mass psychology is the consideration of "Black Consciousness," as written about so eloquently by Poussaint (9).

Black Consciousness subsumes the hotly ambiguous term "Black Power." Psycho-social factors such as I have outlined will force more Negroes to these thoughts. In fact, the modification of the self-image will depend on some sort of positive interpretations of being a member of the black race. Hence Negroes will have to give over more thought and effort, in the next decade and a half, to the question of what can we do for ourselves? What can we do to be proud? How can we dilute all these things that promote dissatisfaction and anxiety? How can we co-operate amongst ourselves in order to be permitted to be better contributors to the society (so that more benefits will return)? Much of the stimulation to answer these questions will come from the segments of the Negro society which have had the most frequent and the most pleasant contacts with the white community, namely the black intellectuals and the black "haves" successful businessmen, professionals, athletes, entertainers).

During adolescent conflict resolution, therefore, the youth will have to develop some philosophy in regard to Black Consciousness. My belief is that this philosophy will be strongly pro-Black Consciousness in those who best succeed in the society. This is not to say there has to be a balancing of anti-white feeling. It is the recognition that by two decades from now our great inner city ghettos probably will not have been razed. We will still be a long way from the operational definition of integration. The great advantage of Black Consciousness will be that it will help to rectify some of the negative imagery given to Negroes in the years since slavery. It will aid in the move up since it will provide a confidence impossible where a self-image is largely negative.

Some economic and social factors will help to promote Black Consciousness feelings in Negro youth who are moving up. The economic factors relate to the growing dissatisfaction about and awareness of the oppressive job market. The social factors have to do with what the youth will see to be the reward system by which white America functions.

In the foreseeable future Negroes will remain twice as often unemployed as whites. In fact, with increasing automation the Negro unemployment rate could rise (even while more Negroes are given opportunity to work at highly skilled positions). During the summer of 1966 the 5-year improvement in Negro employment came to an end while white employment rates soared (5). It should be noted that as usual the Negro was late in getting in on the benefits of the recent national prosperity (1). During the summer of 1966 more white teen-agers got jobs. There was no change for the Negro teen-agers, who already were significantly less able to get employment than whites. The reason for these economic facts might be due to complex issues in economics that harbinger a coming recession. However, many Negroes will wonder in view of the rising employment of whites (all save the unskilled) if the figures reflect a reprisal against the events of the last several summers which were so rife with racial rioting. Whatever the cause of the facts reflected in the figures, the dissatisfaction and anxiety that is provoked will serve to meld Negroes closer together and to make them more "conscious" of their situation, i.e. that whites will not simply hand over "inalienable rights."

As the young adolescent views the social climate of his time and contemplates the stark unfairness of his economic plight (for instance, having more trouble getting a mortgage or having to pay more for credit) dissatisfaction and anxiety will continue to gnaw at his very soul. It may be at this point that the youngster begins to appreciate a couple of factors in the social psychology of the white American.

White America is conditioned to applaud and reward 1) those who help themselves and 2) those who are assertive enough to force their demands. The youngster will not have to be given academic instruction to realize that desegregation has only taken place where there has been applied and constant pressure, usually from the black community. However, in all matters including those which are non-racial, the American establishment, perhaps because of its pioneer background and its philosophy of democracy, always has rewarded self-help. Furthermore, the American people in personal or even international relations time after time give overt approval to and have wide tolerance for the action which overwhelms the opponent. The American psychology is not pacific or passive. Nor does the American reward or cherish the pacific and passive.

Now the cauldron includes dissatisfactions and anxiety from a host of factors, such as the catalyst of Black Consciousness and the awareness of the whites' regard for assertive self-help coupled with a reluctance by the majority to share. Even though many will be moving up because skills are needed and the racial climate is in many places much improved, the inescapable conclusion for most adolescents over the next couple of decades probably will be that only violence and sacrifice will budge certain resistive elements in the white community. These elements will be dispersed generally but will include the less skilled as well as ethnic groups which have more recently arrived in the United States.

Moving up then becomes paradoxically easier and harder than in previous times. Opportunities will be more abundant. More will be able to move up. Yet greater sacrifices and more problems of both subtle and gross confrontation with whites will face those who move. In addition to these pressures which will produce a culture shock, the youth must be prepared to be flexible, adaptive, and opportunistic. Because of automation any youth, white or black, who starts work today faces the need to be re-cycled eight times on his job during his lifetime. If the black youth is to move up he will have, probably, even more re-cycles and readjustments during his lifetime. He should be prepared for such eventuality.

In deciding upon his career still other factors will enter into the thinking of Negro adolescents in he next 15 years. He will look about him to see where Negroes seem to have job opportunities. Some of what he sees might be surprising.

Over the next decade and a half, if current trends continue, the Negro will occupy an increasingly larger percentage of positions in

the armed forces, in hospitals, and in local and national government. Already, for instance, Negroes re-enlist at twice the rate of
whites. Like hospital and government jobs, life in the armed forces
offers the Negro the dignity and self-respect of vocation and usually
represents both a move upward and security. For the white such
jobs often mean mediocrity and no upward mobility. As the economy allows more whites to move up, Negroes will be able to fill
more of such positions.

In addition as time goes on the Negro can expect that the build
up of the suburbs and the re-building of the inner city might promote job opportunities in such areas as construction, finance,
insurance, real estate, and service positions. Service positions will
not mean merely domestic service (which in our affluent, technological society still will require workers) but will include food
distribution, working in stores, marketing, advertising, and computer programming as well as the standard professional opportunities. For the few, yet amazingly many as we think of it in
today's terms, there will be top management jobs and membership
on important boards of directors.

To move up to these positions will mean that not only has the
society made the position available to the Negro but that the Negro
youth will be suitably trained to accept the position. This means,
in general, that the Negro will have to receive a greater quantity and
better quality of education. He will have to be permitted access to
craft apprenticeships and he will have to take advantage of job
training programs. If for whatever reason conditions do not permit
these types of preparation the adolescent will be made even more
dissatisfied about the inequity, anxious about his livelihood, and
angry at the *status quo.*

Nearly all studies indicate that, compared to white peers and
white parents, the Negro youth and his parents are much more
concerned to get as much preparation as their situation will permit.
This cultural emphasis on the value of preparation doubtlessly
will continue and thus will be an important factor in molding
adolescent behavior. The problem of course is that so often one
cannot take advantage of an opportunity because of the duress of
poverty. Such persons will be the potentially explosive ghetto residents of the future.

For those Negroes who do move up, however, one of their major functions will be to re-educate the whites with whom they come into contact. Such interracial dialogues, going on at ever increasing intensity and frequency, will lead to amelioration of racial conflict. As more people get to understand more of each other and rub off each other's angularities and gain access to the other's life compartments, then there will be less friction on the basis of color. A well-known sociological principle stated that, in general, the more people see of each other, the more they like each other. Thus moving up by the Negro will help the American society so that it will become progressively easier for succeeding teen-agers to be welcomed into true interracial living if they can overcome the obstacles to opportunity. In this sense the teen-ager who resolves his adolescent conflicts from years 1 to 5 of this decade will face more problems than the person who begins his adolescent resolution in year 10 of this decade.

The teen-ager of the next decade, therefore, may have fewer of the experiences which now plague the upwardly mobile Negro. My patients reiterate that in personnel offices they are told such things as, " . . . this is not exactly your background . . . your IQ is too high for this job . . . you're too well trained to be happy here." When a person is hungry and told this it is more than aggravating. Such passive discouragement will lessen but the youth may still feel latent discouragement by employers solely on the basis of his color. For instance, even if working and being paid at a level appropriate to his training, he may find clues that lead him to wonder if management gives him excessive supervision or if his bosses are not overly unhappy that he works around white females.

This brings us to the fact that the upwardly mobile, while having interracial dialogues, will have to disabuse whites of some of their myths about Negroes. In addition the white will have to learn what it means to be a Negro. He will consider the latter issue first.

## On Being a Negro: Suppression, Not Denial

It has been written that the Byzantium Roman was too quick to see the hidden rather than the apparent. It seems often times that white social scientists dealing with race problems fall into the same error. I once heard a national authority state to the immense satisfaction of the audience that Negroes were such good athletes because of the way they were carried on their mother's hips while she did her chores. There was no recognition that Negroes know from childhood that where whites let them compete they can win an acceptance which might be capitalized into all sorts of advantages. Also, no one mentioned the joy the Negro and his community feel when a chance exists to undermine the myth of racial inferiority. Thus athletic competition is sought.

Still another example is the case presentation of several hours duration where the professors pointed out that this lady was so passively hostile because of events in her childhood 30 years before. No one mentioned how angry and futile she felt when she had to descend from rickety flights to use an outhouse whenever she wished to urinate. While urinating she could read the large billboard proclaiming the luxurious accommodations (at what was advertised as "reasonable rates") of the deluxe hotel which was within her sight but as far away as another galaxy.

The point is that being a Negro is *being*. It is existing. When one is concerned about today's bread there is not much thought given over to *becoming* in the sense that one can *become* able to eat in a luxury dining room at a reasonable rate. One exists. The white in the lowliest circumstance, unlike the Negro, knows of many instances where people in his situation have risen to the social stratosphere by dint of their own merit.

Even when abject poverty is absent the Negro continues to be more existential. This is because he does not live in an integrated society. Countless thoughts and much energy are needed to search the environment for ongoing racial attitudes. The housewife will wonder if the man at the cash register—be he Negro, Filipino, or white—was a shade abrupt with her because she was a Negro. The sales engineer getting excessive service from an airline hostess will wonder, among other thoughts, if she is doing this just because he is a Negro and she wants to prove she is a decent human being. The child elected by his classmates to speak at the school assembly (if he is one of the 10% in an "integrated" school) will not know, like the beautiful woman, if he was selected merely on the basis of what is skin-deep.

Concerning treatment by whites and their feelings about this treatment, Negroes do not use much denial and repression as so many seem to think. The major ego defense is suppression. No Negro has reached his teens without being aware of his limited freedom in society. Those Negroes who come to maturity over the next decade and a half probably will be even more aware of these limits, even though they see them being pushed back.

Being a Negro, therefore is more than having the knowledge of what it is to be a beautiful woman. It is being highly *existential*. It is knowing that one is abused, degraded, oppressed—one does not have to utilize repression or denial. The most paranoid Negro patient can tell you true and correct reality in terms of past experiences with whites. The most complacent, satisfied, and indifferent middle-class Negro can catalogue his share of harrowing real life experiences. One can walk into any city in the United States and choose a Negro at random and on request receive a recitation, consistent with reality, as to how the whites are kicking Negroes around in the local situation. All suppress their feelings but suppression grows more difficult. The teen-ager of the future may be less patient with what he sees as a futile and ridiculous circumstance. Repression will continue to live somewhere else than in the ghetto.

There are more dimensions to being a Negro. For most it is an environmental soreness as well as being an intrapsychic distress. Whether in a rural or urban area, the bulk of Negroes are condemned to squalor, inadequate recreational facilities, poorer utility services, sub-standard housing, etc. This is the source of the social diseases, such as criminal activity, delinquency, illegitimacy, and addiction, which Knowles states must become more of a concern to the medical profession (3).

All these dimensions of being a Negro will not change suddenly or drastically. For sometime to come the Negro adolescent must still be diligent in attempting to break out of this cycle: inculcation of self-hatred (from all the factors we have mentioned in his environment and psyche) → paralysis of action (so that he is both unable to comprehend success and he fears failure) → low aspirations, low expectations → more self-hatred.

However, as more break the cycle there will be attention focused on more novel aspects of being a Negro. Success in adolescence might bring high and lofty aspirations as it has done for some civil rights workers (8). Here the adolescent feels "omnipotential" and develops desires to be of service to his fellow man. These young-sters will be able to tolerate those in the Negro community who do not exert vigorous effort to better their social conditions. Such youngsters, one may anticipate, will find ingenious ways to deal with those Negroes whose positions make them work to keep segre-gation in order that selfishly they can maintain an area of influence and/or security. As children, more Negroes will have seen whites who will be working in such programs as civil rights movements, domestic peace corps, anti-poverty plans. These whites have a wide variety of motivations to work with Negroes ranging from their own fantasies of rescue to the heavy consciences of their parents. Both racial groups will profit by increased contact with each other.

As more teen-agers attempt to move up they will have to come into contact with an increasingly greater number of whites. An in-evitable consequence of such propinquity will be a larger number of interracial romances and marriages. Easier acquisition of im-proved contraceptives will couple with adolescent curiosity and rebellion to heighten interracial sexual experimentation. Being Negro, for more Negroes and whites, will come to mean a more personal confrontation with a host of white and Negro attitudes about interracial sexuality. These attitudes embrace a totality of fear and fascination on the part of both racial persuasions.

The Negro will be more likely to find that his partner is "sex-ually underprivileged," in the sense that the white may seem to exhibit less freedom of expression. The Negro adolescent may then go on to note other things which are positive about being a Negro. For instance, the Negro may realize that Negro groups are gener-ally less inhibited. Hence there are freer body movements, more spontaneity, and easier interpersonal interaction. These are the racial heritage from sustaining what meagre happiness one could snatch when it was available. Thus *being a Negro is being a ro-mantic*—living the moment and preserving it for the eternity, often times without permitting needless and useless regrets.

With this point of romanticism (despite the bleak environment and intrapsychic seething) one is brought to the consideration of Negritude, in the delineation of what it is to be a Negro. Ultimately, as teen-agers in the next 15 years will realize, the search for a refined definition of Negritude will be the major force in re-shaping the Negro's self-image.

Negritude is the philosophical basic science which of course had to precede, by many years, the shouts of Black Power. Black Power stands as one narrow clinical application of the basic science of Negritude. A Negro intellectual observes that, "Historically Negritude may be given the posture of an intellectual nationalism (4). Currently, cognoscenti artists and scholars are engaged in an important social science polemic. They are comparing and attempting to define the similarities and differences of Negritude in Africa, in Latin America, and in the United States. As this concept is clarified it will trickle down to the masses and force a re-shaping of the Negro's image. The teen-ager's usual pathways of communication are in the mainstream to receive this trickle, e.g. as he listens to current jazz records and as he goes to schools taught by those who have been alert to this frenetic activity to define Negritude for African and Afro-descended people all over the world. The sort of evolution one might predict from such influences to Negro youth in the United States will be a gradual broadening of the idea of Black Consciousness to "Colour Consciousness."

The practical necessity of conjoined political action with all colored people may be one result. In 15 years from now the developing teen-ager may be aware of advantages to be gained by collaboration with Puerto Ricans, Mexicans, Indians, and Orientals. The ultimate goal of Negritude might be transcultural experiences which will help lead us toward a functional one-worldism. Although the Negro will be delighted to accept working interchange with all other races in the pursuit of peace, he will grow more proud of his own individuality. This will eliminate feelings of subservience and promote feelings of relaxed confidence in interracial interpersonal relations.

Among the social science intelligentsia who should contribute their own special theories toward the definition of Negritude are psychiatrists and psychologists. It is here that the hidden truths rather than the apparent might be helpful. This paper will not dwell on an outline of the psychodynamic speculations concerning what it is to be a Negro, since lengthy development of these ideas are presented in many places (10). Black symbolizes the dirty, the impure, the dark, and the dangerous. The black man is different and arouses all the terror that a stranger invokes. The black man is viewed as powerful father (the primal scene occurs in blackness) and vengeful father (who will retaliate because the brother horde has bound together to restrict him from access to the women). The black man is a little brother, to be tolerated in his inept attempts toward maturity as long as he poses no threat to the older sibling.

When the psychiatrists and psychologists show and exchange their "hidden truths" with the truths obtained from the vantage point of such disciplines as history, economics, political science, sociology, literature, and philosophy, a substantial contribution will be made to the definition of Negritude. Such efforts doubtlessly will be consummated in the next decade and the results will spill over to the adolescent age group.

Being Negro therefore ends in the incessant search for a better definition of Negritude in order that one can be a contributing and happy member of the society. In realizing this objective, many young Negroes over the next decade and a half will find themselves acting to disabuse whites of certain of their myths.

Some myths will be corrected with relative ease as whites and Negroes have more contact, particularly as Negritude helps to give the Negro a more egosyntonic self-image. The white will learn, not surprisingly, that Negroes do have feelings, that they can be hurt emotionally, that they are not happy to be obliged to be menials. The white will learn that Negroes are not happy to be outsiders in the society. It will hurt many whites to realize that they do not know all about Negroes and that Negroes may be quite complicated human beings. Even more startling to whites may be the realization that Negroes may know whites better than whites know Negroes.

There is one myth, however, that affects the approach to adolescent resolution as well as efforts to improve the lot of the Negro. This myth concerns how much a Negro is underprivileged. Some whites believe certain fortunate Negroes are not underprivileged. This is not true as long as a Negro knows he is not in a truly integrated society. What is true, however, is that all Negroes, even within the same family household, may not be equally under-privileged.

## LEVELS OF PRIVILEGE: BUT EVERYONE CAN GET HIS HEAD WHIPPED

It will be useful for teen-agers in the next quarter of a century to understand that the degree to which they are underprivileged does not necessarily depend upon their socio-economic class or the standard of living to which they are accustomed. Privilege (and "underprivilegedness") will become more and more a matter of aspirational level and attitudinal emphases for the phase of living that one wishes to achieve. The severely underprivileged will be those who permit themselves to be entrapped in despair, depression, and anger. These feelings will be fruitless and result in a devitalization. On the other hand, the youth who cherishes hope will be much less underprivileged. The sources of hope and its fabric of stability derive from love. Somewhere in the child's intra- and interpersonal experiences he must obtain love and confidence. The usefulness of this concept of the relative degrees of "under-privilegedness" is not limited to guidance of the youth. The adults in the society need such a concept to understand the different problems faced by different Negro youths, for the severely, moderately, and minimally underprivileged Negro have different problems and the solutions require sensitivity to the distinctions. Classification of an individual depends on what success his hopes have fathered (and in turn what successes these hopes father).

### The Severely Underprivileged

Their problem is hopelessness in expecting surcease from the harassment by the majority. These individuals are unable to accept even the possibility that whites do not have to disenfranchise, abuse, and project their own unacceptable id impluses onto Ne-groes. *The solution* depends on the swift relief of legal and economic grievances. Unless such opportunity is afforded and administered, difficulties relating to unemployment (over $\frac{1}{3}$ of employable Negroes are unemployed during a year) or broken homes (nearly 40% of Negroes live in a broken home sometime in their lives) will continue. *The penalty* if there is no solution will be riots, violence, discontent on one end of the spectrum, or apathetic acceptance of defeatism by the Negro with resultant paralysis of a large segment of the population in a time when more skills and more productivity are required.

The social psychiatrist who deals with masses of population and concerns himself with the social factors which lead to maladaptation and illness will see that many of the poverty stricken will fall into this category. Yet he knows that in the clinics which will be more and more available to the poor, that many poverty-stricken youths somehow, from highly individual reasons, will not believe themselves so hopeless. One of the major tasks of the community psychiatrists who staff these clinics will be to help the society locate such individuals and generate and sustain psychic power to move up.

## The Moderately Underprivileged

Their problem is satisfaction with limited opportunity and partial acceptance. Many who move up will find themselves in relatively easy economic circumstances and enjoyng a not undignified life. They may tend to not press or not press in the proper manner for the rights which would move the society toward integration. *The solution* depends on social opportunities being provided so that open housing and open school enrollment are accepted without debate. *The penalty* for failure to solve the problem will be to make insoluble the large issues of the next century, such as urban transportation, air pollution, water supply, manpower shortages, etc. Since the whole world will suffer if the United States permits this to happen while proclaiming democracy, America will be discredited in the world community.

The teen-ager with moderate hope will understand that unless people can live everywhere (and be re-located everywhere) we can not begin to eradicate traffic problems or build aqueducts or find enough secretaries or entymologists. For this to happen Negroes must be given better education and more education so that they can get better jobs. With better jobs and concomitant increased wages, many of the stigmata are removed which are now alleged to preclude chances for open housing or open schooling. Some Negro teen-agers will accept this situation, like many other people in the country. They will live adequately and comfortably in semi-disenfranchisement, while observing the havoc such complacency is bringing. Others will join Negroes of other levels of privilege and because of multiple dissatisfactions and anxieties will be more vociferous about the need for the total society to mobilize to the common danger.

## The Least Underprivileged

Their problem is that, despite their hopes to partake of the best things available in the society, they must live with the uncertainty and frustration that even with high skills and genuine culture complete acceptance is denied. *The solution* depends on providing public and private political opportunity to the Negroes. Here "political" is spoken in the Greek sense of pertaining to "polis." The individual must have freedom (that is, to be at liberty) to help his city-state in whatever manner he can. Only in this way can a Negro gain access to the formal and informal channels of information which will permit him to take part in the decision making of the community. In order for such political opportunity to become available the white must change his attitude toward the Negro and the Negroes' potential to contribute to the society. Thus the white has much work to do on his conception of the Negroes' image as the Negro has to do on his self-image. Cotemporaneously, the Negro youth must see that whites are willing and able to modify their attitudes. The least underprivileged teenager will be most likely to comprehend such a possibilty.

## But the Whipped Heads

Yet over the next decade and a half all Negroes will remain underprivileged because they share certain difficulties. They will have, at all levels, more difficulty in obtaining training so that their hope can be raised. They will be thought of as "psychopaths," who believe laws are not made for them and who permit themselves every indulgence, or as "paranoids," who are too quick to see injury and demand satisfactions. They will be thought of as sexual competitors, whose very primitiveness promotes an unfair advantage and fascination.

The sexual fear of whites is a basic conflict. It may be the factor which will bring about a strong white backlash over the events of the civil rights revolution. The excuse for the backlash will be clothed in some other cliché such as "Black Power is a threat," or "They can't live next to us," or "They can't go to school with my daughter," but the result will be the same. The result will be the white community's permission (and encouragement) to its police force to set severe limits to Negroes. This result in large part will be due to the whites' fear of the Negroes' uninhibited sexuality. Elsewhere I have discussed police-community relations in broad terms of psychodynamic theory (7).

During the civil rights revolution I witnessed in Alabama an unprovoked charge by mounted policemen wielding night sticks onto the heads of the unfortunate peaceful demonstrators. I saw such outrages as a horseman running up onto a porch (without a search warrant) and knocking in a door, on the suspicion that a 12-year-old demonstrator had sought refuge in the house. After the charge large numbers of whites showed their appreciation to the police by offering congratulations for a job well done and even asking for autographs from the police heroes.

At this point I realized that the most privileged Negro, the most cultured Negro, the richest Negro, the most influential Negro, the Negro with the most hope were no different than the 12-year-old boy whose head was bashed in. In common they could all suffer the same fate and the white community would applaud and seek autographs.

Almost always a racial conflagration begins because of some action by a policeman. The policeman can do only what the community will sanction. Unless the white community restrains police forces most teen-agers in the next decade and a half, with all the explosiveness of their awareness of discontent, will reflect the desperation they feel by means of extremist actions.

An important question arises: "What can I do so that teen-agers will not fill the streets with blood and terror?"

## WHAT CAN I DO: EVERYONE MUST DO SOMETHING

During the very week that this chapter is being written I have read heated editorials in newspapers in Providence, Rhode Island, New York City, and Richmond, Virginia, on the issue of local police review boards. In all likelihood in the next decade many cities will establish police review boards and ombudsmen to help, among other tasks, to safeguard minority members from needless coercion and disrespect from policemen. At this time it is difficult to esimate whether such experiments in government will become vital to the American democracy. What every black and white person of all ages in the land can do to help the developng teen-ager is to evaluate these ideas and take an educated stance on whether they should be tried and, if so, under what conditions. In short, such an atmosphere of studious evaluation will tune in the teen-ager to the fact that the community is concerned about his protection from the police) and therefore the chance to live with self-respect). The psychology here is an effort to promote certain political attitudes. It reflects the same philosophy as the open-door policy on a mental ward. By attitude and precept the staff first shows its willingness and confidence that the inmate can operate without the odium of the locked door. The Negro teen-ager, to stave off awful consequences of dissatisfaction and anxiety, must receive the same cues from the society so that he understands, from explicit and implicit community behavior, that it too is willing to give him respect and it is confident that such respect will not be misplaced. Only in this way will a dreadful cycle, now developing, be braked.

This cycle also has gained momentum this very week when, on the heels of the knowledge about the shrinking job market, the Negro teen-ager has observed the defeat in Congress of a civil rights bill for the first time in nearly 10 years. His own analysis of this situation will coincide with that of many white and Negro adults of both liberal and conservative loyalty. He will wonder if a cycle is being put into equilibrium: increased resistance by whites to Negro demands ⇆ increased riots and acts of violence (by both whites and Negroes) → increased demands for justice by Negroes. When such a cycle is in equilibrum, the teen-ager will have intensified dissatifaction and anxiety. Unlike his counterpart of a quarter of a century ago he will have witnessed doors being opened and closed at the same time. In terms of mental stability he will not know what to expect in his adult world (even if his desires and wishes are more sharply delineated and whetted). It is known that mental illness often is proportional to the differences between what one expected his adult life to be and what, in reality, he found it to be.

Ancient wisdom categorized the cardinal emotions as being fear, anger, anxiety, and hope. In clinical psychiatry dealing with the first three may consume an inordinately large amount of time. Yet everything in the therapeutic process says to the patient that the doctor is going to work with him to solve troubles. In other words, intrinsic to any therapy is support, supplied in the guise of hope. The society must provide hope to the next generation of adult Negroes. Thus what each individual must do is to tax his own ingenuity to see how, in his own circumstance, he can supply hope and at the same instance give realistic preparation to the Negro child as to what he can expect in adulthood. This is no small or easy job. The dividends, however, will be handsome for the total society. Two areas where hope plus "reality expectation" can be supplied are 1) in preparing Negro youth for transition to a more tolerant society and 2) in preparing Negro youth to interact with whites and vice versa.

Some years ago I outlined what Negroes might do in helping their youth help the society to become "mature" (6). At that time the American society was considered to be in transition on its way to "maturity." The societies' problems were looked at from the viewpoint of similarity to the problems of the individual's transition to adulthood. All the suggestions for the Negro youth are still applicable. It can be added now that whites in their interactions with Negroes might employ some of these same tools. Further, white children should be told what the Negro child is suffering and what he is being taught. Naturally this must be done with utmost delicacy. The white child must be taught that he will live in a pluralistic world. The company he works for may have a major factory in Japan, members of its board in Africa, major sales effort in South America, technological skills concentrated in Europe, and management know-how in Cedar Rapids, Iowa. To prepare for such an eventuality the white child must learn to live and work in the American pluralistic society.

Each individual can determine how he can aid solutions of the racial problems. There are many contributions that could be made and each new idea will spawn others. Throughout this paper reference has been made to such areas as the need to increase verbal and reading skills of the Negro child, the need to use myths to the advantage of the Negro, the need to transform the white and Negroes' attitude about the Negro image, and the need to find more ways of increasing personal contact. During the next decade civic groups will be rearing Negro children to the responsibilities entailed in home owning or games may be developed to show them how to invest in stocks or how to calculate the cost of credit, etc. Other groups may get citizens to debate the pros and cons of guaranteed income or to collaborate on ways to serve the immigrant populations that will be forced to leave the south because of technological displacement. Other community groups may select areas such as increasing adult literacy or teaching Negroes basic law and civil liberties. Some persons will encourage artistic and literary appreciation and expression. There will be much to be done and much will be done. The adolescent will receive a large share of such benefits.

Some institutions such as the church or neighborhood centres will become community hubs for this sort of adolescent-helping action. Already in Watts in Los Angeles, a Negro community psychiatrist can proudly exhibit the moves being made in this direction (2). What is striking is that in such centres, which look much like traditional settlement houses, the climate is energetic and invigorating. There is conscious emphasis, which all accept, as to the need for education. There is conscious awareness of the need to be proud of being black. There is implicit acceptance that it will usually be necessary for the black to prepare to be *better* than a white counterpart if he is to achieve "equal" consideration. That is, whether one is competing for a position on a football team or whether he is trying to be a certified public accountant, in order to get the job the Negro must show more than a white would have to show in order to get the same job. These manoeuvers permit hope to be projected while reality expectation is undistorted. Of course such centres in themselves play only a small role in ameliorating dissatisfacton and anxiety.

The overall objective will be to give each Negro sufficient self-respect so that he can become a couth, refined, contributing member of the community. All persons can work on general areas for social improvement. At an educational level one can work toward better education. Such work may mean scrapping historical ideas such as the concept of neighbourhood schools and then supplying a more useful system. At an economic level one can labor toward seeing that Negroes have the same job opportunities and income benefits. This may mean getting involved in training schools or tutorial programs, for instance. At a political level each citizen can exercise democratic prerogatives and think through and work for effective legislation. Open housing is a must not only to increase the incentives for Negroes to become couth, refined, and contributing but also to save the inner city. At a psychological level one must see what he can do to promote ideas of dignity and respect between the races. This may mean lecturing one's own children or correcting mass media when they persist in doing things which are ruinous to mutual respect between the races. However, it means more often demonstrating initial trust, confidence, and acceptance to each individual of the opposite race whenever in contact. As more persons prove their humanity to each other, more interracial contacts will be made and more contacts will become meaningful. Our country will be strengthened when it becomes totally democratic.

## PAX AMERICANA: THE ALTERNATIVE TO DISSATISFACTION AND ANXIETY

America must choose between leading the world to an unparalleled period of peace and technical accomplishments or having a labile, volatile youthful segment capable of disrupting the domestic tranquility. Unlike their elders this group will understand the urgency of their situation in terms of immediate redress of grievances before the world passes them by. Unlike their elders they will have knowledge of how civil rights protests led to a definite "protest psychology" which fitted well with both the trends of the time and natural adolescent rebellion and idealism. If some protesting worked in civil rights or resulted in changing higher educational systems perhaps more protesting will lead to a more equitable sharing of the advantages and responsibilities in the society.

To make this choice white America must see that the *sine qua non* for racial relations is "respect." Of course respect is a bilateral channel and Negroes must give it also to Whites. However, direction and leadership for this crucial element must come from the white community. If it does not both races will live in unremitting tension and conflict. America will be paralyzed to solve its basic and vital problems relating to transportation, air pollution, food distribution, waste disposal, improved education, water supply, etc. Perhaps the largest loss is unable to be calculated. Millions of Negroes are not now able to contribute as much as they could (and would like) to making America stronger and better. Now untold energy is consumed by the need to remember one's race and to estimate how race is or will affect even the most minute aspects of daily life. With what energy there is left over many can feel only helpless and hopeless.

Communications and technology have foreshortened the world. More people are fated to have contacts with persons alien to their native land. All of the humankind will become the province of every individual. The Negro teen-ager of the next decade and a half will find it increasingly necessary to defend American social systems.

Everywhere Americans go today they are perplexed by the anti-American attitudes which seem so rampant. As an American I have been equally confused and bewildered—and angry—since I know we are a people with kindly intentions. However, I get an additional communication. I find, to my astonishment, that I am an object of pity. It matters not if I am talking to an African diplomat or a Thai physician or a South American Indian. The message is the same as one given to my family by a Swiss family we chanced to meet on a mountain top in Switzerland. "How," they asked, "can you live in America? Why don't you leave the United States?" they wished to know. Even at the South Pole I was called upon by a New Zealander to defend and explain America's racial policy, which he believed was far more primitive and harsh than the way the Maori are treated in New Zealand. To my astonishment I could not garner sufficient argument or reason to dissuade him of his belief.

If America is to lead the world to peace it must not be placed in a position to answer such questions from friendly, hostile, or neutral host nationals. Opportunities granted to the next generation of Negroes will speak with more persuasion than the tongue of a traveller.

If anyone has read this far he may decide, correctly, that the author believes more has to be done and done quickly and thoroughly to prevent extensive social ugliness. Such a reader also may correctly decide that this essay is too highly biased with the subjective. All that can be answered is that subjective and impassioned bias may be truthful and if so it in no way, in itself, removes the potential national unpleasantness which will have such adverse international effects. Such consequences will influence the lives of white and Negro teen-agers.

Finally, a reader may decide, again correctly, that the author was in the category of least underprivileged persons and that he had the benefit of having a formal education for two and a half decades in situations common only to 10% of our entire population. For this reason, although unhappiness is commented upon, optimism reigns as queen.

As I contrast the opportunities and social regard that were available to Negroes in my father's time with those of the present, I am delighted and pleased beyond words. Having hope, I anticipate that solutions will be actualized and that progress in racial amity will continue on an upward slope despite little declivities on the "sociograph." Having hope, I anticipate that my teen-agers, like all Negro teen-agers in the next decade and a half, will resolve their adolescent conflicts in such a manner that our world will benefit. Having hope, I anticipate that my children, in adult years, will feel accepted (not just tolerated) in whatever community they choose to live. Having hope, I am audacious enough to anticipate that my grandchildren will live in an "integrated" society where no one has an anxious thought any day of his life about the color of his skin. For such hopes to be achieved the Negro teen-ager today needs especially careful attention and guidance. Then a nation which can send a man to the moon will know enough to allow one human being to live next to another human being.

## REFERENCES

1. Bimmer, A. F.: Economic Progress in Black and White. Presented at the Anual Banquet of the Houston Citizen's Chamber of Commerce, January 21, 1966, Houston, Texas.
2. Cannon, J. A.: Department of Psychiatry, U.C.L.A., Los Angles, Calif. Personal tour for the author.
3. Knowles, J. A.: The Medical Center and the Community Health Center, Bulletin of the New York Academy of Medicine, *40:* 713–742, 1964.
4. Lucas, W. F.: Department of Comparative Literature, New School for Social Research, New York, N.Y., Personal communication to the author.
5. New York Times News Service, September 2, 1966.
6. Pierce, C. M.: A psychiatric approach to present day racial problems. Journal of National Medical Association, *51:* 207–210, 1959.
7. Pierce, C. M.: Police-community relations. Mental Hygiene, *46:* 107–115, 1962.
8. Pierce, C. M. and West L. J.: Six years of sit-ins: Psychodynamic causes and effects. International Journal of Social Psychiatry, *12:* 29–34, 1966.
9. Poussaint, A. F.: The Negro American: His Self-Image and Integration. Presented at the 71st Annual Meeting of the National Medical Association, August 8, 1966, Chicago, Ill.
10. West, L. J.: The Psychobiology of Racial Violence. Presented at the 121st Annual Meeting of the American Psychiatric Association, May 4, 1965, New York, N.Y.

# The Puerto Rican— American Teenager in New York City

EDWARD PREBLE

THIS REPORT on Puerto Rican adolescents in New York City is based upon an association with Puerto Ricans in the city over a 10-year period. Except for two special studies, this association has not been part of a systematic research program. The data, observations, and conclusions have resulted from contacts related to direct service programs and from voluntary personal and social relationships which grew out of these contacts.

The Puerto Rican people reported on here are from four different communities in New York City, all of them low-income, slum neighbourhoods. The average median family income for families in these four communities is under $3500, as compared to $6000 for New York City at large. Other average population characteristics for the four communities include: public welfare recipients—four times the city rate; juvenile offenses—three times the city rate; unemployment—two times the city rate; sub-standard housing—two times the city rate; no schooling—two times the city rate; median school years completed—8 years, as compared to 10 for the city.

These figures reflect population characteristics of all people from the four communities, Puerto Ricans and non-Puerto Ricans. The figures for Puerto Ricans alone would reveal a more deprived condition.

This report, then, is primarily concerned with lower-class, socially deprived Puerto Ricans, and the information and conclusions apply only to them. However, since the median family income of Puerto Ricans in all of New York City is only $3800, these people are a fair representation of Puerto Rican culture in the city.

The relationship of the writer to the subjects of this report has been that of a participant-observer, both in the systematic and the natural, informal phases of the study. The essence of the methodology—if it can be called that—is, in William F. Whyte's words, "the observation of interpersonal events" (26). Whenever possible, psychodynamic data were elicited from the subjects by the ultilization of some of the techniques used by Abram Kardiner and his associates in their studies of primitive and modern cultures (8). The central feature of this methodology is the psycho-diagnostic life history interview with individual subjects.

The following is an illustration of this combined approach. A 20-year-old male Puerto Rican was enlisted as a combination research informant and Spanish language tutor for the writer. The lessons and life history interviews took place after dinner in the tenement apartment of the informant's family, a three-room apartment which was inhabited in the evening by members of the extended family, their friends, and a pet chicken. On an average there were six adults and eight children present during these evening visits. The Spanish lesson involved memorizing about 30 conversational sentences which the informant-tutor had written down spontaneously on the previous visit. In addition to their intended use, these lessons produced informative projective material from the subject by way of the "free association" involved in his making up the lesson, a typical unanticipated yield in this kind of research. After his lesson the writer visited and interviewed the other members of the family and their friends. He had other contacts with this family and their friends at weddings, baptismal parties, and other social events.

Along with this formal and deliberate attempt to gain knowledge about Puerto Ricans in New York City, the writer has simply absorbed information through personal and social relationships. For example, one group of about 20 Puerto Rican boys became known to him 10 years ago when he was engaged as a youth worker with street gangs. This professional relationship lasted for 2 years, but the personal association with almost all of these boys has continued to the present day and has been extended to their families, wives, and children. Exchange social visits between the writer's family and the subjects' families have been a regular feature of this association.

## HISTORY AND CULTURE OF PUERTO RICO

Puerto Rico is a small tropical island at the eastern end of the Great Antilles, situated at the approaches to the Caribbean Sea and the Isthmus of Panama. It was discovered by Columbus in 1493. The island was inhabited by the Arawak Indians and periodically by the seagoing Carib Indians. Spanish colonization of the island began in 1508 and the island was held by the Spanish until 1898, when it was ceded to the United States as a result of the Spanish-American War. In 1917 Puerto Rico was made a "Free, Associated State" of the United States, a status which provides United States citizenship.

Puerto Rico has always had an agricultural economy, based largely on sugar production. Other major crops produced are coffee, tobacco, and fruits. Since 1940 there has been a great amount of industrialization, especially in the metal working, electrical, agricultural processing, and textile industries. The growth and production of the economy has, until recently, never been able to keep pace with the high birthrate among Puerto Ricans.

The racial characterstics found among Puerto Ricans are derived from three major sources: indigenous Indians, white Spanish colonizers, and Negro slaves. Combinations from these sources have resulted in many gradations of skin color, hair texture, and facial structure. Five major divisions of racial definition are recognized by Puerto Ricans; these are: 1) *moreno* (black skin, kinky hair); 2) *indio* (bronze skin, straight hair); 3) *trigueño* (brown skin, curly hair); 4) *grifo* (light skin, kinky hair); and 5) *blanco* (white skin, straight hair). Broad facial features are always present in *moreno* and sometimes in *trigueño* and *grifo*. Narrow features are always present in *indio* and *blanco* and sometimes in *trigueño* and *grifo*.

The culture of Puerto Rico is Spanish. The outstanding cultural traditions are the Spanish language, Catholic religion, extended family cohesion, male dominance, double standard, pre-marital female chastity, dignity, and hospitality. Their concern for pride and dignity results in an inordinate embarrassment when they are made to look foolish, either by their own actions or by those, such as family members, whose actions reflect on them. Because of their well-known proclivity for gossiping, any mistake is fully exploited. Referring to the Puerto Rican's love of gossip, one Puerto Rican man said: "Every last one of them gossips. When they were born, they were told, 'this is what you got to do—gossip.' "

Puerto Rican people generally are easygoing and friendly, but they are also quick-tempered. They tend to believe in fate, destiny, and luck, and are consequently undoctrinaire.

The election of Muñoz Marin to the presidency of the Puerto Rican Senate in 1940 marked the beginning of a social and economic development in Puerto Rico which, in one generation, has transformed a 450-year-old culture. Over this period, Puerto Rico has changed from an agrarian colony of the United States to a commercial and industrial partner. The resulting circular migration of Puerto Ricans to and from the United States has accelerated the changes in cultural institutions and behavioral patterns which normally accompany a social and economic transformation.

### PUERTO RICAN MIGRATION TO NEW YORK

Puerto Rican people have been arriving in New York City in large numbers since the middle of World War II, and they now number over 600,000, about 8% of the city's population. They came mainly as a result of the great demand during and after the war for manpower in the United States. The institution of regular air transportation between San Juan and New York at the end of the war made it possible to travel to New York for a fare of $50, which greatly facilitated the migration movement. From 1940 to 1960, the Puerto Rican population in the city grew from 70,000 to 600,000. Twenty percent of all Puerto Ricans now live in New York City. Better than one out of 10 youths in the city between the ages of 15 and 20 years is of Puerto Rican birth or parentage.

There is a natural breakdown of three groups among Puerto Ricans in New York, depending upon when they immigrated. There is the old immigrant group whose members came to New

York as adults before the Second World War and brought their children with them. A second group comprises those who either were born in New York or were brought to New York at an early age. The third group consists of those who have immigrated recently. Sophisticated Puerto Rican adolescents on the street refer to these three groups, respectively, as 1) "Coolo Rican," 2) "Progresso Rican," and 3) "Jivo Rican." "Coolo" is derived from "cool" and implies that these people have been here a long time and are well-adjusted. "Progresso" is derived from "progress" and refers to the fact that these people, being American-born and educated, are in a good position to move ahead fiancially and socially. "Jivo" is derived from the street argot word "jive," which is a term used to describe the act of ridiculing someone.

In New York the first two groups tend to be contemptuous of the third group, whose members must prove themselves in New York before they are accepted. As a rule they must earn this acceptance without help from members of the first two groups. In referring to the refusal of a "Progresso Rican" to help a "Jivo Rican" on a job, one man said: "Instead of 'pulling the guy's coat' (enlightening him) as to what is going on, he didn't do that. Each man is for himself." Besides "Jivo Rican," members of the recent immigrant group are called "hicks," "*jibaro*" (hillbilly), "*acoiris*" (rainbow, referring to the brightly colored clothes favored by recent Puerto Rican immigrants), "*aguacate*" (avocado), and "Marine Tiger" (referring to the Liberty freight ship that transported Puerto Ricans to New York before the institution of regular air travel)—all derogatory references to their native Puerto Rican heritage.

The isolation of recent Puerto Rican immigrants from the established Puerto Rican groups is a prominent feature of Puerto Rican culture in New York City. A common complaint that one hears from Puerto Ricans is that in New York Puerto Rican people do not "stick together." This estrangement also occurs in many cases to members of the same extended family, who have arrived in New York over varying lengths of time. Oscar Lewis reports the case of a family member recently arrived in New York who at the outset was treated hospitably by close relatives who were long-time residents of New York. The newcomer, however, was suspicious of this hospitality and expressed a belief that it would not last for long. She was right. As a rule, friends and relatives recently arrived from Puerto Rico are accepted only if they do not constitute a burden on those already here.

In the Puerto Rican working community in New York there is a similar indifference and hostility on the part of established Puerto Ricans toward newcomers. In the garment factories, for example, Puerto Rican foremen are considered by other Puerto Ricans to be the worst to work for. They much prefer the Italian and Jewish foremen. A Puerto Rican foreman is often referred to as a *jodón* ("ball-breaker").

Toward the Cubans and Dominicans, the other two major groups of Spanish-speaking people in New York, Puerto Ricans have very different opinions and relationships. They dislike the Cubans because, to them, the Cubans appear to act superior and "high-class." Puerto Ricans complain that even now when the Cubans "are down" (referring to the political changes in Cuba), they still think they are better than other Spanish-speaking people, especially the Puerto Ricans. One young Puerto Rican man said of the Cubans, "I have never met one who did not say he had a college education." Toward the Dominicans, on the other hand, Puerto Ricans have a friendly, sympathetic feeling based on the belief that they, like the Puerto Ricans, are "simple people," that is, modest and unpretentious.

### RELATIONS OF PUERTO RICANS TO NON-PUERTO RICANS

As the most recent significantly large minority group in the city Puerto Ricans are objects of suspicion and hostility. That they speak a different language reinforces the predisposition of their non-Puerto Rican neighbors to regard them with suspicion. As one man, a second generation Russian, put it: "You never know what they are talking about; in the old days around here you would hear Italians and Jews talking together in their own language but you would hear a few American words in between and that was okay." One of the derogatory terms applied to Puerto Ricans in New York is "parakeet," referring to their fast-spoken, unfamiliar language. Because of their unusual concern for not making mistakes and "looking bad," Puerto Ricans are especially sensitive about their imperfect English and are easily discouraged about learning.

Another cause of lower-class hostility toward Puerto Ricans is the fact that they are relatively eager competitors in the labor market; they work fast and for minimum wages. In this respect they are known, again in a derogatory way, as "dashers." Italian immigrants in New York, especially in the construction field, were called "zips," for the same reason. A man of Irish descent who had been replaced as a truck driver's helper by a Puerto Rican said: "The Spanish want to work fast because they are hot blooded. They come from a hot climate and all they know is go, go, go. Like me, I take it easy but they want to go, go, go."

The following excerpt from an interview with an Italian informant is a good example of the automatic prejudice directed at Puerto Ricans:

Question: "How did the old timers in the neighborhood react to the Puerto Rican people coming in?"

Answer:    "They didn't like it, what with the crime and all they brought in. They were afraid."

Question: "Do you mean to say there was little crime in the neighborhood before the Puerto Ricans moved in?"

Answer:    "It was the worst. Dutch Schultz and Vincent Cole and a lot more of those guys were around. There was a lot more crime then. They were a bunch of hard killers and all. Dutch Schultz used to use the park over there to dump his bodies in."

### RACIAL IDENTITY IN NEW YORK

Racial identification is a major problem for Puerto Ricans in New York. Although only about 4% of the Puerto Ricans in New York City are listed in official census figures as non-white, the many gradations of skin color, hair texture, and facial structure make a simple distinction difficult. As stated above, there are five major sub-divisions of Puerto Rican racial definition recognized by Puerto Ricans. Their white neighbors are less discriminating; in their eyes all Puerto Ricans, at best, are "half white, half black." Puerto Ricans in New York refer to themselves as "Spanish" rather than Puerto Rican mainly in the interest of avoiding the color stigma.

Although most Puerto Ricans will deny that they are prejudiced about color, close observation and questioning usually reveals a keen sense of color consciousness. This is true in Puerto Rico as well as in New York. The skin color, eye color, and hair texture of a new baby are matters of great anticipation and concern among family members. Of these three features it is the texture of the hair that is most important. It is a common belief among lower-class Puerto Ricans that hair characteristics are determined by the father. Because of this it is a general rule that the man can marry someone with kinkier hair than his, but the woman cannot—all in the interest, in both cases, of "improving the family." In a popular, old song, entitled: "Where is Your Grandmother," a dark-skinned Puerto Rican chides a light-skinned Puerto Rican about the latter's kinky-haired grandmother who is not allowed to show herself on the balcony because of the desire of the family to conceal the "Negro blood" in the family.

When New York Puerto Ricans visit Puerto Rico they prefer to go in the late winter or early spring, when their skin is the whitest. This puts them at a relative "advantage" over their counterparts in Puerto Rico.

In view of these concerns it is an interesting irony that Puerto Rican people, like some other Spanish-speaking people, use the terms *Negro* and *Negra*, or the diminutives, *Negrito* and *Negrita*, as terms of endearment for loved ones, such as, a spouse, sweetheart, or child. On the other hand, the terms *blanquito* and *blanquita* (referring to the color white) are used as derogatory terms applied to those who assume an attitude of self-importance.

Despite the concern about color among their own people, and despite the fact that they suffer discrimination in New York from an identification with the American Negro, Puerto Ricans have a friendly, sympathetic relationship with Negroes in New York. Adolescents, especially, tend to follow the life-style of the Negro with respect to language, dress, music, and dancing. The current language of the street among Negroes and Puerto Ricans is a combination of the "bop" talk of the Harlem jazz crowd of the forties, the "hip" talk of recent years, and a miscellany of terms from the drug addict and prison sub-cultures. In dress, the street fashion leaders study the Madison Avenue models and make up their own outfits, using the same style of clothes but putting them in different combinations. As one boy put it: "They mix up different styles, different colors, different shirts; they dress the model all over again." The music today is "rock-jazz" and the dancing to it is free and spontaneous, erotic but with no physical contact.

A hard test of the relationships between racial and ethnic groups in New York occurs in prison, where group differences, prejudices, and hostilities are greatly magnified. The values, codes, and mores of the inmate sub-culture are based on exaggerated group loyalties. An Irish boy and a Negro boy, for example, may be good friends on the street but when they are in prison together they cannot associate with each other. If they ignore this prison code they are marked as "creeps" by the other inmates and either ostracized or abused. A Negro man explained it this way: "I may know you (a white man) for twenty years. Like I get 'busted' (arrested) with you and all of a suddden you see me pulling away towards my own group. And you might say: 'this dude here he don't want to know me,' but that's not the reason, it's because jail separates you; you feel what you feel, but jail separates you."

This separation of ethnic groups in prison applies to Negroes and Puerto Ricans but in a modified form. Cross-group associations are not automatically condemned, and the one group identifies with the other in a crisis, such as a fight with white inmates, even if it does not intervene. If, for example, Puerto Ricans are fighting non-Puerto Rican whites, the Negroes will not intervene on the side of Puerto Ricans at the outset, but they will "ready up" in case the fight spreads, in which case they will join the Puerto Ricans. The Negroes believe, often correctly, that the cause of such a fight must be a racial slur against the Puerto Ricans, and they identify with their insulted position. As one Negro explained it: "Whatever 'went down' (caused the fight), it's something that we felt before, something that we're sweating for the same reason, something that wasn't correct that we have no power over, like our color or religion or the way we talk, the way we live. Something funny 'went down.'" It is this identification on the basis of color and discrimination which unites the Negroes and Puerto Ricans in New York and which has resulted in an almost common sub-culture, especially among adolescents.

## PHYSICAL CONDITIONS IN NEW YORK

The physical conditions in New York, particularly the climate, have important effects on Puerto Rican people. In contrast to the tropical climate of Puerto Rico, New York is considered cold by Puerto Ricans for much of the year. A common complaint is about the "pain in the bones" due to the cold weather. There are temperamental as well as physical reactions to the cold. A character in the Puerto Rican play "The Ox Cart," by Rene Marques (12) expressed a common belief about the effects of the New York climate on Puerto Ricans when she said: "It must be that the cold oppresses a person's heart. Grandpa used to say that the heart can dry up like an old bean. But here it don't dry up. It freezes. It freezes up like ice. And that's even worse." Puerto Ricans say that in New York one's blood turns to ice, and that the icy blood of "Americans" accounts for their (imputed) passivity with respect to sex, fighting, and other emotional expressions.

There are also important secondary consequences of the cold weather, a main one being that the children stay in the house much of the time and interfere with the privacy of the parents. In Puerto Rico the children play outside most of the time and are not around the house—as one woman put it—"to hear all the family troubles." On a typical cold day in New York—even in the fall or spring—the family will all be inside being warmed by supplemental heat from the open gas burners on the kitchen stove. Kettles of water are put over the burners to produce steam for the apartment. This practice is the cause of many tenement fires.

Neighborhood settlement patterns in New York present problems to Puerto Ricans which they did not have in the urban areas of Puerto Rico. Because of financial limitations—at least in the beginning—and because of discrimination, Puerto Ricans from different family and class backgrounds live together in the same neighborhoods. Although this integration is seen by liberal and sophisticated Puerto Ricans as an improvement over the community segregation between the classes in Puerto Rico, the average Puerto Rican complains that "the good are thrown in with the bad, and the good suffer." This is a reference both to the exploitation of working people by criminals and delinquents and to the susceptibility of young people to the delinquent activities of "the street."

In addition to the major problems of race, hostility, discrimination, language, climate, housing, and employment, Puerto Ricans also experience the discomforts and irritations shared by all New Yorkers, such as the noise, dirt, crowdedness, and hurried confusion. A recent juke box song, "47.50"* (the price of an airplane ticket to Puerto Rico) sums up a common Puerto Rican attitude about New York:

Forty seven fifty for the aeroplane
Forty seven fifty for the aeroplane
Forty seven fifty for the aeroplane
If I had the money I go home again.

(1)

I was born in Puerto Rico
In the mountains near the sky
When I think how sweet my country
I so sad I almost cry.

(2)

Here they push me in the subway
Why they angry all the time?
When I go for employment
Make me go in back of line.

(3)

You are laughing at my English
I don't blame you man it's true
When you come to my island
You got funny accent too.

(4)

In my country there is sunshine
Everybody singin' songs
If you skin has some colour
They ain't gonna treat you wrong,
If you skin has some colour
They ain't gonna treat you wrong.

* Reprinted by permission of G & F Music, Inc. (© 1965, G & F Music, Inc., ASCAP).

## EDUCATION AND EMPLOYMENT

Over 60% of the employed Puerto Rican males in New York City are either factory operators or service workers, a condition which is reflected in the median income for Puerto Rican males of $2900. Ten percent of the male Puerto Rican labor force is unemployed. A significant factor in this economic picture is that 93% of the male Puerto Rican labor force in New York City were born in Puerto Rico and most of them received either no education or inadequate education in the United States. The most important educational deficit for those born and raised in Puerto Rico is their lack of competence in the English language.

With adequate education and training in New York a young Puerto Rican man or woman can find employment, and with further training and experience he or she can move up to a position of responsibility which is personally satisfying and financially rewarding. Few Puerto Ricans will deny that, with the qualifications, there are satisfactory job and career opportunities in New York. But those who had the opportunity for an adequate education here, whether they took advantage of it or not, constitute perhaps 10% of the total Puerto Rican labor force.

Because of the proximity of Puerto Rico there is an opportunity for circular migration which most immigrant groups in the United States have not had. This has had an important effect on the economic adaptation of Puerto Ricans both here and in Puerto Rico. On the positive side, those who have little opportunity in Puerto Rico to save money for security or capital investment can, with patience, ability, effort, and sacrifice, save the money here and return to Puerto Rico with the means to improve their lives there. On the negative side, there are those less patient who become discouraged with what they consider to be their "bad luck," either here or in Puerto Rico, collect a week's pay, and buy an airplane ticket, with about the same expectation with which, in Puerto Rico, they buy a lottery ticket or, in New York, play "the numbers." The opportunity to gamble which cheap circular migration affords, has a negative effect on sustained adaptational effort.

Evidence of the extent of circular migration is found in the hybridization of language by Puerto Ricans. Spanish words are made out of Enlish words—*el caucho* (couch), *la furnitura* (furniture), *cigarillos con filtro* (filter cigarettes), *el roofo* (roof), *la marqueta* (market), *hangiando* (hanging around), *cheatión* (cheater), *parqueate* (park here). Sentences and phrases often contain both Spanish and English words—*el otro way* (the other way), *no lo trusteès* (don't trust him), *vota la garbage afuera* (throw the garbage out). Sometimes a Spanish idiom will be patterned after an English one, such as the phrases, *te veo* (see you) and *cojelo suave* (take it easy), which are used in taking leave of someone. *El hombre* (the man) refers to the police, as does *la Hara*, which is supposedly derived from the name of a well-known, unpopular policeman by the name of O'Hara who worked in a Puerto Rican neighborhood. *"Cuidado! la Hara!"* ("Watch out! The police!") is a common cry on the street.

## THE FAMILY IN NEW YORK

The most significant result of social, cultural, and economic conditions in New York for Puerto Ricans is the downgrading of the Puerto Rican male. The disadvantages of the Puerto Rican man compared to other men with regard to employment and social acceptance in New York have important consequences for all members of the family. In order to survive in New York, the average husband-wife pair with children must jointly contribute to the family income or obtain welfare assistance. The tradition of male dominance in the Puerto Rican family is difficult to maintain in the many cases where the female members of the family are contributing at least an equal share of the financial support. The man can remain as head of the family only if he is bringing the money home. The Puerto Rican male's sense of pride and self-esteem is, to a large extent, dependent upon his culturally prescribed dominant role in the family. The sudden reduction and, in some cases, reversal of this role in the family can cripple his confidence and self-esteem and render him ineffective as a family figure. A frequent result of this development is that the man of the family leaves the home, either voluntarily or under pressure from his wife. When this occurs the wife either goes to work or obtains welfare assistance, or both, and, more than likely, improves the financial condition of the family. With two or more children, for example, it is possible for a woman to receive welfare benefits amounting to over $60 a week, which is more than the take-home pay of many Puerto Rican factory and service workers. A Puerto Rican woman being supported by welfare assistance will say, often proudly, "I am living with "Wilfredo" (a common male Puerto Rican name), jokingly referring to the city Welfare Department. In a Puerto Rican neighborhood in New York, the 1st and the 15th of each month are known as *dia de las madres* (mother's day) because those are the days that the Welfare Department checks arrive in the mail. These days are also known as *dia del fenómeno* (the day of the phenomenon).

One-fifth of the adults and one-third of the children in the study areas are on the Welfare Department rolls. One of the worst humiliations that some Puerto Rican men suffer occurs in those cases where the man is living with a woman who has represented herself to the Welfare Department as living alone, and he must either stay away from the house during the day, or hide, in order to avoid detection by the Welfare Department investigator.

Puerto Rican men sometimes say that they live *a la cañona* (under the gun) in New York, referring to conditions of social constraint. This phrase also refers to acts which result from a contrary impulse generated by frustration and desperation. Thus a man who suddenly acts out his rage against someone or something will say later, "I did it *a la cañona*."

A study by Malzberg of first admission rates of Puerto Ricans to New York State mental hospitals showed that over a period of 2 years the admissions of males over females were 22% higher (11). A different but impressive kind of evidence for the relatively unfavorable impact of New York immigration on the Puerto Rican man can be found in New York City Puerto Rican folklore. In the song "America"† from *West Side Story*, a polemical dialogue between Puerto Rican boys and girls takes place regarding the features of New York life. In this dialogue, the girls have all the positive lines and the boys have all the negative lines about Puerto Rican life in New York:

† Reprinted by permission of G. Schirmer, Inc. (© 1957, L. Berntstein and S. Sondheim).

Girls:  Everything boom in America, industry
        boom in America.
Boys:   Twelve in a room in America.
Girls:  A new house with more space.
Boys:   Lots of doors slamming in our face.
Girls:  I'll get a stylish apartment.
Boys:   Better get rid of your accent.
Girls:  Life can be bright in America.
Boys:   If you can fight in America.
Girls:  Life is all right in America.
Boys:   If you're all white in America.
Girls:  Here you are free and you have rights.
Boys:   So long as you stay on your side.
Girls:  Free to be anything you choose.
Boys:   Free to wait tables and shine shoes.
        Everything grime in America
        Look at the crime in America
        Terrible time in America.

The symptomatic behavior of Puerto Rican men in New York tends to be aggressive rather than depressive. Drinking, gambling, fighting, and promiscuity are common manifestations of attempts to maintain their *hombria* (manhood). Puerto Rican women are usually aware of the compensatory nature of this behavior. They say that in New York, Puerto Rican men become more promiscuous than they were in Puerto Rico, because they are trying to "prove something." Even though they may understand the motivation behind the promiscuity, Puerto Rican women in New York are not inclined to be as tolerant about it as they were in Puerto Rico, where they were dependent upon the man for support. Here they can find employment or go to the Welfare Department for support. One young Puerto Rican man was surprised when his wife left him because of his association with other women: "I felt that wasn't a good enough reason for breaking up our marriage; you have to expect that from a man: I felt that as long as I did everything for my family—no matter how much I 'messed around' on the street—that it would never lead to anything important." In New York, a married man is a *picaflor* (ladies' man, lit. "hummingbird") at the risk of losing his wife.

As the father loses his authority in the family, the mother and the children are likely to exploit the situation by engaging in social activities outside the house. The woman may join a social group on the "stoop," in the beauty parlor, or even in a bar; the children join cliques on the street and in the candy stores. In the case of a socializing mother or adolescent daughter, the father becomes the object of neighborhood gossip, which diminishes his pride, dignity, and self-esteem.

The breakdown of the hierarchial, paternalistic, and self-centered family traditions among Puerto Ricans in the immediate family also applies to the extended family and to the institution of the *Padrino* (godfather) who, in Puerto Rico, is a key figure iin the cohesion of the family. A similar lack of mutual responsibility and respect extends to the immediate community of the family as well. In Puerto Rico it is expected that unrelated neighbors in the family's community take responsibility in the parents' absence for caring for and disciplining the neighbors' children. This is not true in New York, where the tendency is to "mind one's own business." A 36-year-old Puerto Rican man said: "In my time when I was a kid it was hard for a kid to get into trouble, because kids had a lot of respect for older people. Like say you're a neighbor and you know my father, and you see me doing something wrong; you come up to me and say, 'that's wrong, you don't do this.' I would obey because I wouldn't want you to tell my father because then my father would beat me up."

Any latent dissatisfaction and hostility that Puerto Rican women may have as a result of their former subjugation in Puerto Rico can develop freely in New York. Recent female immigrants are regarded suspiciously by long-time female residents of New York because of the belief that the newcomers are overly eager to exploit their newly found freedom in a reversal of the double standard and they do not appreciate the competition. This is an exaggerated fear, but it has some foundation.

Although the women and the children in the family may experience an initial sense of relief and freedom with the collapse of male authority in the family, they pay a price for their emancipation. An absent or ineffective father leaves a void which cannot be filled. This disadvantage weighs most heavily on the adolescent male in the Puerto Rican family. He has lost a pattern for his male respect and identity and, in many cases, is encouraged to identify with the mother. Even in Puerto Rico there is a tendency for the women to teach children to depend upon the mother and to distrust the father.

There are also problems for adolescents in these cases where the father is able to maintain his dominant position in the family. Both the women and the children observe around them in New York the relative freedom which their counterparts have, and in this new cultural context experience a dissatisfaction which they had not felt in Puerto Rico, where the culture at large supported the tradition of male dominance. Under these circumstances the mother and the children often conspire to evade the rigid attempts of the father to control them. In the case of an adolescent girl, a mother will frequently become a partner to the girl's attempts to establish relationships with boys outside the home. For example, the mother and daugher, under the pretense of taking a walk or going to the store, will meet a boy at some appointed time and place and the mother will conveniently disappear. In these cases, it is usually obvious that the mother, besides helping her daughter, enjoys some vicarious satisfaction from the conspiracy. One strict Puerto Rican father who discovered such a conspiracy referred to his wife and adolescent daughter as *bandidas* (bandits). Mothers who perform this function for their daughters are commonly called *alcahuetas* (pimps).

In the case of the strict, old-fashioned families it is the girl rather than the boy who suffers the most social and psychological pressure. At the courtship age she commonly has three choices: she can stay "upstairs" (in the house), she can attempt to deceive the parents regarding her activities outside, or she can marry at a young age. One girl who spent part of her adolescence in Puerto Rico and part of it in New York preferred Puerto Rico, because there the houses are usually only one story high and one can escape out the window, whereas in New York one is usually several stories up. In those cases where the home is several stories up, the parents in an old-fashioned family will always sleep in the room which leads to the fire escape, thus preventing a surreptitious exit by the children. A girl in this situation does not have an opportunity for free and honest associations with her peers, both male and female. She may, with permission, bring a boy home to meet the family (an act known as *la entrada*) but when she does this it constitutes an announcement of their intentions to marry. In some families, if she does not marry the first one she brings home, she does not get a second chance for a family-approved marriage.

The social alternatives of the adolescent Puerto Rican girl are determined more by the family than is the case with the boy. If she is from an old-fashioned family and does not try to evade the strict family authority, which in effect prohibits social relationships outside the home, she waits for the opportunity to get married, which she usually does at an early age. In this case, the adolescent period of social experimentation common to American culture is denied her. She becomes a housewife and mother and her future depends, to a large extent, on the kind of man she marries. One girl who is determined to avoid such an early marriage said: "I don't want to end up like my sister. My sister got married when she was sixteen, the age I am now. Right now she looks three years older because of all the suffering she has done. She is only very young. No matter what this life we have here, it is to suffer. We always have problems, but I don't want to start now, I want to start from eighteen up." When another young woman raised in the old-fashioned way was asked if she were happy staying "upstairs" during those adolescent years, she answered: "Sure, I wasn't happy, I wasn't sad; I didn't have no choice."

A girl from an old-fashioned family who rebels and finds devious ways periodically to escape the authority and surveillance of the family is likely to get into more trouble on the streets than are Puerto Rican girls raised in any other way, because she is overly eager to show her peers, both boys and girls, that she is "hip." Referring to such a girl, another girl who had been raised in a liberal family stated: "These are the ones that always get out of line. You know, they drink and if you would give them a pill they would take it just so they could show you they ain't scared or anything like that. They want to be big shots and they always turn out the wrong way. You know, like they will take anything that a guy will give them."

The girl with the best chance for a successful personal and social adaptation is the one raised in an intact family which has some flexibility regarding an acceptance of the different cultural and social traditions of American culture. She has some freedom to experiment personally and socially without being forced into a premature marriage and without being pressured to convince everyone in a hurry that she is "hip."

The adolescent boy in the old-fashioned Puerto Rican family does not have the disadvantages of the girl. He has a strong father as an identification figure and, at the same time, he is encouraged by both parents to become a man—*el hombre*. It is understood that his place is "in the street." In other words, the concept of the double standard operates in these families with the customary benefits to the male. Aggressiveness and independence on the part of a boy enhance the reputation of the family; on the part of a girl, they damage it.

In selecting a Puerto Rican marriage partner, a Puerto Rican boy used to prefer a young, recent immigrant from Puerto Rico a *Jivo Rican*), the primary consideration being that it was a good chance she would be a virgin *(señorita)* and unknowledgeable about "the street." In recent years, however, because of extensive circular migration and the resulting transmission of American customs to Puerto Rico, a young woman from Puerto Rico is not regarded, *prima facie*, as a virgin. Today a boy believes that a "good girl" can just as well come from New York and that it is the family background that counts. When a boy marries a girl who is believed by the family to be a virgin, one of the parents of the girl, usually the mother, takes the boy to a private room and explains to him that the girl is not experienced in sex, as he is, and that he must be patient and considerate.

The Puerto Rican girl tends to prefer a boy who has lived in New York for a long time (a *Progresso Rican*) because he is more likely to be in a position to earn a good livelihood and to have acquired the cultural traits ascribed to the American man, namely, a less authoritarian attitude toward women and a greater sense of equality and consideration. In referring to these "Americanized" Puerto Rican men, Puerto Ricans will say: *"Los sienta en el baúl"* ("they sit on the trunk"), an old phrase used among all classes to describe men who stay in the home, help the wife, and are not promiscuous. It is usually used in a jokingly derogatory way, one man to another.

Many young Puerto Rican women prefer an American man to a Puerto Rican man, and such marriages are becoming more frequent. It is the common conviction of Puerto Rican women that Puerto Rican men are by nature polygynous and liars; even if American men may lie, they say, they are not good liars, and you can at least catch them at it.

Jewish and Italian men are the most common out-marrying partners for Puerto Rican women in New York. There is a situational factor involved in this trend, in that Puerto Ricans have moved into neighborhoods which were predominantly Jewish and Italian, such as the Lower East Side and East Harlem. Because of their relatively close neighborhood association with Italians, many Puerto Ricans refer to all white New Yorkers—no matter what their ethnic background—as "guineas," which is a slang name used by other people only for Italians.

Jewish men are favored by Puerto Rican women because of their "tolerant" attitudes, their loyalty to the home, and their economic enterprise. American Italians are preferred by those Puerto Rican women who want a husband who is American but has some traits and values in common with Puerto Ricans. Extended family cohesion, sociability, expressive style of life, and the Catholic religion are the major factors. The patriarchial tradition among Italian men is also a value for Puerto Rican women, if, as is likely with American Italians, it has been tempered by American customs.

Recently there have been a number of cases of Puerto Rican women marrying Chinese men, who now probably rank third as out-marrying choices for Puerto Rican women.

Young Puerto Rican men are attracted to American girls but they do not marry-out as often as the Puerto Rican girls. One boy explained this by saying: "There are too many obstacles; first you have to win the girl, then her friends, and then her family." American girls are referred to as "fay" girls, which is a Negro slang term coined from the "pig Latin" translation of "foe" (originally, "ofay.")

## THE ADOLESCENT BOY IN THE COMMUNITY

It is outside the family that the Puerto Rican boy must meet the tests of personal and social adaptation. In New York his main adaptive alternative is to join the "hips" or the "hicks"; that is, to adopt the current street style and behavior of delinquent-prone Americans or to maintain a strict cultural integrity incongruent in many ways with the new environment. Faced with this alternative many Puerto Rican youths in a slum community choose the "hip" way of life, whether that means gang membership, as it did in the fifties, or the aloof, unaggressive indifference of today's "hipster." The Puerto Rican boy who does not join the current mode of street life, with its characteristic style of dress, argot, social behavior, and manner of walking, is ridiculed by the "hip" Puerto Rican youths. The chances are that he will isolate himself from New York City culture at large and live exclusively within a narrow Puerto Rican sub-culture in the city. This relegates him to a marginal existence as a $60-a-week laborer.

The boy who has the strength to withstand the initial social pressure, without withdrawing, has a chance to work his way toward a more successful adaptation than is inherent in the "hip" or "hick" alternative. He can gradually adopt an American style of life without renouncing the basic values of his Puerto Rican heritage. This kind of boy is known in the street as "quiet," a term of respect even when used by a "hipster." It does not refer to one who has retreated from the pressures of the street but to one who has successfully resisted them. In the street-fighting days he was known as one who "don't know nothing unless you bother him and if you bother him he knows everything," or briefly, "he don't know nothing."

Young Puerto Rican men with the qualifications for employment beyond the most menial jobs are usually those who were born in New York or who came here at an early age. The major factor in their relative success is their knowledge of English, which enabled them to progress in school. Puerto Ricans who come to New York as adolescents are at a serious disadvantage. Because of the language disability they are placed in segregated, slow-moving classes where even a well-motivated student can become discouraged and frustrated. Many drop out of school, even before the age of 16 (the legal age at which one can withdraw from school), often with the consent or advice of parents, who believe they might as well get a job which brings some money into the family rather than waste time in school. For many boys, however, a low wage is an insult to their pride and they think it more manly to "hustle" on the street. Having chosen the "street life," they engage in criminal activity for money and may become involved in drinking or use of narcotics.

Street gang fighting was a popular activity for such boys in the late forties and early fifties, but over the last 10 years it has disappeared. The cessation of gang fighting occurred around 1956 and coincided with the rapid spread of heroin use among adolescents on the street. Prior to World War II the use of heroin by lower-class people in New York was relatively limited, being more or less confined to certain musicians and "show people" and to a criminal sub-culture consisting of small-time racketeers and hoodlums, burglars, petty thieves, pickpockets, prostitutes, and procurers. After the war a new market of potential narcotic users existed among the expanded Negro and Puerto Rican population in New York. Between 1940 and 1950 the Negro population of the city almost doubled and the Puerto Rican population quadrupled.

This new market was quickly exploited by the narcotic industry, beginning in 1947. Narcotic use on a large scale among Negro and Puerto Rican adolescents began around 1955 and replaced gang fighting as the "hip" thing to do. Over the past 10 years, the use of narcotics and the crimes committed to support it have become the major delinquent activities of street adolescents. Puerto Rican youths, along with Negroes, the Irish, and Italians, have been especially vulnerable to narcotic addiction. The migration of Puerto Ricans from New York back to Puerto Rico has resulted, in recent years, in a serious narcotic addiction problem in Puerto Rico.

## CONCLUSION

Since the 19th century, New York City has been the major point of entry to the United States for immigrant groups from the world's lower, displaced classes. All of them minority groups when they arrived in the United States, they included, in the early 19th century, the English, French, and German; in the middle 19th century, the Irish and still more German; in the late 19th century, the Italians and Jews; and, after World War I, the Negroes, both from the West Indies and—as in-migrants—from the southern states.

The most recent immigrants—the Puerto Ricans—have been here in large numbers for only one generation, which accounts for the negative features of Puerto Rican life in New York reported above. A comparison with other cultural groups after one generation of immigration would show that the Puerto Ricans have adapted relatively fast. There are many indications that they will become integrated into American life in the United States with progressive facility. Over a 10-year period (1950–1960) the percentage of Puerto Rican men in New York who work in the operative and service industries dropped 18% with a correlative rise in the semi-professional, clerical, and sales fields. Puerto Rican men have shown that with adequate education and training in the United States they have the motivation and ability to improve their economic status. With this improvement they will be able to assume their proper roles as family heads, with resulting benefits to their families and to the community.

The main justification for this optimism is to be found in the Puerto Rican's zest for life, his sociability, sense of pride, and emotional warmth. It is very easy for anyone to become friendly with Puerto Ricans. They are eager to establish relationships with "Americans" and quickly respond to friendly overtures. Of the four adolescent ethnic groups with which this writer has worked and associated in New York (Negro, Irish, Italian, and Puerto Rican) the Puerto Ricans have been the most responsive and co-operative. They are relatively non-defensive and unsuspicious at initial encounters and are interested in sustained personal relationships.

A good test of the Puerto Rican's friendly and co-operative attitude is to have an automobile failure in a Puerto Rican neighborhood. Soon after the hood of the car has been raised, a band of volunteer mechanics will be on hand to give advice, assist, and provide tools. This does not always benefit the automobile, but it does promote good-will, respect, and understanding.

## REFERENCES

1. Bender, L. and Nichtern, S.: Two Puerto Rican Boys in New York. In *Clinical Studies in Cultural Conflict*, edited by G. Seward, Part IV, Spanish Legacy, Ch. 10, The Ronald Press Company, New York, 1958.
2. Berle, B. B.: *Eighty Puerto Rican Families in New York City*. Columbia University Press, New York, 1958.
3. Brameld, T.: *The Remaking of a Culture*. Harper & Brothers, New York, 1959.
4. Chenault, L. R.: *The Puerto Rican Migrant in New York*. Columbia University Press, New York, 1938.
5. Glazer, N. and Moynihan, D. P.: *Beyond the Melting Pot*. The M. I. T. Press and Harvard University Press, Cambridge, 1959.
6. Handlin, O.: *The Newcomers*. Harvard University Press, Cambridge, 1959.
7. Hanson, E. P.: *Puerto Rico: Ally for Progress*. D. Van Nostrand Company Inc., Princeton, 1962.
8. Kardiner, A.: *The Individual and His Society*. Columbia University Press, New York, 1939.
9. Kardiner, A. and Preble, E.: *They Studied Man*. The World Publishing Company, Cleveland, Ohio, 1961.
10. Lewis, O.: *La Vida*. Random House Inc., New York, 1966.
11. Malzberg, B.: Mental Disease among Puerto Ricans in New York City. Journal of Nervous and Mental Disease, *123*: 263–269, 1956.
12. Marques, T.: *The Ox Cart (La Carreta)*, translated by C. T. Pilditch, unpublished, 1966.
13. Mills, C., Seniot, C., and Goldsen, R.: *Puerto Rican Journey*. Harper & Brothers, New York, 1950.
14. Opler, M. I.: Dilemmas of Two Puerto Rican Men. In *Clinical Studies in Cultural Conflict*, edited by G. Seward, Part IV, Spanish Legacy, Ch. 10, The Ronald Press Company, New York, 1958.
15. Padilla, E.: *Up from Puerto Rico*. Columbia University Press, New York, 1958.
16. Rand, C.: *The Puerto Ricans*. Oxford University Press, New York, 1958.
17. Rogler, L. H. and Hollingshead, A. B.: *Trapped: Families and Schizophrenia*. John Wiley & Sons, Inc., New York, 1965.
18. Rothenberg, A.: Puerto Rico and Aggression. The American Journal of Psychiatry, *120*: 962–970, 1964.
19. Sexton, P. C.: *Spanish Harlem*. Harper and Row, Publishers, New York, 1965.
20. Srole, L. Langner, T. S., Michael, S. T., Opler, M. K. and Rennie, T. A. C.: *Mental Health in the Metropolis (The Midtown Manhattan Study)*. McGraw-Hill Book Company Inc., New York, 1962.
21. Steward, J. M.: *The People of Puerto Rico*. University of Illinois Press, Champaign, Ill., 1956.
22. Stycos, J. M.: *Family and Fertility in Puerto Rico: A Study of the Lower Income Group*. Columbia University Press, New York, 1955.
23. Tumin, M. M. and Feldman, A. S.: *Social Class and Social Change in Puerto Rico*, Princeton University Press, Princeton, N.J., 1961.

24. United States Bureau of the Census: Subject Reports. Puerto Ricans in the United States. Final Report P C (2) — 1A. In *U.S. Census of Population: 1960*. U.S. Government Printing Office, Washington, D.C., 1963.
25. Wakefield, D.: *Island in the City*. Houghton Mifflin Company, Boston, 1959.
26. Whyte, W. F.: *Street Corner Society*, rev. ed., University of Chicago Press, Chicago, 1955.

# Adolescent Identity Crisis in Urban Mexican Americans in East Los Angeles*

ROBERT L. DERBYSHIRE, Ph.D.

I N AMERICAN SOCIETY, culturally divergent ethnic categories and adolescents have much in common. Both are minorities lacking adequate access to economic, political, and social power; both are excluded from the mainstream of American adult culture, and both are strugglng toward acceptance yet having difficulty locating adequate and functional acculturative frames of reference for culturally integrated participation. Functional relations between simultaneous membership in socially and culturally excluded minorities and their effect upon adolescent identity crises is the subject of this paper. Indications of adolescent identity are based upon data gathered from Mexican American adolescents residing within the most economically depressed area of East Los Angeles. Identity crisis, with its subsequent strain resulting from role-conflict (28) which is stimulated by the adolescent's desire to identify with family, peer, and greater adult worlds (3) and which is concomitantly influenced by the dominant culture's lack of acceptance of Mexican American cultural diversity and the role-conflict it engenders, suggests that adolescence for Mexican Americans in an urban setting is vulnerable to deviant behavior.

Terminology (14) difficulties are inherent within minority populations who are citizens of the United States of America. All

* This research was supported through National Institute of Mental Health Grant MH-01539-01, Welfare Planning Council, Los Angeles, California. Acknowledgement for co-operation in the study is made to Professor Georgene Seward of the Psychology Department and to Professor William R. Larson of the Computer Sciences Laboratory, both of the University of Southern California, Los Angeles, California.

73

members of minorities, either born or naturalized in the United States, are American citizens first. Aside from American citizenship, however, there are certain ethnic characteristics which promote or inhibit human interaction and relationships within the United States culture (21). These differences are based upon physiognomy, i.e. hair structure and color, nasal index, height and weight, eye color and eye fold, and skin color. There is no conclusive evidence that physiognomical characteristics of ethnic categories determine their behavior. However, determinants of behavior are related to gross cultural differences, linguistic nuances of persons from varying backgrounds, and societal reactions to physiognomical differences. When these differences interact with the dominant white, Protestant, "capitalistic," Anglo-Saxon "democratic" culture of the United States, prejudical and discriminatory behavior often occurs. In other words, differences in behavior among ethnic groups are the result of at least two major phenomena: 1) the "right" and "wrong" of behavior as a result of socialization supporting the dominant values (38) within one's culture and 2) these behaviors in interaction with the United States culture which views minority persons and their behavior as "alien."

The term "Mexican American," without the hyphen, is used to identify the minority population with whom this project is related. Although we recognize that numerous identity conflicts exist within the community of East Los Angeles, it is not the intention of this research to alienate, determine consensus, or ameliorate feelings of group identification. Although other Spanish-speaking populations, i.e. Cubans, Puerto Ricans, and other South and Central American nationalities, reside in East Los Angeles, statistical analysis of the community indicates that the bulk of the population originally migrated from Mexico. Overtones of group identity problems are not dismissed. Self-reference labels of Latin Americans, Americans of Spanish descent, Americans of Mexican descent, Mexican Americans, or Spanish-speaking Americans, and others are frequently heard in East Los Angeles. Because of the lack of consensus over semantic identification problems we chose to use the abbreviated form of identification, i.e. Mexican Americans without the hyphen. The persons described in this research are Americans who by virtue of their Mexican ethnicity receive differential and inferior treatment. One teen-ager stated, "Mexican American means bicultural and bilingual a little more than other Americans."

After this issue of terminology we can examine the following issues related to this study. The East Los Angeles Mexican American's cultural environment and socio-economic status will be described. Minority status interacting with majority control and its resultant minority identity crisis will be presented. As minorities seek acculturation and adolescents move toward adulthood both encounter the marginal process. Marginality as it relates to Mexican American adolescence will be discussed. Data from a recent investigation of adolescents in East Los Angeles will be analyzed in terms of these theoretical constructs.

## The East Los Angeles Mexican American

East Los Angeles, the unincorporated area in which our study was carried out, lies east of Boyle Heights, south of City Terrace and Alhambra, west of Monterey Park, and north of Commerce and Montebello. Those census tracts which supply the greatest amounts of family disorganization, juvenile delinquency, crime, drug addiction, dilapidated housing, poverty, and other indicators of community pathology are surrounded by four huge concrete and steel freeways. Apparently these freeways tend to limit the ecological mobility within the area. The Long Beach Freeway on the east, Santa Ana Freeway on the south, San Bernardino Freeway on the north, and the Golden State Freeway on the west provide a man-made wall which segregates the most economically deprived Mexican Americans.

On a clear day, when smog neither settles in this basin nor nestles against the San Bernardino Mountains, snow-capped Mount Baldy is seen as it overlooks Los Angeles County. On humid days, yellowish smog is a devastating hazard to the health of this community.

Although a university, state college, and junior college are located in this area few residents join its student body. Fewer natives of the area are members of the faculties. Statistics on junior high and high school dropouts are the highest in the County.

The "Serape Belt," as East Lost Angeles has been designated, was at one time a predominantly Jewish neighborhood. Today, however, main thoroughfares, Brooklyn Avenue, 3rd Street, and Whittier Boulevard, display advertisements in Spanish, *Cantinos*, corner fruit stands, motion picture theatres with Spanish-speaking movies, and Anglo merchants who display signs reading "hablo Espanol." Many merchants and some physicians' offices keep the Spanish language television station on during the day. Tortillos and tacos are sold in small sidewalk carry-out shops. Signs designating the office of a "curendero" (a folk curer or medicine man) and "abagado" (a false lawyer) are frequently seen.

From secondhand furniture and clothing stores filter the sounds of Spanish language radio programs. People on the streets more frequently speak Spanish than English. On Friday evenings the dark complexioned faces of older males in the cantinos reveal the rugged manual labors of the week. While women are frequenting the shops and stores, groups of young men are visible on several corners. Although clothing is worn and tattered, yet it is neat; hands, face, and eyes appear fatigued; a massive pride is characterized by the erectness of body posture and lightness of gait.

Houses in East Lost Angeles are small, and colorfully painted, with dilapidated fences and small flower gardens. Much of the housing is rented, not owner-occupied. In many neighborhoods the interdependent atmosphere of the Barrio (small community) exists. Females, particularly mothers and wives, are often busy with local church and neighborhood affairs. Children frequent the streets for companionship and peer activities. Local settlement houses as well as more recent poverty programs provide some recreational and social facilities.

The sheriff and his deputies and the state police are avoided when possible. Church and its responsibilities are taken most seriously by females, while males pay lip service. Immigration officers are well known and avoided. Unknown Anglos asking questions in the neighborhood are viewed suspiciously. Middle-

and upper-class "Chicanos" (slang for Mexican Americans) are also viewed with trepidation for fear they are investigators for Anglo institutions.

Although families in this ghetto appear to be patriarchal and matricentric, there is excellent evidence that male strength and dominance exist only because females feel it is best to play the subordinate role. Females frequently verbalize dissatisfaction with their husbands' and fathers' position in the family but give and promote family respect out of deference to his loss of status in Anglo culture. Among families interviewed by one of the researchers, there was an apparent role-deception by females to provide a foundation for the emasculated if not lost "machismo" of their Mexican heritage. This was most frequently revealed through the wives' lack of condemnation for their husbands' extra-marital sexual exploits. Praise was often given for the males' lack of fear and his physical combativeness outside of the house. Although sexual and aggressive behavior was seldom condemned, most mothers and wives were able to verbalize to the interviewer that these actions were dysfunctional for getting ahead in Anglo land. "The poor man fights so much adversity everyday that the least I can do is support him in the ways of his father."

Child-rearing practices are punitive and severe. Girls are protected while boys are encouraged to be aggressive. Gang life is most usual for boys. "Pachuco" gangs have their distinct dress and speech patterns (14). Gangs frequently attack isolates, dyads, or triads of their rivals. Large gang warfare is seldom encountered although it does exist. These gang disagreements most frequently involve territory or females. Although East Los Angeles, no doubt, produces a variety of family belief systems, most older persons give lip service to the Mexican family prototypes. This has been described by Oscar Lewis.

"According to the ideal pattern for husband-wife relations in Tepoztlan, the husband is viewed as an authoritarian patriarchal figure who is head and master of the household and who enjoys the highest status in the family. His perrogatives are to receive the obedience and respect of his wife and children as well as their services. It is the husband who is expected to make all important decisions and plans for the entire family. He is responsible for the support of the family and for the behavior of each member. The wife is expected to be submissive, faithful, devoted, and respectful toward her husband. She should seek his advice and obtain his permission before undertaking any but the most minor activities. A wife should be industrious, frugal and should manage to save money no matter how low her husband's income. A good wife should not be critical, curious, or jealous of her husband's activities outside the home" (19).

This ideal type of interaction with the dominant American culture and its influences upon adolescent identity crisis will be discussed later.

TABLE 1

*Selected population characteristics* (25)

| Characteristics | Los Angeles County | East Los Angeles |
|---|---|---|
| Total 1960 population | 6,038,771 | 105,464 |
| Persons/ square mile | 1,479 | 12,379 |
| Population increase 1950—1960 | 45.5% | 15.4% |
| Age classifications | | |
| Youth (0—19 years) | 35.5% | 42.9% |
| Productive ages (20—64 years) | 55.3% | 50.0% |
| Aged (65 years and older) | 9.2% | 7.1% |
| Ethnic categories | | |
| White | 80.8% | 29.1% |
| Negro | 7.6% | 0.0% |
| Spanish surname | 9.6% | 67.1% |
| Other | 2.0% | 3.8% |

According to the 1960 Census, 83.9% of the Spanish surname foreign-born in Los Angeles were born in Mexico. These 99,000 Mexican-born immigrants represent a 41% increase over 1950 (11). Nevertheless, the greatest proportion of the 15.4% population increase described in table 1, apparently results from "natural increase," i.e. an excess of births over deaths, rather than from immigration. As "Age classifications" indicates, this is an extremely young population, with a male-female median age of 22.3 years. Because the 125% increase (between 1950 and 1960) for ages zero to 14 a high dependency rate of 100 productive adults exists for the East Los Angeles Mexican American population. Therefore, each productive adult between the ages of 20 and 65, on the average, supports one person in addition to himself (Table 2).

In three census tracts (5305, 5310, and 5311) in East Los Angeles, where our sample of adolescents resided, the Spanish surname population exceeds 90%. Each of these tracts reports large households (3.79–4.46 persons per household) and a large number of "other relatives" (over 17%) per household. Problems associated with over-crowded conditions (delinquency, incest, out-of-wedlock pregnancy, etc.) are frequent. Twenty-seven percent of all dwelling units have over 1.01 persons per room.

TABLE 2

*A comparison of East Los Angeles and Los Angeles County on seven parameters of socio-economic stability* (11)

| Parameters | Los Angeles County | East Los Angeles |
|---|---|---|
| Family income: $4,000 or less | 19.1% | 29.6% |
| Employment: Unemployment males | 4.5% | 6.0% |
| Education: 8 years or less | 13.2% | 38.1% |
| 1 year college or more | 24.2% | 6.8% |
| Family status: Families as households | 77.2% | 85.0% |
| Separated and divorced | 7.1% | 9.2% |
| Housing status: | | |
| Dilapidated and deteriorated | 7.8% | 29.0% |
| Productive ratio: Youth and aged/100 adults in productive ages | 80.8 | 100.0 |
| 1962 youth status: Neglect/1,000 | 1.7 | 1.0 |
| Pre-delinquent/1,000 | 4.5 | 6.1 |
| 1962 youth status: Delinquent/1,000 | 11.2 | 13.4 |

While nearly 30% of these families have incomes of less than $4000 per year, 10% have incomes below $2000. Fewer than half (47%) of all Spanish surname persons own their own home. Over 54% of all dwelling units occupied by Mexican Americans in East Los Angeles were built prior to 1940, while 30% of all units were considered in 1960 to be dilapidated and deteriorated.

These difficulties and a lack of indegenous leadership have kept upward mobility and self-help at a minimum. Upward mobility in

East Los Angeles is generally concomittant with out-migration. According to *Background for Planning*:

> "In addition, families that leave the ethnic neighborhood may change their names, and become assimilated into the Anglo-white community. The relative ease with which members of this minority group may become a part of the dominant group acts as a detriment to the entire Spanish surname population. The most able and successful members of the community are most likely to move first. This leaves the parent group without adequate leadership and, in addition, the group becomes more and more identified with its least successful members in the eyes of the total community" (25).

Data of this nature indicate the difficulty East Los Angeles Mexican Americans have maintaining a cultural identity while simultaneously participating in the mainstream of the United States way of life. One can participate if one avoids his cultural heritage. To participate significantly in the Mexican American heritage automatically excludes one from access to the benefits of middle-class Anglo society, e.g. education, employment, and housing.

### MINORITY GROUP STATUS AS A SOURCE OF IDENTITY

The uniqueness yet ubiquitousness of intergroup relationships, which depend upon the social structure peculiar to individual association, is one of the fundamental assumptions underlying the basic premise of sociology. Individuals behave in terms of others; that is, the pressure of group conformity is extremely significant in determining individual behavior. Similarly, associations, groups, and institutions strongly influence the behavior of individuals and other groups. The direction and extent to which any individual or group reciprocates will be directly proportionate to the status, authority, and power of the external association. This is an inescapable reality when considering minority-majority relationships.

Minority behavior and status can be understood only in terms of the majority. The American ethos is fundamental for understanding majority-minority relations. Robert Schermerhorn's definition of minority adequately and precisely defines the position of the Mexican American minority in the United States.

"Minorities are subgroups within a culture which are distinguishable from the dominant group by reason of differences in physiognomy, language, customs, or culture patterns (including any combination of these factors). Such subgroups are regarded as inherently different and 'not belonging' to the dominant group: for this reason they are consciously, or unconsciously excluded from full participation in the life of the culture" (31).

American minorities lack adequate access to the sources of community power. Exclusion from culturally significant behaviors limits the minority's functional repertoire of problem-solving modalities (4). The extent to which a minority lacks problem-solving techniques is related to influence over and reciprocity with the social institutions of middle-class America. Minorities which appear to have the least access to power and are the most excluded are the most socially visible. Social visibility influences social interaction and its outcome. It is characterized by racial phenomena, language, religion, and behavior patterns (especially those governing human growth and development, e.g. food, drink, affection, child rearing, education, etc.). In the United States there is an inverse correlation between social visibility and access to social power and significant cultural items. The more visible minorities (e.g. racial) must overcome laws and institutions in order to seek acceptance while less visible minorities (e.g. ethnic and religious) need to deal with folkways and mores which interfere with acceptance.

While racial minorities (this is particularly true for Negroes and Indians) are likely to have their inferior status confirmed by law and institution, ethnic and religious minorites (Jews, Mexicans, Catholics) find their minority status more frequently in the folkways and mores. Variations of these patterns exist, of course, depending upon density, recency, and similarity factors (21). The greater the numbers, the more recent the immigration; and the more divergent the cultural and physiognomical characteristics, the greater the acculturative difficulties. Therefore one major functional property of a minority is its lack of influence.

This lack of influence establishes a devaluation of one's culture. To devaluate one's culture creates a negative or at best an ambiguous and conflicting identity. Such devaluation of the minority culture by the majority establishes the matrix of culture conflict. Seward states:

"Turning to ethnic groups in process of acculturating, the value discrepancies between in-group and core culture are a constant source of stress for their member. The severity of the stress is a product of degree of divergence and rate of culture change. The resulting social role conflict is differentially expressed in neurosis "choice" (34).

Role-conflict precipitates strain. Parsons has distinguished four principal types of reaction to strain (27). These four reactions which may occur simultaneously assist the organism to adjust to its conflictful social situation. Each is well-known and each seems to stimulate a relatively common complaint from members of the majority toward the minority. It is not unusual to locate stereotypes of minorities at the core of which is the minority's use of fantasy, anxiety, aggression, and defensiveness.

In an earlier study Mexicans were viewed by middle-class, college-educated, southeastern American Negroes as dirty, passionate, dishonest, unintelligent, passive, slow, humble, weak and beautiful (8). Another attitudinal investigation suggests that native-born (United States) Mexican American students view themselves significantly different from foreign-born (Mexico) Mexican Americans on all parameters except they each agree that they are "short, fat and dark" (9). Native-born Mexican Americans see themselves as significantly more emotional, unscientific, authoritarian, materialistic, old-fashioned, poor and of low social class, uneducated, mistrusted, proud, lazy, indifferent, and unambitious. The high degree of stereotype similarities between native-born Mexican Americans and Negroes with a lack of agreement for foreign-born Mexican Americans establishes the influence of the dominant American value orientation upon native-born Mexican American self-acceptance and self-stereotyping.

In a cross-cultural pilot study of concepts of social sex roles, Seward (35) compared small groups of late teen-age, middle-class, Caucasian, Mexican American, and Negro males on 12 scales from Osgood's semantic differential pool. In general, these sub-cultural comparisons yield dominant images of the father in the case of the

Mexican American, and of the mother in the other two groups. Since these tentative findings fit the traditional conceptions but not recent reports on lower-class groups, the study should be replicated with large samples from different social strata.

Kluckhohn and Strodtbeck have compared the value orientations of dominant American culture and native Mexican culture (17). The Mexican orientation to nature views misfortune as a product of sin and change is only possible with strict discipline, while the same American value orientation sees man as a pliable product of his environment. Man's relationship to nature is seen by Mexicans as fatalistic or as one of "subjugation" to nature, while the dominant American theme is to conquer nature. Mexicans are present-oriented and "manana" will take care of itself. However, Americans spend most of their energy planning for the future. This future orientation can be seen in economic, educational, and political behavior patterns. The orientation to activity for Mexican core culture is spontaneous or "being"—oriented, while Americans are achievement-oriented. Non-achievement in American culture is almost unAmerican, while achievement in Mexican culture is viewed with suspicion. Orientation to relationships in Mexican culture is linear and is expressed in the dominance-submission patterns of the family. American culture, on the other hand is individual-oriented.

These conflicting value orientations perpetuate identity conflicts for Mexican Americans. Carolyn Zeleny (23) suggests the slow rate of assimilation for Mexican immigrants is related to the fact that the southwestern United States, at one time was a part of the Spanish Empire and Americans have really only taken over Mexican territory. The feeling is frequently stated that if Mexicans were in Southern California before Anglos, then why should Anglo culture discriminate. Should not Anglos acculturate Mexican ways? Carey McWilliams suggests the slow assimulative rate of Mexicans is due to the lack of abrupt, well-defined national boundaries. For European immigrants to the United States " . . . the Atlantic crossing was of the utmost psychological and sociological importance, it was a severance, a crossing, an abrupt transition. But Mexican immigrants have seldom ventured beyond the fan of Spanish influence in the borderlands (23). . . ."

Oscar Lewis states that in Mexico "middle class machismo is exressed in terms of sexual exploits and the Don Juan complex, whereas in the lower class it is expressed in terms of heroism and lack of physical fear" (18). Celia Heller (14) also recognizes the importance of machismo. However, in her study of Mexican American youth she emphasizes the machismo complex to include sexual prowess, physical strength, courage, adventurousness, male dominance, self-confidence, and verbal articulation. Older brothers frequently have the role of guardian and protector of sisters and younger brothers. This is viewed as an extension of father's role, while in the United States the brother's role is most often linked to the outside world which he represents. This creates father-son conflict.

Honor is important. One must have an inner integrity, a sensitivity to insult, and extreme politeness. The concept of La Raza, the spiritual and cultural bond of the splendid and glorious destiny of all Latin Americans, is manifest and familism is emphasized. Parents give unconditional love and stimulate little initiative. Resignation and fatalism are highly related to religion and home training.

Heller suggests that her sample de-emphasizes eductional and intellectual values. Since education is not viewed as a means to success, school dropouts are more frequent than among Anglos. Although gang life is meaningful, the majority of Mexican American youth are not delinquent.

These values are antithetical to upward mobility striving and the development of an achievement identity. Recently, Heller's Los Angeles study of an "ambitious" sub-group of Mexican Americans suggests that at least one segment is moving toward improving their status. Mexican American high school graduates between 15 and 19 years expect to achieve higher status than their fathers, although Mexican Americans is the only group that fails to show an intergenerational increase in socio-economic status. Unusual homogeneity is partly due to separateness in locale and language as well as to discriminatory occupational patterns. Heller suggests a recent shift in values with emphasis on deferred gratification, future orientation, mobility strivings and with higher goals than those of father. This trend is reflected in Heller's Los Angeles study, ". . .

which shows that only 4 percent of the Mexican American male high school seniors expected to be in unskilled or semiskilled occupations, whereas 42 percent of their fathers worked in such occupations. Conversely two percent of the fathers were in professions or semi-professions, but . . . 35 percent of the sons aspired such occupations" (14). School integration is the major factor associated with ambition in Mexican American youth. High school graduation separates those with the American dream from others.

Another recent investigation by Zurcher *et al* (39), uses Anglo, Mexican American, and Mexican bankers to support Parsons and Shils' hypothesis (28) that culture influences the value orientation of particularism. Particularistic individuals also appear to be alienated from work in a universalistic organization. If the validity of this hypothesis can be carried over to other institutions outside of work then it is relatively easy to understand why Mexican American adolescents choose "deviant behavior" as a solution to role-conflict precipitated by universalistic-particularistic value orientation. If a Mexican American adolescent must choose, because of his definition of the situation, between universalism (duty to community, organization, society) and particularism (duty to friend) his choice will be influenced by his perception of his parent culture.

A dominant value in American culture is universalism. Universalism puts the group before the individual. The basic premise of American institutions including the family leans heavily toward the universalistic end of the continuum. It implies that decisions are made on the assumption that those who work toward group conformity must do so on an impersonal level. Universalism highly supports role and status, role-performance, and institutionalized mechanisms for role-supports. Although universalism is the dominant value in the United States, and no doubt is supported more by the middle class and above, it does not mean that particularism or particularistic interests have no influence. It goes without saying that when decisions are made on an impersonal basis, certain particularistic or personal phenomena are a part of the final decision. For example, when a large institution is deciding to hire an individual to fit into a certain position in the system, this individual must first meet the specified requirements for the role. This, of course, means that he must have a certain experience, education, as well as a specific knowledge for performing that role. However, when the institution has a series of persons who equally fit the role, a choice must be made on other phenomena. Therefore, in the last phase of selection such phenomena as race, ethnicity, religion, personal characteristics, and friendship patterns do take precedence. These increase the degree of fit between the personality of the individual to be hired and his supervisor or the perceived personality of the entire institution.

A particularistic point of view, on the other hand, states that decisions are made on a personal level. Friendship patterns and associations become more important to choices under this view than does ability to perform the role. This type of phenomena can be found in American culture to some degree in family businesses. However, this is not always the case. Other social conditions permitting particularistic forms of hiring may evolve during times of societal stress. For example, during the Second World War when large industries were subsidized by federal funds, some industries had funds for which there were no allocated positions. It was not unusual, under those conditions, for some employers to establish positions for which the role was not clearly defined. Most frequently these positions were filled by persons who were friends or relatives of higher echelon personnel. This is also currently evident in some federally-funded poverty programs.

The universalistic value orientation fits most adequately to the free enterprise, capitalistic economic system and the democratic political system. Because of the profit motive it is almost impossible for an organization to hire individuals who inadequately perform their roles. Therefore, from this point of view, American institutions are structured and organized with little interest in a personal or particularistic orientation. It also becomes apparent that the universalism-particularism continuum has different implications depending upon one's social class in the United States culture. For example, it may be hypothesized that there is a correlation between occupation, source of income, and education and the universalistic point of view. In other words, although particularism may be more a point of view of lower classes in general and in particular our lower-class Mexican American, probably it is related to differences in education, income, occupation, and the values of Mexican culture.

Adolescents also have a particularistic investment in peer relations. In American culture particularism is probably most important during adolescence. It is at this time when the roles of responsible citizen, "good student," and "willing family member" are often in conflict with peer and gang associations. Not only does the Mexican American have the cultural problem of particularism versus universalism but this is more strongly accentuated by a similar social problem during adolescence. This social problem is a functional part of the adolescent identity crises. Rubel states in relation to this value orientation that Chicanos are dyadic, close-kinship-centered, seldom achievement-oriented, and apprehensive of Anglos (30).

When the majority forces the minority to accept the dominant culture (e.g. language, institutions, etc.) or be excluded, it is in effect establishing culturally supported role-conflict. The resultant strain and adaptive defense mechanisms which are frequently inadequate, set the stage for identity conflict. Identity conflict for minorities is particularly severe, but to be an adolescent in this minority doubly burdens the identity formation processes. This paper examines the relationship between the cultural minority status of being Mexican American and the social minority status of adolescence and its reciprocal influence upon identity crises.

The reader must be aware that we are dealing with numerous interrelated socio-cultural and psychological phenomena. Adolescence, lower-class status and cultural diversity interact to create the unique identity crisis. Some problems associated with lower-class status for Mexican Americans must be assessed.

Since 1954 Mexico has provided more permanent visa immigrants to the United States than any other nation (26). Most of these persons move into rural communities of the United States southwest or slum ghettos of large cities (e.g. Los Angeles). Legal permanent immigrants, together with temporary farm migrants (braceros), visitors and students, and illegal entrants comprise a sizeable population, a majority of whom find themselves, because of lack of marketable skills, cultural diversity, and Anglo discrimination, at the bottom of the economic, social, and political systems.

Persons at the bottom of the social structure, whether they are of Mexican ancestry, Negro, Anglo, Oriental, Indian, or others, find themselves excluded from access to full community participation (4). Most frequently, the excluded are members of national, racial, and cultural minorities. These include American Indians, Mexican Americans, European immigrant categories, American Negroes, Puerto Ricans, and Oriental migrants. Aside from these racial and ethnic minorities is a large category of social minorities; these include the unskilled, the unschooled, the unemployed, and the transient. There is much overlapping, since minorities are not mutually exclusive categories. Therefore, concomitant with large populations of racial and ethnic minorities are excesses of the unschooled, unskilled, and unemployed.

To exclude means to shut out. Persons who are barred from participation in the culture represent the excluded. Exclusion implies setting up a barrier effective for keeping a person or class of persons from what is open and accessible to others (7).

Indices of exclusion are many. Rates of illness, both physical and mental, are an important index. Illiteracy, arrest, poverty, illegitimacy, suicide, narcotic rates, and many others give clues to the quality and quantity of exclusion. Utilization rates of institutionalized services, education, health, welfare, etc., are also an index of exclusion. The under-utilization of culturally approved services, (e.g. education) and the over-utilization of socially sanctioned but negatively valued agencies, (e.g. clinics, police, and welfare) is an indication of the degree of acculturation toward American ways of doing things. The Mexican American population of East Los Angeles is representative of this socially excluded category.

## ADOLESCENCE, IDENTITY FORMATION AND IDENTITY CRISIS

Several theoretical prepositions derived from observations of minority-majority interaction for adolescents in the United States society are apparent.

1) The minority adolescent's "sense of identity" is a function of his relationship to others. It first develops in a dyadic system of infant and mothering person. An extension of this, prior to and during adolescence, is membership in a family system and later

both peer association and the adult social world. These groups provide socially meaningful experiences (10). Differential social relationships learned through interaction are a result of a family system, social structure, dominant and subordinate value orientations, social class, and communication as restricted and developed by each bio-physical organism.

2) There is a tendency to interact with persons who a) have similar physiognomical characteristics (2), b) a shared communicative network (language), and c) shared socially significant symbols (culture and social class).

3) These interactional choices: a) personally serve need gratifying and anxiety-reducing function, and b) maintain as well as reflect self-perception and his status and role in the social system.

Adolescence is the process during which the identity of the unweaned family member changes to the weaned individual (3). The chances of the unweaned family member to have marital, occupational, psychological, and relational problems leading to deviant behavior is high. Bossard and Boll suggest the difficult problem of integrating the family world (with its intangible guilt-ridden blood bonds), the peer world (with its conformist pressure for achieving status on the basis of appropriate homosexual and heterosexual behavior), and the non-family adult world (of responsibility to neighbors, mass media, transient associations, economic, political, recreational, and religious institutions). As Bossard and Boll state:

> "This, then, is the perennial sociological problem of the adolescent, that he must live in three worlds, each distinct in many respects from the others, each changing with the passage of time, and each changing in its meaning and importance to him. However intriguing, however romantically expectant, this is not an easy stage in the life span" (3) .

Adolescence is a period for achieving independence, choosing and preparing for one's life employment, learning an appropriate and rewarding sex role, working toward intra-generational acceptance and planning and evaluating marriage and family tasks. Kenkel states:

> "Perhaps the most obvious task facing him in the interim is the need to become an autonomous person, no longer emotionally dependent on his parents and freed from the need for direction from

parents or other adults. Adolescents must reconcile societal demands, family expectations, and their own personality needs in
such a manner that they emerge with a realistic masculine or femin-
ine sex role. Adolescent boys and girls alike must come to grips
with the economic realities of the society in which they live and
select and prepare for a role in the economic system. Ultimately
the normal adult is expected to be able to marry, so at the adolescent stage preparation for marriage and family living must be in
the picture. A further developmental task involves the ability of
the adolescent to find a place for himself among his age-mates"
(16).

Puberty is generally indicative of adolescence inception. Demands and desires of boys and girls during this time are seeking
parental emancipation. The dominant social control of parents is
sometimes fought successfully; sometimes not. Adolescent crisis is
the strain stimulated by the role-conflict produced by independence
demands. Adolescence in our society is considered terminated
when the adulthood goal of self-support, independent of one's family of orientation, is gained.

Johnson states (15):

"Identification with one's sex role may or may not be complete
or 'wholehearted.' The likelihood of successful identification is
greater (1) if the main model for a boy's sex role (the father) shows
affection for the boy; (2) if the boy's acquaintance with the role
model is intimate and prolonged; (3) if other important persons
(notably the mother) encourage the boy to take his father as a
model (in which case the boy will be doubly rewarded; first by the
father and then by the mother); and (4) if the role model treats
the boy's mother well (for then the boy, who presumably loves his
mother, will want to be like him). Obviously, the reverse of any of
these conditions will tend to have the opposite effect. For example,
if the boy's mother has contempt for her husband, the boy will be
in conflict about the goal of becoming a man, lest he become 'contemptible," like his father" (15).

Sears et al (32) support these assumptions in their recent work
on identification and child rearing. While examining several parameters of identification one underlying principle cut across most,
"When the parent of the opposite sex rewards dependency, the
child develops behavior characteristics of that sex."

One's personal identity affects the way one defines and reacts to social situations. Identity is one major factor in understanding behavior. Shibutani writes:

> "The comprehension of what a man does requires a record of (1) his definition of the situation, (2) the kind of creature he believes himself to be, and (3) the audience before which he tries to maintain his self-respect" (36).

The identity question in Shibutani's terms is: What kind of creature does the Mexican American adolescent believe himself to be? This, of course, is the central thesis of this paper. It will be analyzed in terms of adolescent lower-class Mexican American responses to a questionnaire. What is identity and how does one acquire it? Although there is some question whether personal identity and self are the same, they will be used interchangeably. The question is legitimate, in that personal identity could be viewed as a part of self, while self is personal identity plus other components.

According to George H. Mead, "The self . . . is essentially a social structure and it arises in social experiences (24). This social experience establishes a "generalized other." The generalized other Mead considers to be the interactive groups to which the individual feels he belongs. These feelings of belongingness, Mead claims, are fundamental to personal identification. Charles Cooley has stated a similar premise with his theory of the "looking-glass self." Cooley asserts each individual sees himself as he interprets how others see him (6).

> "Cooley meant that each person's orientation toward himself is a reflection of the manner in which he is treated. He imagines how he appears to someone else, imputes a judgment to the observer, and reacts with pride or mortification to the imputed judgment" (20).

It is these reflections of the looking-glass self which determine where and how one locates himself in reference to the rest of humanity. In terms of American minorities it might be suggested that Mexican Americans should develop two selves or identities, one for the Mexican world and one for the social world of Anglos

(36). According to Mead and Cooley, self-formation comes about through interpreting the responses of others toward the self as an object. Interpretations from two cultural worlds toward the same object (in this case, self) must be different by virtue of the social definition of minority status. "Early in life a child learns the importance of responding to intention" (28). The intentions to which the adolescent must respond are different for Mexican and Anglo social worlds. The dual social system maintains separate sets of characteristically expected responses. Not only are the expectations of these two different, but Mexican Americans are frequently excluded, because of cultural diversity, from close emotionally reciprocal interaction, from which many important nuances of social life are distributed. The ghetto provides a meaningful generalized other for personal identity, whereas the school system and other Anglo institutions submit Mexican Americans to an obscure, distorted, and often meaningless generalized other.

Parsons recognizes that the generalized motive to become similar to another is the core of the identification process (28). He carries Mead's and Cooley's concepts further. Mead and Cooley suggest that individuals receive self-denunciation and self-gratification from how the individual feels others feel about him. Although they do not explicitly mention that "ego" wishes to be like "alter" who sends "ego" self-gratifying messages, the maintenance of "ego's" organism is based upon receiving gratification from others, which can only be obtained simultaneously with or after the gratification of "alter's" needs. In the Mexican American ghetto, if "ego" desires to be similar to Mexican prototypes, "ego" receives ambiguous support from the generalized other of the Mexican culture depending upon his sex. If "ego" is male, "alter" prototypes are seldom available, but if "ego" is female, "alter" prototypes are encouraged. However, "ego" receives no support from the generalized other of the Anglo social world, because "alter" communicates deprecatory meanings to Mexican Americans.

Another point made by Parsons, pertinent to identity formation is: ". . . identification results in the internalization not only of moral standards (the superego) but also the cognitive and expressive features of the parent and through him the culture as a whole" (28). Parsons places importance upon the parent as interpreter and synthesizer "of the culture as a whole." Identity for lower-class Mexican Americans becomes confused because of 1) the parents' inadequate knowledge of Anglo culture; 2) a pride in Mexican culture, and 3) the confusion elements of available dominant social institutions (e.g. schools, church, police, etc.).

"When a man places himself in a well-defined category, his behavior is thereby circumscribed, but it becomes easier for him to identify himself as a particular kind of human being," states Shibutani (36). It is difficult for Mexican Americans to place themselves in an unambiguous category. If they see themselves as Americans, the Anglo social world seldom reinforces this identity, except possibly during time of national crisis. If they identify themselves as Mexicans they have a cultural heritage, a common way of being treated to reinforce this definition. Mexican American adolescents are forced through normal social intercourse to interact with the values and institutions of the Anglo social world, if not its immediate representatives. Because of the quality of social interaction encountered by Mexican Americans, they are seldom, if ever, able to approach familiar situations in the Anglo world with confidence. Shibutani makes the following assertion:

> "Thus, each person's sense of identity is constantly being tested in social interaction and repeatedly reaffirmed as other people live up to expectations. Furthermore, the more frequently and consistently such confirmations are forthcoming, the more he can take his assumptions about himself for granted and approach familiar situations with confidence.
> "Men approach one another with hypotheses about themselves. By virtue of the fact that he is who he is, a person expects others to treat him in a given way; if, the anticipated responses actually take place, his hypotheses are confirmed, and this reinforces his conception of himself" (36).

Personal identity is internationalized through the interactive process. As Shibutani states "Personal identity, then, constitutes one's only tie with the rest of society, each person has a status in a community only in so far as he can identify himself as a specific human being who belongs in a particular place" (36). Each person's status is based upon his social roles and their performances. The learning of social roles is defined as the socialization process. All learning is not included in socialization, but only that learning which is significant to role-performance and role-identity.

The importance of group membership as a determinant of self or ego identity has been presented by Erikson:

> "The growing child must at every step derive a vitalizing sense of reality from the awareness that his individual way of mastering experiences . . . is a successful variant of a group identity . . . ego identity gains real strength only from the whole-hearted and consistent recognition of real accomplishment, i.e. of achievement that has meaning in the culture" (10).

Adolescents must experience this accomplishment within their family, peer, and non-family adult worlds. One barrier to the last is an extended period of marginality through which Mexican American adolescents have difficulty passing.

## Socio-Cultural Marginality and Identity Crisis

This analysis of marginality is concerned with the interrelations of sub-aspects of both the dominant and subordinate systems and with the socio-psychological consequences for its constituent parts due to participation in the system (12). The major concern is with one consequence of majority-minority relations as it is relevant to the Mexican American in the United States. This consequence has been referred to as the process of marginality or the marginal state. Marginality is a significant social phenomenon for Mexican Americans. As long as the social system establishes differential treatment for Mexican Americans, marginality is a functional system due to cultural hybridization (22). As migration to urban areas increases, a larger number of individuals, to whom the term marginal might be applied, are recognized. They seem to be on the advancing "edge" or "margin" of their own socio-cultural group as it is in contact with representatives of the surrounding power-holding Anglo society. Such an individual is characterized by incomplete acceptance by members of his own group and by whatever personal conflicts accompany such lack of acceptance. On the other hand, he may experience certain rewards from members of the larger group with whom he is in contact, although here, too, only partial acceptance is usually postulated.

Antonovsky has described marginality as a *state* or condition in the following terms:

"1.   Two cultures (or subcultures) are in lasting contact.

"2.   One of them is dominant in terms of power and reward potential. This is the non-marginal of the two. Its members are not particularly influenced by or attracted to the other, the marginal culture.

"3.   The boundaries between the two are sufficiently permeable for the members of the marginal culture to internalize the patterns of the dominant culture as well as that of their own.

"4.   These patterns, in their entirety, cannot be easily harmonized.

"5.   Having acquired the goals of the non-marginal culture, members of the marginal group are pulled by the promise of the greater rewards offered.

"6.   The barriers between the two tend to be hardened by discrimination from the one side, and by pressure against "betrayal" from the other.

"7.   Marginality acquires particular intensity when the clash persists through more than one generation" (1).

Antonovsky's description includes a number of elements which may be considered as *functions* in that they are *consequences* (for individuals or groups) of existing in this state or condition for a period of time: 1) the acquisition and integration by the subordinate or marginal culture, of signficant elements of the dominant culture; 2) the stimulation to greater achievement on the part of marginal group members which follows the acquisition of dominant group values; and 3) a reactive intensification of intergroup barriers. Antonovsky does not make it explicit, but it would seem to follow that this intensification may be a result of increased anxiety on the part of non-marginal members of the two groups about the loss of their social identity.

Limited acceptance by two cultural worlds (Mexican and United States) and a lack of stable integrative techniques for family, peer, and non-family adult worlds creates extensive difficulties for Mexican Americans so that they can locate neither unambiguous non-marginal identity models nor participate freely without fear in the Anglo world.

A majority of the 800,000 Americans with Spanish surnames who reside in Los Angeles County are of Mexican ancestry. Until the early 1960's many of these persons had maintained a rural, agrarian, Mexican belief system. A by-product of the Mexican cultural tradition is the close-knit family. Mexican family tradition gives cultural support even after meeting the extremes of an industrial, highly urbanized megalopolis, e.g. Los Angeles. If the traditions of Mexican culture, in the United States, are maintained through this highly integrated family, then one can hypothesize that Mexican American adolescent crises arise not only from the expected turbulence and instability due to physiological, age-sex role and peer demands but these conflicts are compounded by the impact of American social structure on the Mexican family system.

Adolescence, in American society, is an extended period during which United States youngsters desperately and sporadically desert childhood while seeking adult social world acceptance. At best, adolescence in America is a relatively haphazard process. This identity "no-man's land" is a prolonged process in the United States. Although puberty and its physiological concomitants, no doubt, influence behavior, cross-cultural data indicate that an extension of the adolescent process, without institutionalized puberty rituals, a lack of social function and status, and a tendency for the community to isolate and alienate the adolescent, all are important facets contributing to the dysfunctional behavior frequently attributed to adolescents.

Middle, upper middle, and upper-class Americans generally provide guidance and adequately defined institutionalized means for converting adolescence into adulthood. For example, since formal education is a value to be cherished, American culture extends minimal education approximately to the ages of 20 to 22. Youngsters in the upper classes have an opportunity for psychological and financial support as well as the external and internal motivation for participation in educational institutions during their extensive journey through no-man's land into adulthood. The socio-economic milieu of these persons makes early entrance into the occupational and economic institution unnecessary.

Lower middle- and lower-class American adolescents, because of a lack of psychological and social supports, the need to earn a living, and the need to become "somebody" and get out of the social situation where they find themselves, more frequently grasp at the available overt significant symbols provided by their limited adult-world experience. Smoking, automobiles, drinking, leaving school, going to work, sexual acting-out, narcotics—all are attempts, frequently unsuccessful ones, at integrating and synthesizing the complex social world of adults.

However, some dysfunctional aspects of legal social control over adolescents exists. Concomitant with the value on extended education are Child Labor laws which make it legally impossible for adolescents to earn a living until they are of age 16 to 18. Legal restrictions on property ownership, however, follow the assumption that one must be 21. Control over one's political destiny also is infrequently obtained until the 21st birthday. Participating in such highly visible adult-like behaviors, e.g. drinking alcoholic beverages, being free from local curfews, assuming complete responsibility for one's own behavior, being free from family restrictions and others, hinge on sex and age (18-21) restraints. Adolescence in American society frequently perpetuates two messages. One message based upon the legal institutions, stresses chronological age as the important factor to acceptance in the adult world, while child-rearing patterns, the educational institutions, and the community insist upon "mature behavior patterns." Seldom is there a socio-cultural and psychological integration of the chronological age with totally accepted behavior patterns.

To straddle the two worlds of adults and children, with simultaneous feelings of rejection from both and acceptance from neither creates role-conflict. During this process adolescent individuals are desperately trying to be relieved of the dependency upon one world, while struggling for autonomy and acceptance in the other.

Adolescents dealing with this ambiguous, marginal process, for the extended period of time upon which the United States culture insists, find themselves in no-man's land, engaged in sifting the ever-increasing role-models for supporting an unambiguous sense of identity. A meaningful sense of identity, with its behaviorally adaptive techniques, is a result of the integrative processes drawing upon an adequate and socially meaningful childhood with its familial and peer experiences, adolescence with its peer, family, and educational implications, and young adulthood with its educational, work-related, and familial associations. It is the interaction of these associations and the growing child's ability to integrate and perceive them in terms of adaptive modes of behavior that presents the matrix for his identity.

The absence of a formal declaration of adulthood in American culture establishes ambiguous, idiosyncratic methods for finding its beginnings. Therefore, the responsiblities and rewards for being adult are seldom fully realized until several years past the legal status of adulthood. This is when complete independency from family ties is prominent in the young person's life. Adult uncertainty is difficult in itself, but to approach adulthood by being a member of two divergent cultures, yet maintaining dependency upon the dominant one, establishes the unique variation of Mexican American adolescent identity crisis.

Identity crisis experienced in adolescence is more dramatic in 1) societies which extend the period while ignoring puberty rites and other cultural mechanisms of certainty, and 2) excluded segments of the society where cultural supports and institutionalized means for beginning and ending adolescence are less clearly defined. Therefore, adolescents in the American society who reside in the cultures of poverty and subsistence have greater difficulty dealing with cultural authority in relation to their self-perception than those adolescents who live in cultures of affluence.

For persons who are born and reared through many generations in the lower classes of the urban complex, adolescence is difficult. When the incorporation of adult social world values becomes meaningful, the difficulties of this process are compounded by membership in an ethnic minority. This is particularly evident where family values of the ethnic social world are in conflict with those of the American system.

Adolescent members of minorities not only straddle worlds of childhood and adulthood but simultaneously must cope with the identity difficulties extended through the knowledge that one's culture is devalued and ignored in the culture in which one finds it necessary to live, play, work, and love. The devalued minority culture then becomes a parallel to the less valuable childhood social system while the majority culture has much in common with the adult world.

Adolescent crisis under these circumstances is most traumatic. This is significant when the American value system pays lip service to, but belittles, the values, religion, superstitions, and the cohesive family of the Mexican minority's native land. The Mexican American learned these values in close communication and interaction with significant others; therefore they are sacredly held. The American value system, on the other hand, with its upwardly striving, high production-oriented value system, frequently alienates minorites because of the devaluation of their cultural system.

Belief and participation in age and sex role changes gives meaning to life developmental processes while simultaneously allowing for less role-conflict, greater integration, and more adequate and accurate resolution of crises. A lack of participation and understanding of age and sex role development leads to social system conflict.

American social structure permits adolescent Americans of Mexican descent only limited access to American social norms and behavior. It gives rewards for obtaining United States behavior patterns while simultaneously paying little homage to the Mexican or Mexican American social system and values which are significant to the adolescent. The compounding of cultural diversity, inaccurate and inadequate participation in age and sex roles, the majority belittling significant beliefs of the minority, and the fracturing of language as it relates to one's world view makes this research of adolescent identity crisis imperative.

## ADOLESCENT IDENTITY CRISES RESEARCH

During the initial data gathering phase of this experiment we were fortunate to receive the willing aid and support of an East Los Angeles teen center and its leader. During the first Friday evening while approximately 30 subjects were completing the questionnaire, a rival gang invaded the teen center. Not only was the experiment interrupted but many of the forms were destroyed which extended the data gathering period several months. After this unfortunate incident, adolescents were brought in two at a time to complete the 34-page questionnaire.

### Purpose

This research purposes to examine the relationship between Mexican American culture and adolescent identity crisis. Problems associated with identity crisis for adolescents will appear differentially (when holding sex and social class constant) depending upon the degree of identity wih Mexican culture.

In an earlier work Seward suggested ". . . the paradoxically sounding assumption that the more firmly an individual is embedded in his primary ingroup the better integration he may be expected to make with the dominant culture" (33). Peak writes, "The great differences in philosophy of acceptance and resignation, passivity, dependency, etc. between Mexican and Anglos have been the cause of much misunderstanding of Mexicans by the Anglo population who misinterpret Mexican philosophy and see these people as indifferent, lazy or unambitious" (29). These differences are accentuated during adolescent crisis. Since Mexican values are the antithesis of the American adult ego ideal, then unless Mexican American adolescents find congruence in, and lack ambivalence toward, their sub-cultural values, transition into adulthood may be filled with identity conflict.

The dominant pattern in Mexican families is to develop in the growing child obedience, humility, and respect for elders (13). Adolescent crisis is turbulent with problems of authority and self-determination. An intensification of ambivalence toward obedience, humility, and respect is encountered at this time for most Mexican American adolescents. We hypothesize that this is particularly evident for youngsters who have not adequately internalized the dominant Mexican values.

Associated with these difficulties is the humility of the older generation. A lower-class Mexican lady indicated, "When my teen-age children do wrong I blame nobody but myself for not being more strict." In response to being asked how she felt when the children lived up to her expectations she stated, "I thank God for making them that way." The Mexican American adult with his extreme humility associated with success and self-punishment associated with failure, establishes a psycho-social situation within which the developing child, when in contact with the Anglo world, finds difficulty integrating the concepts of responsibility, aggressiveness, authority, and independence. To manifest a world view that, "man can do only 'bad' things and God can do only 'good' things" is functional only with strong cultural support and a lack of interference from outside cultures. Culture shock for Mexicans is apparent when the Anglo world suggests that man is responsible for both his "good" and his "bad" deeds. This establishes for the growing child a conflicting situation, creating ambivalence toward the Mexican value system, while concomitantly supporting acceptance of the Anglo culture which is more functional for upward mobility and has only limited usefulness for self-preservation. Since adolescence is a time for breaking away from authority, both parental and religious, the Mexican American youngster who has ambivalent feelings toward his culture easily strikes at his parents through deviant acts without offending God.

Mexican American informants in East Los Angeles indicate that youthful gangs are most frequently those boys with extreme feelings of ambivalence toward the Mexican culture.

According to Erikson's assumption, the mastering of future life experiences for adolescent Mexican Americans depends upon the success with which they mastered their own culture and later the Anglo culture. It may be hypothesized that if one successfully gains "whole-hearted" cultural support for his Mexican identity, then later success at coping with incongruent Anglo modes of behavior is functional for political and socio-economic success, yet not necessarily dysfunctional for ego identity. If, as it is suggested by other investigators (37), the Mexican American family has been, during the last generation, moving away from overt father-dependence to the American pattern of individualism, then the strong, dominant father and passive, submissive mother of the Mexican cultural pattern are no longer functional as a "successful variant of group identity." As stated by Seward, "This change has had a disorganizing influence on family structure and adversely affected the personalities of family members, often resulting in antagonism between eldest and younger sons, and becoming manifest in delinquent behavior" (34).

In a series of investigations with American Negro college students, children, and mental patients and their families, it was hypothesized that problems of identity formation, identity conflict, adolescent crises, and marginality are results of the absence of a distinguishable culture (5). If identity is most difficult for a culture-less minority, then it can be postulated that those members of a cultural minority who view their culture with ambivalence and see it as incongruent, will have greater difficulty with adolescent crises than those adolescents who receive strong cultural supports.

## Hypotheses

Our broad working hypothesis is: Mexican American adolescents who strongly incorporate Mexican culture into their belief system are better able to organize, synthesize, and generalize with less conflict from the behaviors and values of both the Mexican and Anglo world and these adolescents are more adaptive to adolescent crisis than Mexican American adolescents who deny or demonstrate ambivalence toward Mexican American culture.

More specifically the hypotheses to be tested through the use of a questionnaire are as follows. 1) Identity conflict and unresolved adolescent conflict (as measured by our instrument) will be statistically significantly greater for Mexican American youths (13–19 years of age) who deny, reject, or display ambivalence toward Mexican American culture. 2) Because of less incongruence between Mexican and Anglo female sex role-behavior, Mexican American females, when controlled for social class and age, will display significantly less identity conflict than Mexican American males.

## Methodology

The sample consists of 89 adolescents of Mexican American background living in the low income area of East Los Angeles. These young persons, 42 males and 47 females, were between the ages of 13 and 19. Each youngster anonymously completed a 34-page questionnaire. This included 10 pages of objective information covering a personal and family history as well as subjective feelings and attitudes toward persons and values significant in the life of adolescents.

Together with these face sheet data was a series of 24 concepts followed by 19 Osgood semantic differential scales. These scales were selected to personally reveal concept differences for male-female roles and American and Mexican value orientations (e.g. proud-humble, dark-light etc.). Each concept concerns itself with personal identity in that each relates to persons who may present problems of ego integration during adolescence (e.g. Mexican, Father, Mother, bullfighter, etc.).

*Findings and Discussion*

Although there are no differences between males and females in terms of age, country of birth, length of time lived in Los Angeles, religion, or education, the males in the sample have significantly more fathers who were born in Mexico than do the females. The education of both mother and father, for males and females, is not significantly different. Males, significantly more frequently than females, failed to answer historical and opinion items. Apparently, males have less information concerning family background or they are more reluctant to answer questions concerning them. Ability to answer or not in terms of understanding based on educational level should not be significantly different. No significant difference exists, between males and females, on the basis of where mother was born. Mother's education is also the same for both categories. The boys in the sample had an average of six and one-half siblings at home while the girls from this population had five and one-half siblings at home.

Twenty-six questions concerning some pertinent facts about their lives as well as their opinions were asked. All those questions which show significant differences at the .05 level of confidence between males and females will be mentioned. Females more frequently attend church. Both males and females feel that they have little or no control over what happens to them. Both males and females also feel, and strongly so, that God is a powerful, omnipotent being.

Fathers in both groups are infrequently employed. Girls, significantly more than boys, see their father as participating in family life. All subjects know their mother loves them. Mother is viewed as one who keeps the family together. Both males and females feel that the family means more to them than anything else. Although both groups speak Spanish quite frequently, their reading of Spanish newspapers is extremely infrequent. Boys in this sample attribute illness to themselves more frequently than do the girls. Girls feel more strongly than boys that when they do something wrong the whole family suffers.

Another major difference between males and females is in response to their reason for working. Boys disagree more frequently than girls to the statement, "The reason for working is to save money for the future." Both boys and girls believe that sickness is punishment for bad deeds. The parents of girls most frequently seek help with problems from members of the family. Boys' families do also, but not as frequently as the girls' families. A *curandero* seems to be the least frequently used by these youngsters' parents for assistance with personal problems.

Both males and females in this sample indicate that their families utilize friends or the priest for assistance when someone is mentally ill. Females also feel more frequently that mother should obey father and protect the children. Obedience to father apparently is not as important to males. The "gang" apparently is important to the same degree for both males and females, although it appears unimportant to the majority of them.

Based upon the 19 semantic scales used in this experiment, there is no significant difference between the way male adolescents identify with their fathers and female adolescents identify with their mothers. All differences are reported where the T exceeds 2.0 representing a significant difference at .05 or better. There is identification congruence between the way these adolescents view self and parent of the same sex. Girls see self and mother similarly on all scales except they feel mother is braver, more leading, more beautiful, and wiser than self. Males view self and father alike on all scales except they see father as more active and harder. When females compare self to father they see signficantly more difference than males. Father is braver, stronger, more leading, more beautiful, more intelligent, and harder than self. Boys identify as closely to their mothers as do the girls. Boys see mother as more sober, more virtuous, lighter, and more beautiful than self. Females do not display significantly less identity conflict than Mexican American males. Therefore, our second hypothesis is invalid.

When these adolescents compare self with how they would like their parents to be, mother, it seems, is the person whom they wish to change. Girls would like their mothers to change on 11 items. That is, they desire mother to be more proud, virtuous, leading, superior, sober, strong, beautiful, intelligent, active, wise and kind. Boys also would like their mothers to be more sober, virtuous, light, co-operative, beautiful, intelligent, and kind. Females would lke their fathers to be more brave, virtuous, strong, leading, beautiful, active, and wise. Males, however, would like their father to be more brave, sober, virtuous, leading, and kind.

When comparing the self-concept of males with that of females, they differ significantly (Z < .05) on only three items. Boys are more brave, leading, and ugly. When "self" is compared with "self as I would like it to be" males and females desire to be different on the same perameters. Both males and females desire to be significantly more brave, virtuous, strong, leading, beautiful, intelligent, and wise. Girls feel that they also should be more active and superior; however, boys do not. Boys on the other hand desire to be more hard, while the girls do not.

Males and females both view social workers, medical doctors, teachers, and boss on similar parameters, all of which are different than self. Boys view wife as more virtuous, light, humble, beautiful, and softer than self. Males evidently perceive themselves as more marriageable than girls perceive self. Males state the only significant difference between self and husband is that husbands are more humbly. Humble is considered by these adolescents as a negatively valued behavior pattern. Females note that husbands are more brave, excitable, leading, beautiful, wise, and hard than self.

Both sexes were readily able to discriminate significantly wide variations between self and crazy persons, babies, and God. Males see themselves as completely comparable to a bullfighter except on one parameter; bullfighters are more virtuous. Boys see themselves as different from Mexicans on only three parameters; they feel Mexicans are more dark, rash, and unfriendly. Girls, however, see themselves as similar to Anglos on all scales except three; Anglos are more competitive, leading, and unfriendly. Males, however, see Anglos as more rash, humble, weak, ugly, and passive. Male negatively valued concepts, i.e. police, Anglo, medical doctor, social worker, teacher, and boss all have clusters of negatively valued adjectives which described these persons as significantly different from the Mexican American youth participants in this study. Females, on the other hand, had fewer and held less intense feelings against the two categories of police and crazy person.

The total group was divided on the basis of responding to statement 41, "When I do something wrong, my whole family suffers." This statement provided greater differences between groups. The phenomena of family suffering for the wrongs of an individual is a Mexican cultural trait. None of the other 20 questions revealed as strong differences between Mexican and American culture identification. Although there is no difference in religious preference between the two groups, the highly Mexicanized category attended church much more frequently than the highly Americanized category, and this is particularly true for the females. Also, the fathers of highly Mexicanized adolescents participate in family life much less frequently. Although mothers for both categories are seen as loving, fathers for the highly Mexicanized category, when angry toward the child, elicit sympathetic feelings from mother for the child much less frequently than do those with an American identity.

Self-blame when things go wrong is significantly more frequent among those with a Mexican identity than those with an American identity. School failures, at this point, are more frequent for the highly Americanized adolescent than for the adolescent with a Mexican identity.

The ability to read and speak Spanish is apparently greater for youngsters with a Mexican identity; yet, adolescents who identify with the American culture read significantly more Spanish newspapers. In response to the statement, "When sick, I blame myself," adolescents who identify as American respond significantly less frequently in this manner than do those adolescents who identify as Mexican. Although both adolescent categories feel that mental hospitals help sick people, the highly Mexicanized significantly more frequently believe that when a person is mentally ill, he cannot help himself. Neither category desires to live in Mexico.

Youngsters with a Mexican identity believe that sickness is a punishment for a bad deed. An interesting finding is that highly Mexicanized youngsters, significantly more than the Americanized adolescents, feel that school teaches one how to get ahead and gives one skills for doing so. Youngsters with a Mexican identity are more likely to agree that human beings are sinful by nature.

To the statement, "Sex before marriage is okay for boys," Mexicanized boys almost unanimously agree, while Mexicanized girls divide evenly between agree and disagree. However, Americanized boys also disagree to that statement, but the Americanized girls are more likely to agree with it than disagree with it. On the other hand, in response to the statement, "Sex before marriage is okay for girls," the Mexican identified boys split half in agreement and half in disagreement, while the majority of the Mexicanized females disagree. Adolescents with an American identification, however, indicate to this same statement that the boys agree that sex before marriage is okay for girls, but the girls highly disagree with this.

Americanized boys find the gang to be significantly more important than do the Mexicanized boys. There is no difference, however, between the girls. Although both groups highly agree that crazy people deserve to be punished, Mexicanized adolescents agree to a significantly less degree than do Americanized adolescents. Girls with a Mexican identity, much less frequently than girls with an American identity, disagree with the statement, "When there is misfortune, I seek a means of control."

On the basis of these data, it appears as if the Mexican American youngster who more highly identifies with the Mexican way of life is more educationally minded, is more sympathetic and adaptable to deviants, maintains more respect for authority, and is more adaptable to conflicting situations. These data indicate that, at least for this population of lower-class Mexican American adolescents, the maintenance, perpetuation, and integration of the Mexican heritage and culture is important to the maintenance of a stable sense of identity while growing up in the United States. Also, in terms of the number of failures in school and arrests for these lower-class youngsters, a Mexican identification acts as a buffer and protects against hostile relations created within the American social structure.

## CONCLUSION AND SUMMARY

On the basis of the data gathered from these 89 Mexican American adolescents of Los Angeles' Serape Belt it is apparent that boys have greater conflict over their identity and social role than girls. Neither males nor females in this sample identify with the Mexican family role-prototype. Role-relations and behaviors of mother, father, wife, and husband do not match the Mexican family described by Oscar Lewis (19). Girls more closely identify with the Anglo female and mother roles while boys identify more closely with the "machismo" and husband roles of the Mexican culture. Females desire that their mothers should fit more closely the Anglo mother prototype. Interestingly enough, males also would like their mothers to behave more as Anglo mothers.

Minority group status for these Mexican Americans can be related to the schism between male and female identities. Role-conflict is engendered by a marginal status between the cultural need for maintaining the identity of one's heritage and the social necessity for maintaining one's integrity and economic stability in a culturally hostile environment. Both girls and boys who must closely identify with Mexican culture (i.e. language, religion, family structure, and values) appear to have less identity difficulties and less conflict over family roles. On the other hand, male and female adolescents who more closely identify with Anglo proto-types appear to maintain greater identity incongruence between how they see themselves and how they would like to be. Also, these same Americanized adolescents see greater role-conflict in what mother and father are and how they wish mother and father would be.

It appears that Americanized adolescents (those who least value Mexican culture) are in greater conflict over choosing appropriate behaviors for adequate functioning in the family, peer, and greater Anglo or Mexican American adult worlds (3). If as Parsons (27) has suggested role-conflict produces strain which can be recognized through deviancy, then according to our data Americanized Mexican American adolescents are more vulnerable to deviant behavior depending, of course, upon their ability to cope with reactions to strain.

According to this investigation forced acculturation of minorities by the dominant group may be dysfunctionl for adequate and accurate integration of dominant value orientations and behaviors. Pride in one's cultural heritage appears functional as an integrative technique for reducing adolescent identity and role-conflict.

## REFERENCES

1. Antonovsky, A.: Toward a refinement of the marginal man concept. Social Forces, 35: 57, 1956.
2. Blau, P. M.: Patterns of choice in interpersonal relations. American Society Review, 28: 41–55, 1962.

3. Bossard, J. H. S. and Boll, E. S.: *The Sociology of Child Development*. Harper & Brothers, New York, 1960.

4. Brody, E. B.: Cultural exclusion, character and illness. American Journal of Psychiatry, *122*: 852—858, 1966.

5. Brody, E. B.: Color and identity conflict in young boys. Psychiatry, *26*: 188—201, 1963.

6. Cooley, C. H.: *Human Nature and Social Order*. Charles Scribner's Sons, New York, 1922.

7. Derbyshire, R. L.: The sociology of exclusion: Implications for training adult illiterates. Adult Education, 3—11, 1966.

8. Derbyshire, R. L.: United States Negro identity conflict. Sociology and Social Research, *51*: 63—77, 1966.

9. Dworkin, A.: Stereotypes and self-images held by native-born and foreign-born Mexican Americans. Sociology and Social Research, *49*: 214—224, 1965.

10. Erikson, E.: *Childhood and Society*. W. W. Norton & Company Inc., New York, 1950.

11. Frendenberg, E.: *Social Profiles: Los Angeles County*. Welfare Planning Council, C-3, 1965.

12. Golovensky, J. R.: *Marginal man concepts. Social Forces, 31*: 333-339, 1952.

13. Guerrero, R. D.: Neurosis and the Mexican family structure. American Journal of Psychiatry, *112:* 411—417, 1955.

14. Heller, C. S.: *Mexican American Youth: Forgotten Youth at the Cross-roads*, Ch. 1, Random House Inc., New York, 1966.

15. Johnson, H.: *Sociology*. Harcourt, Brace & Co., New York, 1960.

16. Kenkel, W.: *The Family in Perspective*. Appleton-Century-Crofts Inc., New York, 1960.

17. Kluckhohn, F. and Strodtbeck.: *Variations in Value Orientation*. Row & Peterson & Company, Evanston, 1961.

18. Lewis, O.: Marriage and the family: Husbands and wives in a Mexican village: A study of role conflict. American Anthropology, *51*: 602—610, 1949.

20. Madsen, W.: *The Mexican Americans of Southwest Texas*. Holt, Rinehart & Winston, New York, 1964.

21. Marden, C. F.: *Minorities in American Society*. American Book Company, New York, 1952.

22. Martindale, D.: *The Nature and Types of Sociological Theory*. Houghton Mifflin Company, Boston, 1960.

23. McWilliams, C.: *North from Mexico—The Spanish Speaking Peoples of the United States*. J. B. Lippincott Co., Philadelphia, 1949.

24. Mead, G. H.: *Mind, Self and Society*. University of Chicago Press, Chicago, 1959.

25. Meeker, M.: *Background for Planning*. Welfare Planning Council, Los Angeles, C-3, 1964.

26. Mexican American Study Project. Progress Report, Division of Research, Graduate School of Business Administration, U.C.L.A., Los Angeles, April 1965.

27. Parsons, T.: *The Social System*. The Free Press of Glencoe, Inc., Glencoe, Ill., 1951.

28. Parsons, T.: and Schills, B.: *Toward a General Theory of Action.* Harvard University Press, Cambridge, Mass., 1959.
29. Peak, H. M.: Search for identity by a young Mexican American, *In Clinical Studies in Culture Conflict,* edited by G. Sewards, The Ronald Press, New York, 1958.
30. Rubel, A. J.: *Across the Tracks: Mexican Americans in a Texas City.* University of Texas Press, Austin, 1966.
31. Schermerhorn, R. S.: *These Our People.* D. C. Heath and Company, Boston, 1945.
32. Sears, R. R., Rau, L., and Alpert, R.: *Identification and Child Rearing.* Stanford University Press, Stanford, 1965.
33. Seward, G., editor: *Clinical Studies in Culture Conflict.* The Ronald Press, New York, 1958.
34. Seward, G.: Sex identity and the social order. Journal of Nervous and Mental Disease, *139*: 126–136, 1964.
35. Seward, G.: Personal communications to author.
36. Shibutani, T.: *Society and Personality.* Prentice-Hall, Inc., Englewood Cliffs, N.J. 1961.
37. Spiegel, I. P. and Kluckhohn, F. R.: Integration and conflict in family behavior. GAP, No. 27, 1954.
38. Williams, R.: *American Society.* Alfred A. Knoff Inc., New York, 1960.
39. Zurcher, L., Meadon, A., and Zurcher, S.: Value orientation, role conflict and alienation from work. American Sociological Review, *30*: 539–547, 1955.
40. Progress Report, Mexican American Study Project, Division of Research, Graduate School of Business Administration, UCLA, April, 1965.

# Identity Conflicts of Chinese Adolescents in San Francisco

STANLEY L. M. FONG

WHEN VISITORS come to San Francisco, one of the first sights they want to see is Chinatown. When they walk along Grant Avenue after a morning of shopping at Macy's, Roos-Atkins, and the City of Paris, the street suddenly narrows and they see swaying strings of Oriental lanterns, dazzling Chinese signs, and curving pagoda roofs. To many, Chinatown seems picturesque and exotic, a city within a city—a feeling of being in the Orient. It is populated by some 36,000 Chinese, but at night, surprisingly, it seems to be peopled by tourists. The strollers shop in the numerous curio shops, eat in Chinese restaurants, some finely decorated in modern Chinese, and walk by a few impressive banks with Chinese motifs and plate glass doors and walls. But they rarely see or are aware of life behind these buildings. It is on this that this article will focus.

To get a good perspective, one has to go back into the pages of time to the origin of Chinatown. The very first Chinese pioneers to California were merchants, selling food and Chinese goods such as tea and silk. Their early success, in the 1840's, prompted others to follow, but their numbers were still small. Then the cry of gold was heard and the rush was on. At seaports, Chinese clamored and crowded into the ocean-going vessels of the day. Hitherto, the trans-Pacific passage had been one of trade in goods; henceforth, human cargo was to form a large part of the trade. But unlike the immigrants from Europe, most of these men were married, leaving their wives and children at home; those who were unattached were often quickly married off under the auspices of their parents before they set off to sea. Thus, parents hoped to ensure the return of their

111

sons to the land of their ancestors. They dreamed of finding gold, free for the taking, and returning to China to retire in luxury. "Gold Mountain" was the name they gave to America. Many did not find it. After the gold rush was over Chinese continued to come. This time it was the call of the transcontinental railway to lay down tracks, and tens of thousands of Chinese "coolie" laborers came. (Chinatowns were often started by men who left the tracks in various parts of the country.) Then the depression came and agitation against Chinese miners and laborers grew. Many laws were passed against aliens to keep them from staking claims or to trouble them in other ways, and many Chinese left the mine fields throughout California and withdrew in the Chinese ghetto. A great many returned to China and the population of Chinese in America started to decline. Others stayed and hoped to glean a small fortune, by peddling or washing clothes, before returning to their father-land—this was to take a lifetime for some. But a fortune was made by some and they returned to live the lives of wealthy gentlemen in their villages; others, when money ran out, left for America to make more for the next visit, often taking a growing son to help out. The habit of sending their savings across the sea followed.

What are the reasons at home that brought about the immi-gration of the Chinese? To begin, it is important to say that these Chinese did not come from all parts of China but from one in particular. This was the coastal province of Kwangtung, of which Canton is the best known city. It was once a prosperous area, but it became the most densely populated region in China. In the last century its population outran its food supply and famine and poverty followed. There were also floods. In the north, a most terrible flood occurred in 1847 when the 3000-mile long Yangtze River overran its course. There were also floods in the rivers to the south. Hundreds of thousands of peasants were left homeless and flocked to the cities to find relief and new means of sustenance. The cry of gold on the other side of the Pacific was heard and stirred up great hopes.

After a few decades in America it became popular for Chinese to send for their wives or acquire, with the aid of relatives, picture brides. Slowly families began to appear on the Chinatown scene, a ghetto once geared for units of homeless men. The family has always been the center of Chinese society for millenniums and has a great influence on all spheres of life. But the Chinese family differs, in many respects, from the surrounding American pattern and the key to the problems of Chinese adolescents in America may lie here. A look at the family pattern is essential.

## THE FAMILY

In the traditional Chinese family the father is considered to be the head of the house and has authority over the family members. The wife is considered to be subordinate to the husband. It is for the wife to serve also as a servant to her in-laws. Her status is improved immeasurably when she gives birth to a son, although some recognition does come from giving birth to a daughter. The offsprings are taught to respect their parents and show obedience in the form of filial piety. The children are also taught to respect their relatives near and far. It is the custom of the culture to venerate the elders. In fact, the husband is expected to yield to the authority of his parents and older relatives. In the extended family system of the Chinese, the reach of the family is far-reaching, so far so that it is the parents who arrange a marriage for the son, often without the son having knowledge of whom the bride is until after the wedding ceremony and the bride unveils her face. Many of the older generations in Chinatown were married in this fashion. The phrase that the Chinese are "under the ancestor's shadow" is appropriate. "The son owes to his father absolute obedience, and he must support his parents, mourn for them, bury them according to social station and financial ability, provide for their needs in the other world, and take all necessary steps toward insuring the male line. The younger man is obliged to do these things not only because of his duty to his parents but also because he is indebted to his and his father's common ancestors. Thus, from the point of view of kinship organization as a whole, the father-son identification is merely a necessary link in the great family continuum, with numerous ancestors at one end and innumerable descendants at the other" (10, pp. 236–237).

A closer look at the father-son relationship is useful. The Chinese " . . . admonished the male, as soon as he is able to understand, to obey his parents, especially his father, to the fullest extent;

that it is bad behavior to question his wisdom or decisions; that it is good to do whatever he wants done without the slightest regard for one's own feeling; that it is not desirable to commit one-self to any independent line of action; that it is sinful to do anything which disturbs his father in any way; in other words, that he is to keep himself ready at all time, as long as he lives, to please him, and to be of all possible service to him" (10, pp. 244–245). Traditionally, "The paternal authority does not stop when the younger person has come of age, but is continued as long as the father is alive" (10, p. 258). Ideally, the younger man has no complaints against the arrangement as such because his turn will come when others will have to submit to his authority. "Then the younger man takes the father's place in the great family continuum. In this way the thing of primary importance in shaping personality is the ancestral authority. The more reliance upon this authority the individual shows, the better adjusted he becomes throughout life. This authority over him and prearrangement for him run through every aspect of his life and work, including his marriage and means of livelihood. At every turn the individual is confined within this prearranged framework" (10 p. 258).

The obligations of a daughter are not as great, for the ties with her parents will be severed when she marries into another family. The females, then, ". . . are not as responsible as are the males for following in the shadow of their ancestors" (2, p. 299).

In general, parental authority is a major theme in Chinese culture. What is the effect of this type of training on personality development? "As far as the overt behavior is concerned, the first outstanding quality is an explicitly submissive attitude toward authority" (10, p. 260). In a typical Chinese village there are very few choices and very few uncertainties. "All routes are, so to speak, barred except one, that which follows the foot-steps of his father, his father's father, and the whole line of his more remote ancestors. Along the established path, life is agreeable; all other trails lead to misery and self-destruction. . . . He tends to be apprehensive of any departure from the beaten path" (10, p. 260). This passage is immediately comprehensible when it is mentioned that some villages are controlled by one clan, which may occupy an entire village.

But the social structure of the villages, as mentioned already, was being undermined by famine and poverty. Many of the younger men went abroad to find other means of livelihood. Meeting some success in their endeavors, many encouraged their brothers, uncles, and cousins to come to America and share in the available opportunities, for mutual dependence is a central theme of Chinese society. With decades of this practice, networks of relatives in America began to develop.

Undoubtedly, the family image these immigrants brought over with them was based on the Chinese model. The child-rearing practices in Chinatown were patterned after this traditional ideal. The growing number of relatives in Chinatown helped maintain the extended family to some extent. But the kinship system was never completely duplicated in America, for such personages as the grandparents and other elders were left behind in the old country. Coupled with this, there were other social forces in the ghetto which made it difficult to preserve, in all aspects, the traditional form of primary family relationships. In moving from the past to the present, from a village setting to an urban one, the style of life changes. In Chinatown the common man usually works over 8 hours a day, 6 days a week, as cook, waiter, dishwasher, and clerk, which are the chief occupations in the ghetto. The work entails working into the evening and it is common practice for employees to eat supper at work, away from their families. The wages are low, and often mothers, especially ones with large families, need to work in a sewing factory to supplement the meager family income. There are about 170 garment factories in Chinatown which make use of this source of labor, hiring about 3000 women in all (5). (Attempts to unionize the garment factories in the ghetto seem doomed to failure as it would endanger their thin thread of existence. They are grateful for their little extra income and are fearful that their employers would not be able to compete successfully with the larger society if labor cost goes up.) The conditions of life in the ghetto, thus, make it difficult for many parents to perform their roles as agents of socialization. (The case is quite different in a village community.) Family life is weakened even further by the fact that the children go to Chinese language classes, after coming home from American public schools, and do not return until after seven o'clock in the evening. Fatigue may set in and it is not surprising that a large number of Chinese youths resent going to Chinese school. It seems, at times, that "they are seldom home except to eat and sleep" (14, p. 115). But most Chinese parents want their children to learn the language, customs, and manners of their ancestors. In a manner, they have given the Chinese school the task of socializing their children. Many of the youths react negatively to this experience. Mischief in school is not uncommon and playing "hookey" is a recognized pastime. Only a small number complete all six grades of Chinese elementary school and a handful finish the Chinese junior high program. The ancient methods of learning by rote and recitation prevail in the Chinese classroom and do not appeal to the children who have been exposed to the modern American approach. The problem is compounded by the fact that the Chinese teachers speak a more "sophisticated" dialect than the local one the youngsters are used to and this makes for some communication difficulties. The irony of the situation is that these teachers do not occupy a very high status in their students' eyes. It is not uncommon, because of low wages, for these teachers to take outside jobs as waiters, clerks, and handymen.

A sojourner described the Chinese school in the following manner: "Discipline is practically unknown, and mischief expresses itself in multiferous ways: from dirty jokes scrawled on blackboards to practical jokes. . . . A near sighted teacher once told me that he would rather 'teach a group of monkeys than a bunch of them little devils.' He said it with a bitterness born of experience. No sooner had he put his spectacles on the desk one evening than a "little devil" sneaked up and grabbed them. His helplessness in his blindness made the boys laugh and the girls giggle. . . . When he resigned, he swore he would never again teach American-born Chinese even if he starved. A friend of mine who holds two American university degrees, and helps in his father's store in Chinatown, had a similarly unpleasant experience. He was asked to substitute for a teacher for two weeks. The first day, the pupils, boys and girls, greeted him in chorus with: 'You are not a teacher. You are only a store clerk. We have seen you packing boxes of canned goods. You can't teach us anything" (14, pp. 118–119).

The Chinese in America who have gone to language schools

when young may smile when they read this passage. I suspect that, in school, even the more timid ones found secret delight in observing such activities. For it is understandable that children who are young and energetic would rather be at home and play. The conspicuous few who misbehave are probably "acting out" their rebellion against their parents or parental substitutes. Typically, the father—whose authority is not to be challenged—is the one who insists that the boy or girl attend Chinese school. The mother is likely to be more sympathetic. On the Chinese school ground, the conflicts between youths and authority figures may be re-enacted. Unable to express their differences to their parents, who give them no choice in the matter, they may displace their angry feelings onto their language teachers. Unless they are skilled teachers, they may have a problem on their hands, either in the form of mischief or large scale indifference. The latter, a form of passive-aggression, is rather common and includes not doing homework or not preparing for exams—girls do much better than boys as they tend to be more submissive. This is not surprising, as passive-aggression is proverbial in Chinese culture, a culture where a plain disobedience or expression of hostility toward one's elders is strictly tabooed.

On the whole, though, the respect and obedience that Chinese children give to authority figures elsewhere are, to a large extent, observed in schools also. In the American school system, Chinese children rarely misbehave. They have the reputation of being the best behaved pupils in the city, as teachers at Commodore Stockton Elementary School in Chinatown will attest. Evidently, the attitudes of many youths toward Chinese and American schools are different. The appeal of the Chinese classroom is much less than the American one. Some resent going to Chinese classes when they see a few peers who do not, such as boys and girls from more westernized homes or their American playmates. A number of children develop very strong feeling against learning Chinese. In fact, Hsu spoke of a few " . . . . Chinese children raised in the United States who spat at anyone who dared to talk Chinese to them" (9, p. 97).

When the child goes to American public school, he learns a new language, and he acquires greater facility as he goes through school.

The time will soon come when he speaks mainly in English with his peers. He speaks English increasingly at home with his brothers and sisters. The parents may soon find that they are losing contact with their children and some communication problems develop. Many parents at this point try to learn the new language to keep up with their children. At school, the child also learns new skills and social values which may be foreign to those of the parents. At this age, the school teachers begin to serve as respected models of social behavior. These behaviors which the child observes and learns may, however, be different from those at home. It is common, in the American culture, to teach the child to fend for himself, to make his own decisions, and to stand on his own feet. Instead of being led by an authoritarian figure, the pupil is encouraged to be self-reliant and independent. In fact, the child may be encouraged to assert himself. I can remember an episode in my grammar school days. I heard a boy crying and turned around. The lady teacher rushed up and yelled at the bully to stand still and asked the small one to hit him back. The little boy stopped crying immediately and shook his head slightly, and a faint smile grew on his face. When I looked back on this, he must have been just as astonished as I was. His smile must have been one of surprise at such a novel approach to discipline. A traditional child would have been told by his family to run home when there is danger and let the family take care of matters through the proper channels.

The seeds of cultural conflict may be sowed, then, at a very early age and the mind of the sprouting child may be bent, at some point, by the winds of perplexities. In a more psychological language, the child may develop some conflict-laden identifications with two social worlds, the one of parents and the other of teachers and peers. In most instances, as the child grows older, the peer values grow stronger and override many parental sanctions. One of the common complaints of Chinese parents is that their child does not obey them—at least not as submissively as before. One wonders if the desire of Chinese parents to enroll their children in Chinese school is to some extent to maintain cultural continuity with their children.

With some immigrants, who are in the lower rung of the economic ladder, they may feel insecure in their tenuous position; the incipient loss of the formerly strict obedience of their children may threaten their status even more. To reinstate their prerogatives, the parents, usually the father, may even demand greater obedience. It may be recalled that in Chinese culture, the behavior of the child reflects on the parents, who will be accused of not having taught their children to behave properly. Hence his status is intimately tied into the behavior of his offsprings. The child, on the other hand, is growing to be more American and independent. Authority based on arbitrary grounds, to the child, is not well received. This area of conflict with his parents may lead to inner turmoil for the child. In speaking about another ethnic group, Erikson mentions that the "weakest relationship . . . seems to be that between the children and their fathers, who cannot teach them anything and who, in fact, have become models to be avoided" (6, p. 160). In turn, the parents may feel helpless, isolated, and insecure with the disintegration of a former way of life which they have left behind in China. The rapid change in social roles may be damaging to the self-image of these parents. The parents may turn their hopes to the Chinese schools and take greater interest in the progress of their child. However, the report cards are often a shock to even the most sympathetic parents (14).

The reaction of the American-born children to the boys and girls who are born in China is interesting. At the American public schools the China-born children, a number of them recent refugees from Hong Kong, find it natural to communicate with one another in Chinese and occasionally may be seen reading Chinese comics. The American-born children regard these overseas boys and girls with disfavor and call them "China-bugs." In retort, the China-born call the American-born kids "Bamboo knots"—i.e. hollow in the inside and similar to the American slang, "knuckle-head." In other words, the heads of the American-born are empty of Chinese thoughts and language.

When parent-child relationships are not close, the child often turns to his peer group for his social needs. In traditional China, one need not turn to playmates outside of the extended family, for villagers usually live side by side with relatives. An old saying inspired Chinese not to wander far from their place of origin. (In fact, it was customary for the old sojourners to have their bones shipped back to their villages for the final resting place.) In contrast, the United States is characterized by great social and physical mobility. Erikson calls attention to the American creed, that of faith in the magic liberation by going places (6). Although this may be so for parents, this mobility often throws the child in a new group where he is the stranger. This experience of aloneness is an anxious event for adolescents. To alleviate such a state there is a strong flow to merge into a peer group. It seems that Americans conform to the prevailing styles and standards to anticipate group acceptance as rapidly as possible. In contrast, the Chinese still have intact kinship ties, as may be seen in the large number of relatives who appear at weddings and banquets in Chinatown. But family ties are loosening, and there is a growing tendency to form a strong peer-group ties.

## STREET CLUBS AND GANGS

A case in point is the growing number of street clubs or gangs in Chinatown. Many of these teen-agers come from families where both parents are working or perhaps bereaved, or from a disturbed family. Instead of going home to an empty house, physically or emotionally, they loiter in coffee shops, street corners, or pool halls. These street clubs separate into the American-born boys and the foreign-born boys, the latter group which includes mostly new arrivals from Hong Kong. There is animosity between these two sorts of Chinese teen-agers and they do not have much to do with each other. They do not even speak the same language. The American-born, mostly second generation youths, speak English and the China-born speak the Cantonese dialect. The American-born clubs go by the name of "The Raiders," "The Sultans," and "The Immortals" and may be identified by their club jackets. The group of about 150 China-born boys is called the "Bugs." The Bugs made the news lately for their part in burglarizing stores, both in and out of Chinatown, by crawling through narrow transoms.

Occasionally, these American-born and China-born clubs get into a "rumble." The Agency of Youth for Service steps into the role as a mediator. Mr. Wong, a staff member, says "We use unorthodox tactics to prevent juvenile delinquency. I know their hangouts. I go there and when I see a fellow with a club jacket on,

I just say 'Take me to your leader.' A lot of these kids don't like to fight. They only do it because they are challenged. They can't back down without being called 'chicken.' But we, the agency, can tell them not to fight. With us as mediators, they don't have to fight" (13, p. 44).

Mr. Wong's life is a telling one and reflects the personal histories of some of the club members. He was expelled from Galileo High School for insubordination and habitual truancy, after having threatened the life of the Dean. An interview tells that "After that, still being under age, he went to continuation school which he did not finish. Because he 'liked to fight a little,' he freelanced from one street club to another, leading him eventually to the other side of the law. His own juvenile delinquency and his past record for burglary qualify him to speak about the young rebels from personal experience. Since finding himself and reforming, he has recruited about 150 teenagers after the service began last July. Their subsidiary programs include 'Good Citizenship,' 'Knocking on the Big Door,' which gets dropouts back to school, and the 'Neighborhood Youth Corps' which pays boys to work, such as picking up cans on beaches at $1.35 an hour" (13, p. 44).

The Youth for Service may succeed in providing suitable role-models for these youths to identify with, models which may be missing at home. Delinquents from other minority groups have also been benefiting from the leaders provided by the agency.

Juvenile delinquency is attracting the eyes of others in China-town too, with posters in store and shop windows announcing a radio series on this problem. A look at police records, from the years 1961 to 1964 (5), shows a growth in juvenile delinquency. The number, however, is still small, the second lowest in the city (the lowest is the Japanese). About 160 delinquent Chinese a year go through the halls of the San Francisco Juvenile Bureau. Most of these cases (75%) are either dismissed or placed under informal supervision. Typically, the anti-social behavior of these youths does not involve phyiscal assault, as is true of many other groups, but it does involve stealing, either from home or from stores. The girls usually steal from home (could this be a token attempt to get something of value from the home, i.e. affection which is usually given to her brothers first? Or are they so desperately trying to find an identity that a negative one is better than none at all?). For both boys and girls, the trial observation of Abbott (1) is interesting: in the delinquent group, about half of the youths have working mothers, away mainly in sewing factories to make ends meet.

The growing rate of delinquency in Chinatown will probably continue. It may be informative to look at the Chinese community a number of years back. Twenty years ago most of the Chinese lived inside the boundary of Chinatown because of housing barriers in the larger community. This made the Chinese enclave more tightly knit, and it was not uncommon for people to run into each other on the streets. Anti-social behaviors by youths were likely to be observed by some related persons, who would report them to their parents or reprimand the youths themselves. Also, a young Chinese got little, if any, support from his fellow peers. If they did, they met the same fate too, for it was perfectly legitimate for relatives to discipline children in the Chinese culture. After World War II, housing barriers began to fall and the exodus out of the ghetto began. They moved out from cramped quarters to more adequate housing in outlying areas. The better established Chinese moved out and the web of relationships in the Chinese ghetto began to loosen. Coupled with this, the older generation was getting along in years and their voices faded from the Chinatown scene. Hence, the control the ghetto Chinese once exerted is diminishing.

The signs seemed to suggest that the Chinese ghetto, as a living quarter, would disappear and become just a tourist center. But the recent influx of refugees from Hong Kong and Southeast Asia gave a new cycle to Chinatown. With the mushrooming of strange and new faces, there is greater anonymity in Chinatown than there was 20 years ago. To these new immigrants, the old problem of making a living came along with them. Since many cannot speak English and have no vocational skills, they can only filter into the available jobs in the ghetto. Many of these refugees had experienced long periods of unemployment previously because of the scarcity of jobs in Hong Kong and so have been idle for a long time. The situation may be a little better in Chinatown, but the future is not much brighter.

To the unsuspecting tourist, Chinatown presents a picture of swarming activities and growing prosperity. Behind its facade of glittering signs and modern front, however, it has many social and economic problems. It is considered a slum by the city and receives aid from the Anti-Poverty Act. It is short on housing and many rooms are over-crowded. It will be recalled that the Chinese ghetto was mainly a community for isolated, homeless men and was built along these lines. Today many of these tenements are condemned by the Public Health Department and a number of owners are trying to sell their property instead of trying to renovate them because of the extensive repairs needed. These strains contribute to the adjustment problems of refugees in America.

It is interesting to note that in Taiwan and Hong Kong, areas which are undergoing extensive westernization, the juvenile delinquents pattern themselves after two different models (12). Some of them are dressed in western fads and the others style themselves after the traditional Chinese cloth and hang out in temples. One may speculate on these two opposing modes of identification.

A cue may be provided by Erikson's analysis of Germany before the outbreak of Nazism. He described the image of a divided Germany. "The German image of disunity is based on a historical feeling of discomfort which may be called the 'Limes complex.' The Limes Germanicus was a wall—comparable to the Chinese wall—built by the Romans through western and southern Germany to separate the conquered provinces from those which remained barbaric. This wall was destroyed long ago. But it was replaced by a cultural barrier which separated the area in the south, influenced by the Church of Rome, from that of Protestant northern Germany. Other empires (military, spiritual, cultural) have thus reached into Germany; from the west, sensual and rational France; from the east, illiterate, spiritual, and dynastic Russia; from the north and northwest, individualistic "protestantism and from the southeast, oriental easygoingness." All conflicts between east and west, north and south, were fought out in the battle somewhere in Germany—and in the German mind.

"Germany's desperate paradoxes led to those extremes of German contradiction which—before Hitler—were considered to constitute two different Germanies. In reaction to the sense of cultural enrichment one type of Reichs-German became, as it were, too broad, while the other became too narrow. That other nations have analogous conflicts between cosmopolitanism and provincialism does not remove the necessity of understanding the German version of this dilemma. The 'too broad' type denied or hated the German paradox and embraced the whole encircling 'outer world,' he became cosmopolitan beyond recognition. The 'narrow' type tried to ignore foreign temptations and became 'German' to the point of caricature. The first was always glad to be mistaken for an Englishman, a Frenchman, or an American; the second arrogantly overdid the narrow inventory of his few genuine characteristics" (6, pp. 347–349). (Does this describe the fact that the China-born boys called themselves the "Bugs," after being christened "China-bugs" by the native-born Chinese?)

In late adolescence, the American-born and China-born Chinese still continue to keep their distance from each other. Across the bay from San Francisco, at the University of California, the distinction is institutionalized. There are two Chinese student clubs, one for the American-born group and another for the China-born group.

## SOCIAL LIFE

Among Chinese youths, there is a detectable tendency to provide or create social responsiblities for each other. A Chinese student club may be found in any college which has a sufficient enrollment of Chinese. Since educational attainment is traditionally valued in Chinese culture, a high proportion of the youths attend colleges and universities. During the spring recess, the Chinese student clubs join efforts and sponsor the Chinese Students' Intercollegiate Organization (CSIO) Conference. Here, Chinese students from all over the state come to enjoy themselves. There is a queen contest with girls representing 15 Chinese student clubs. The fellows and coeds participate in various activities such as an icebreaker, fashion and talent shows, oratorial contests, athletic tournaments, coronation ball, banquet. Then there is the Chinese Student Association in the San Francisco Bay Area, consisting of China-born students, and it has started an annual affair. For the non-college people, there are many church groups in San Francisco Chinatown, representing all major religions from

Protestant to Catholic, to Mormons, to Buddhists, which, in addition to their regular services, hold independent and joint retreats, such as the Lake Tahoe Conference and Asilomar Conference. There is also a Pacific Coast Conference for both college and working people, which meets annually over the Labor Day week end. (To these may be added the various social and athletic clubs in Chinatown.) These organizations often hold dances and other social functions throughout the year to get publicity and to provide opportunities to renew acquaintances and make new friends.

These groups usually hold discussions in their conferences. It would be helpful to look at some of the matters which are of interest to them. The topics, taken from such meetings, include the following: "Chinese Attitudes towards America"; "Does the American Image of the Chinese Stifle the Chinese's Aspirations?"; "The Place of Chinese Tradition in a Modern Industrial Society"; "Cultural Conflict and the Marginal Man"; and "The Withdrawn Chinese in Western Society." There are also talks on such topics: "Are Dating Habits and Morals Changing for Today's Chinese College Students?"; "Anatomy of Morality"; and the "Quest for the True Values in Life." From this catalogue, there seem to be undertones of anxiety over their minority status and problems of identity. The undertones may be loud for some Chinese and inaudible for others, but they do seem to exist.

According to one announcement, "The programs set up for the conference are topics that affect the students because they are students and because they are of Chinese ancestry. The subject matter has been chosen because of the direct affect they may have and thus give a new and more personal direction and attitude to the problems that face us" (3). Hence, indications are that Chinese youths may consider themselves to be marginal to the wider society. But more important, they also feel marginal to themselves, to other fellow Chinese in America. The discrimination between the China-born and the American-born has already been mentioned. There are other distinctions among the Chinese. At this point, a look at the experience of a Chinese girl, a foreign student, would be highly enlightening.

"Even at the universities, I discovered that the distinctions among the varieties of Chinese are no less strictly observed. At Stanford University, around the corner from the campus Post Office is a small wooden structure which houses thirteen Chinese Nationalist students. Most are graduate students in engineering. They sleep and eat there, and study apart from the rest of the University. Each takes a turn cooking for the whole house (which includes five more students who just dine there) every two weeks. In this way, they are able to eat in the accustomed Chinese style and talk to each other in Mandarin.

"When I entered Stanford University as a freshman, the Chinese Club gave a party to welcome new Chinese freshman girls. I looked forward to the event hoping to meet several other Chinese girls as well as boys. As it turned out to my surprise at the party, there were only four Chinese girls, including myself. What a poor harvest we were for the men students there when among us, not one was a "typical" Chinese girl. Two of the girls were born in San Francisco and Hawaii and could not speak any Chinese at all, which disqualified their social acceptability by the Nationalist Chinese students. The third girl being from Hong Kong, spoke Cantonese which also disqualified her. Since I was the only one who grew up in Taiwan and spoke Mandarin, I was acceptable except for the fact that I dated Caucasian boys.

"At the time, I was taking my liberal education seriously at college and saw no reason to discriminate against Westerners—especially when I enjoyed the casualness of dating American and European students. And if this made me less socially acceptable to the Old Guard Chinese students, I wasn't greatly concerned. Nonetheless, a Nationalist Chinese student told me, 'You are still all right. You still have *some* Chinese in you, but they (the American-born Chinese) are not Chinese.'

"I asked him frankly, 'Why don't you take out American-born Chinese girls? Since there are so few Chinese girls around, it would improve your social life if you accepted them. After all they are Chinese too.'

" 'No,' he was adamant, 'When you say "Chinese" you mean something—the same language, same custom, same interest. The American-born Chinese have different language and values from us. They imitate the way Americans behave. We are not the same kind' " (13, pp. 47–48).

By the same token, the American-born Chinese consider the foreign-born students to be too "Chinese*ee*" or "Chinafied" (terms equally applicable to immigrant parents but this is never done. Old-fashioned is the word.) Like the foreign-born students who discriminate among themselves, such as differences in dialect, the American-born also tend to make distinctions among themselves but on a more subtle basis. Some of the out-of-town Chinese, from other states, get the impression that the Chinese in the city are surprisingly clannish. Coming from an area where there were a few Chinese, they had expected that the Chinese would welcome them with open arms or at least be more cordial in "breaking the ice." In any event, there seems to be weight to the argument that some of the groups in Chinatown are cliquish, e.g., church and social groups. The various cliques may have been together for a long time and their history may go back to grammar school days. The existence of such closely knit social groups may demonstrate some need to maintain a closed circle. These youths may have been together when they were starting the painful break away from the traditional values at home. By coalescing with peers of like minds, they may alleviate their feelings of being marginal to the world. Erikson has said, "It is important to understand . . . such intolerance as a defense against a sense of identity confusion. For adolescents not only help one another temporarily through much discomfort by forming cliques and by stereotyping themselves, their ideals, and their enemies; they also perversely test each other's capacity to pledge fidelity" (6, p. 262). This mechanism of defense is a fragile one though, for the group must constantly guard against the protrusion of strangers into the "closely" knit group.

Excluding people on grounds of some pre-conceived or petty differences, they are better able to define themselves. It helps them answer the question, "Who am I?" They know "who they are" and, ruefully, "who they aren't." So, it is easy to see that the intrusion of outsiders upsets this tenuous definition of the group—or, in other words, a piece of their social- or self-identity. One can see this plainly in the sharp separation between the American-born and the China-born Chinese. Although such broad distinctions are helpful, more refined definitions are needed and so they must also differentiate among themselves too (sub-cliquing) in order to get closer to a definition of their own personal identity.

It is significant to note that these Chinese groups do not include people of other oriental extraction, such as Japanese. Once in a while some members may bring up the question of inviting other Orientals into the group. Such suggestions usually create some tension and then the matter is dropped abruptly. Some members have mentioned that if they started to let in a few non-Chinese more may join and the club may no longer be one for Chinese.

At first, the multitude of clubs and organizations for Chinese youths may come as a surprise. This really need not be if one looks at the behavior of their forebears in Chinatown. One can see a plethora of ethnic organizations at an early time. They consist of family associations, which number about 60 in Chinatown. The family associations open their doors to people with the same sur-name and encompass all Chinese in Chinatown. There are also territorial associations and membership is based on place of origin in China. It may be mentioned here that 90% of the Chinese came from the four most backward counties in Kwangtung Province (9). Together, all these associations make up the grand organization called the Chinese Consolidated Benevolent Association, more commonly known as the Chinese Six Companies. These associa-tions performed many functions in the past: helping the sick and needy, taking care of immigration, arbitrating disputes, and main-taining peace. But these aging associations now have a dwindling membership and have eliminated many of their previous activities. Many are now largely social in nature and sponsor family picnics in the summer. Today, the new arrivals from Hong Kong, when they see the scores of family association halls in Chinatown, are amazed for they have never seen anything quite like it in Hong Kong or China. However, these associations had once served the needs of the early immigrants and gave them status in society at a time when the surrounding society was harboring anti-Oriental sentiments. In short, these associations were creations of the times —created by uprooted men to replicate a social order, somewhat exaggerated though, which was geared to their mutual needs and to which they were accustomed, i.e. the extended family with its nucleus of primary human relationships. These associations, in essence, preserved the identity and self-esteem of these men and gave them a place in a new world.

This is a persistent problem, of becoming isolated from the larger whole, not only for the immigrant Chinese but also for their descendants who will follow them, and it will be more acute as the extended family continues to decline in our modern era. The traditional and tight bonds that once gave the family members a feeling of security and belonging will be untied. The Chinese individual, moving away from his ancestors' shadow, will soon face the world as a separate entity. Alone, he may experience isolation, insecurity, and a feeling of powerlessness. In his desolation, he may seek the refuge of clique relations to see him through the chilly winds of loneliness. Such new ties may diminish his potentialities as an individual, as Fromm (6) has pointed out, but in any event they give him security. He feels that he belongs, and this is important. "He may suffer from hunger or suppression, but does not suffer from the worst of all pains—complete aloneness and doubt" (8, p. 51). Perhaps as he grows older and more sure of himself, he may develop his potentialities to a greater extent.

## IDENTITIES

It should be clear by now that the Chinese youths are a rather heterogeneous crowd. They differ widely in their feelings about becoming involved with the larger society, which range from none to complete participation (7). In a simple way, a Chinese individual may be classified according to the degree of "identity" he manifests toward Chinese and American culture. Some of the types suggested are familiar. One consists of those Chinese who are highly identified with their own ethnic group and orbit entirely around their ethnic enclave. They may be imperious to, or even ignorant of, the social barriers in the larger society. They may be rather contented and satisfied with their lot and rarely need venture outside of the coterie of their China-born friends. The foreign students at Stanford University are examples. Such isolated behavior is typical too of the older, entrenched ghetto Chinese. The opposite extreme would be those who reject their own ethnic group and attempt to identify wholeheartedly with the larger society. Their orientation may lead them to achieve a higher degree of social integration than others of their own ethnic group. But as ethnic minority members are not totally accepted by all segments of the larger society, their intense orientation toward finding their identity exclusively in the American society may lead to further frustrations and greater insecurities. Unsuccessful attempts to integrate with one segment of the majority society may often force the anxious and obsessive adoption of new role-performances to enter the in-group of another segment. Still, a third way may be to renounce both the ethnic and dominant cultures. These people probably find that they are unable to choose between sets of values, beliefs, attitudes, mores, etc. originating from, to them, irreconcilable ways of life. Such persons may withdraw from both cultures and find a niche in some alienated groups in society, such as "beatniks." Perhaps the most enriching orientation involves the capacity to live in both the dominant and minority cultures without undue doubt and conflict. While the most potentially rewarding solution of all, it is by no means easy to achieve for a scrutiny of inner values is involved. It is in this group, perhaps, that "We will eventually witness the evolution of an individual whose empathic insights into the minority, marginal and majority societies will result in unique creativity" (4, p. 11).

However, each of these developing identities may be threatening to others who follow a different orientation. We have seen some Chinese who want to maintain their cultural identity as much as possible, such as the China-born, and others who want to put on the trappings of the American culture as much as possible. Yet each of these ways may have its own kind of conflicts. Some of the American-born Chinese, for example, may feel guilty when they look at the China-born individuals for these are often people their parents would have liked them to be. On the other hand, the China-born, who suffer some cultural disadvantage in their adopted country, may sometimes envy the qualities of their more westernized brothers. Thus, the existence of Chinese who choose a different pathway may be a threat to the emerging, but incomplete, identity of the others. But the differences do not stop here. Even among the American-born, the very Americanized ones who live in integrated campus dormitories, for example, may feel that the ones in the Chinese fraternity may be too clannish. In turn, their fraternity brothers may feel that the dormitory boys "think they are too good for us." The varying orientations tend to cut them up into small dissident groups and each with problems of their own. One Caucasian social worker, for example, commented about the sensitivity of some American-born Chinese to be called Chinese instead of Chinese-Americans. Interestingly, one Chinese sociologist, Rose Hum Lee, insisted that the Chinese should be called *American-Chinese* (11). This is surprising and humorous to some Chinese but not at all to others. The above social worker, while talking to the author, apologized quickly when he referred to me as a Chinese instead of Chinese-American and said he hoped that I was not offended. This surprised me as I always say Chinese when I speak of the same. But come to think of it, some Chinese have questioned me if I am referring to the American-born or China-born Chinese, to the Chinese-Americans or Chinese-Chinese. I guess it is worse when a white person says the word Chinese, for some listeners may be offended because they feel that they have been relegated to a minority status and their position as full-fledged Americans is not fully recognized. Needless to say, not all Chinese feel this way.

Like many Americans today, the Chinese suffers, at one time or another, " . . . under the problem of what he should believe in and who he should—or, indeed might—be or become" (6, p. 279). Many have, fortunately, integrated the strands of two cultures into well-functioning personalities. How these identity conflicts are resolved is another story in the American pageant and deserves future studies by social scientists.

## SUMMARY

The traditional family ties of the Chinese are loosening in America. The youths are turning more to their peers for emotional and social support. In the transition from one way of life to another, the process of self-definition may be a confusing one for Chinese adolescents. The spectacle of life goes on. The Chinese are many and they point to different directions. The voices in the Chinese crowd are at odds when the question is raised: "Who am I?" or "Where am I going?" The dust of the debate is unsettled.

For the different camps of Chinese adolescents are motley and dis-harmonious. On the one side are the China-born; its constituents, a cacophonous one: Cantonese and Mandarin speakers, southerners and northerners, rice-eaters and wheat-eaters. On the other side are the American-born, a cleavage of bilinguals and a lesser number to whom the Chinese tongue is a foreign one. In wrestling over their identity—their place in the world—they are grappling with each other. A number of them, fortunately, emerge from the fray with a clearer definition of themselves. It has been said by Kipling, "East is East, and West is West, and never the twain shall meet." But the twain shall meet, in the minds of the Chinese youths.

## REFERENCES

1. Abbott, K. A.: Personal communication to author, 1966.
2. Abel, T. M. and Hsu, F. L. K.: Some aspects of personality of Chinese as revealed by the Rorschach Test. *Rorschach Research Exchange and Journal Projective Techniques, 13*: 285–301, 1949.
3. Chinese Students' Intercollegiate Organization Conference, 1964, March 1964, Berkeley, California.
4. Derbyshire, R. L. and Brody, E. B.: Marginality, identity and behaviour in the American Negro: A functional analysis. International Journal of Social Psychiatry, *10*: 7–13, 1964.
5. DeVos, G. A. and Abbott, K. A.: The Chinese Family in San Francisco: A Preliminary Study, A group masters' thesis under direction of G. A. DeVos and K. A. Abbott, University of California, Berkeley, Calif., 1966.
6. Erikson, E. H.: *Childhood and Society*, Ed. 2, Norton & Company, Inc., New York, 1963.
7. Fong, S. L. M.: Assimilation of Chinese in America: Changes, in orient-ation and social perception. *American Journal of Sociology, 71*: 265–273, 1965.
8. Fromm, E.: *Escape From Freedom.* Avon Books, New York, 1965.
9. Hsu, F. L. K.: *Americans and Chinese.* The Cresset Press Ltd., London, 1955.
10. Hsu, F. L. K.: *Under the Ancestors' Shadow.* Columbia University Press, New York, 1948.
11. Lee, R. H.: *The Chinese in the United States of America.* Hong Kong University Press, Hong Kong, 1960.
12. Lin, T. Y.: Two types of delinquent youths in Chinese society. *In Culture and Mental Health*, edited by M. Opler, pp. 257–271. The Macmillan Company, New York, 1959.
13. *Sun, S.*: Cracks in the Flower Drum. *San Francisco Magazine, 8*: 36–48, 1966.
14. Yun, L. G.: *Chinatown Inside Out.* Barrows Mussey, New York, 1936.

# Japanese American Identity Crisis

JOE YAMAMOTO, M.D.

With the great Civil Rights Revolution of the present decade, we have been inclined to assume that oppression, racial discrimination, and prejudice are invariably causes of low self-esteem, poor performance in school, crime and delinquency, breakdown of families, and hard-core poverty. These assumptions have been based upon a comparison of visible minority groups, for example Negroes or Mexican Americans, with the general population. There is no question in my mind about the possible deleterious effects of being treated as if one were a second-class citizen. The evidence that these deleterious effects occur are all too frequent in the statistics of crime and delinquency and all the other measures of social problems.

Because the Orientals have proved to be exceptions to these generalizations we shall examine some of the differences which may explain why there are different problems. Caudill for example in his study of 1948 showed that Japanese Americans were well-accepted in Chicago; evaluated as being better workers than their Caucasian cohorts, they were often promoted and at times placed in supervisory roles over Caucasians (1).

The Japanese in America comprise a tiny proportion of the population. The best estimate is that 0.1% are of Japanese extraction. They, along with the Chinese who preceded them, were encouraged to immigrate to America to supply cheap labor. The vast majority of the Japanese immigrated to the United States prior to the passage of the Oriental Exclusion Act in 1924. They brought with them a distinctive culture, basically rural, feudal, and Oriental, which they then combined with Victorian and post-Victorian values cherished in America, often with vigor. Despite

133

great discrimination in all areas such as segregated housing, segregated schools, limited occupational opportunity, social exclusion, and legal discrimination in such matters as ownership of land and interracial marriage, the Japanese have thrived. There is little crime or delinquency, no hard-core poverty, low school dropout rates, and few divorces. The level of education is higher than that of the general population, and the Japanese try to be over-achievers. This was a finding mentioned by Strong when he commented on the superior performance of Japanese students, a difference which was not correlated to intelligence test results which showed that they were average. (Of course this may of itself not be an accurate measure since most of the Japanese grew up in bilingual homes, and the original language was often Japanese. This may have made it more difficult to score well on tests in English.) Strong pointed out that the Japanese may be more conscientious or better able to please their teachers (cited in l).

For many decades the Japanese in America were kept in ghettoes, well-delineated and self-contained islands where Japanese was the only language necessary. There they lived, worked, married, bore children, and dreamed of returning home to parents, relatives, and townsfolk as wealthy repatriates home to the farms and villages. Toward this end, the first-born children were often taken back to the paternal grandparents to receive a proper Japanese education. Japanese was the original tongue learned by the child and with the beginning of school, the child was also enrolled in *Nihon-Gakko*, where he learned Japanese in the afternoons after public school and on Saturdays. The Japanese manners, celebrations, values, and attitudes were altered only with the incorporation of American Victorian and post-Victorian values. Japanese Americans learned to *Ojigi*, to know one's place in the social structure, to be patient *gah-man*, to be concerned about the family and groups rather than to be selfish *wah-gah-mah-mah*, to work hard and excel with the Japanese spirit *Yamato-Damashi*, and to be quite concerned about the reactions of family and peers that one would be laughed at, *minna-warau*.

Let me give a few examples of how this molds behavior. Despite the door being closed to white collar jobs because of prejudice and discrimination, the Japanese were more often high school and college graduates just for the sake of being educated. Even though men with college degrees could only obtain work as gardeners and as fruit stand vendors, they still went to college. Great emphasis was placed on education and knowledge which were considered virtues. One could be respected for what one had learned and knew regardless of one's occupation or material rewards.

During the Second World War, I was interned first at Santa Anita, California, and later at Heart Mountain, Wyoming. After 8 months, I was permitted to leave the camp and resume my pre-medical studies in St. Paul, Minnesota. Just before the war ended, I applied to the University of Minnesota Medical School. The FBI interviewed me for a security check, and the agent asked if I was loyal to the United States. I told him, "If by loyalty you mean do I agree with the evacuation of the Japanese into camps, the answer is NO. If you mean would I fight for the United States the answer is YES." I asked the agent what he thought about my loyalty, and he was non-committal. When I was accepted for medical school, I felt determined to excel. Being the first Japanese-American student accepted as a freshman, I felt obligated to show how well I could do.

Other Japanese were showing the way in the 442nd Regimental Combat Team, the most decorated unit in the Army with most of the GI's earning purple hearts. Their motto was "Go for Broke." This was a segregated group which out-performed their cohorts at a time when integration was being advocated to restore the morale of Negroes in the services.

When I was in analysis, I arrived to lie on the couch one day to tell with much fatigue and anguish how I had been hip deep in rain water and mud, cleaning the waterway next to our house. I told my analyst that my mother had put some tree branches over the waterway. She did this because she was concerned about our dirt going onto our neighbor's land downstream. In her social concern she had effectively dammed the waterway causing the flood, the mud, and debris! My analyst's monocle popped out and he could not get over the great concern my mother had shown for our neighbor.

These stories, I believe, illustrate how the Japanese were raised to have pride, yet behave humbly, be patient and hard working, be ambitious with emphasis on education, loyal to family, group, and country, be socially concerned, meticulously courteous, and scrupulously clean. All the while ties were maintained with Japan. Even the descriptive term for each generation demonstrates this: *Issei*, first generation away from Japan: *Nisei*, second generation; and *Sansei*, third generation.

The Japanese values, combined with the American Victorian and post-Victorian values, stood the Japanese in America in good stead. They were able to work hard, to save, to educate their children, and to dream of ultimate return to parental Japan. So far I have spoken only of the ways in which the cultural values have combined with those extant in America with positive results. What then have been and will be the problems of the second generation Japanese, the *Nisei*? Although the *Nisei* have done well, it has been at the price of flexibility and freedom. The stress on family, group, and nation have been so well inculcated there is less room for individuality. Because of this, initiative and creativity have been less emphasized. Along with this, there has been a too rigid adherence to the letter of the law, with the loss of a feeling of freedom, for example, about sexual pleasures. This is surprising since the Japanese had brought along a cultural value of enjoyment of bodily experiences. This however conflicted with the Christian feeling that the body is sinful, lustful, and evil. The Japanese in America thus became less able to enjoy themselves. This was very recently brought home to my wife Maria and myself. We were at a New Year's Eve party with all Japanese friends and at the stroke of midnight there were many joyous greetings of "Happy New Year" but nary a kiss. As a matter of fact, I kissed Maria but with a slight feeling of inhibition since no one else was kissing anyone— all this despite cocktails and the salubrious effects of champagne to toast the New Year. Both Maria and I were aware of the contrast of kissing at another party with our Caucasian friends.

Despite the rigid adherence to old customs and values, the Japanese community has changed. The effects of World War II and the concomitant evacuation of the Japanese to inland camps have had lasting effects. Unlike the trail of tears with its devastating effects on the Seminole and Cherokee, the evacuation of the Japanese had mixed blessings. It had a positive effect in permitting the

Japanese to return to the Pacific Coast to a less emotionally charged atmosphere with less prejudice. I believe this is so despite Senator Inouye's reminiscence about returning from combat, having lost an arm, and still in uniform with his combat decorations. He went to a barber shop where the barber asked "Are you a Jap?" After a discussion in which Senator Inouye had to admit he was of Japanese ancestry, the barber told him that he would not give any "Jap" a hair cut.

There are cutting reminders that not all is rosy in the diminution of discrimination and prejudice. However, there are undoubtedly changing attitudes about Orientals in the Pacific Coast states. For example, 15 psychotherapists were recently asked which ethnic minority groups experience prejudice and discrimination in Los Angeles (2). The minority groups listed were Negroes, Japanese-Americans, Jews, Chinese-Americans, and Mexican Americans. Five psychotherapists felt that Japanese-Americans and Chinese-Americans are not oppressed or discriminated against in the Los Angeles area (1). It may be that these therapists are from other parts of the United States with different patterns of prejudice.

An example of this was my own personal encounter with anti-Semitism. I was invited to join a medical fraternity in 1946. This was a big change since all the medical fraternities had rules excluding non-Aryans from memberships. I joined and subsequently had the peculiar experience of hearing my fraternity brothers heatedly debate the invitation of another student because he was Jewish. This was a shocking situation to me. I was accustomed to anti-Oriental prejudice, but this sort of racism in an integrating fraternity reminded me of the different patterns of prejudice there. They could accept me, a Japanese-American, right after World War II but had much more difficulty in accepting a Jew. I was convinced of the variation in ethnic prejudice and how even World Wars may not disrupt the established patterns of oppression.

Just as geography makes a difference in the groups selected for discrimination so too does geography significantly alter one's personal role and reaction. In 1957 I attended a meeting in a Los Angeles hotel. My reaction was quite different from the reaction to hotels in Minneapolis, Chicago, Cincinnati, or even San Francisco. In Los Angeles I felt a certain uneasiness and wariness. I was vaguely troubled as if I might be thrown out. This was due to having been taken out of Los Angeles in April 1942. I am pleased to be able to report that my personal reaction of anxiety has lessened in Los Angeles hotels, just as I hope that it is now less popular to be prejudiced toward any other person because of his race, religion, or ethnic origin.

What are those features which have fostered Japanese behavior? I assume that there are roles, values, attitudes which Japanese assume, learn, and adopt because of experiences from early childhood through maturity. As Caudill has shown, the Japanese baby is more intensively mothered in early life, the child more often sleeps in the same room, and there is a greater physical intimacy in the parent-child relationships (3). The Japanese child learns to be courteous, ambitious, hard working, patient, neat, clean, obedient, and to be concerned about the responses of those around him. This is an important difference, the degree of concern about others and the strength of family ties. The father is the leader, the patriarch; the family comes first, then the neighbors and extended groups, and then the nation. Along with these factors is the feeling of pride in being Japanese. The spirit of the *Yamato Damashi* permeates all Japanese activities. Literally translated, this refers to the Japanese Spirit and explains in part the over-achievement of the Japanese as students, workers, family members, citizens, and soldiers. The *Yamato Damashi* is armor against racial oppression, discrimination, and prejudice. The spirit permits one to feel better than those who are oppressive—all in all a positive prejudice toward Japanese and things Japanese. Those outside the circles of family, neighborhood, and nation are viewed with less acceptance.

It is the thesis of my presentation that all these factors combine to contribute to a positive sense of identity which transcends the individual and is most often group identity, with the family and national groups as the critical variables. Indeed, living in ghettoes, the parents continuing to speak Japanese, the prejudice toward and rejection of people and things not Japanese all tend to promote a Japanese identity. In addition, the family, the Japanese school, the *Ken-Jin-Kai* (Prefectural Associations), and the Japanese community all engage in maintaining ties with the Japanese culture and values. One enduring value has been the *Yamato-Damashi* which suggests a Japanese standard of performance, demands the extra exertions, the pursuit of excellence, regardless of non-Japanese values or opportunities, and conscientious performance of duties, responsibilities, and the payment of obligations incurred not only by oneself but by all members of the family.

Thus within the clearly defined roles in the community, the Japanese individual grows up with positive feelings about himself, his groups, with values that permit him to excel in productive endeavors as long as these fall within prescribed fields and are not in conflict with the Japanese values. The emphasis is on the accepted, the predictable, the traditional. Novelty and innovation are not prized. What are the consequences of all this? I believe that there will be negative aspects because of these very strong emphases on the traditional, the accepted, the conservative.

One example of this is in the large number of Christian converts among the Japanese in America where the majority are Protestants. In Catholic countries, the majority of Japanese Christians are Catholic. While in Japan, despite 100 years of missionary efforts, only 0.5% of the population are Christian! Along with these accretions of the values of the majority, there are suggestions that the conservative attitudes have been too well learned. This is shown by the most distressing poll taken in 1964 before the elections. The issue was the repeal of the Rumford Act. Repeal meant that property owners would be able to discriminate and refuse to sell to individuals because of race, religion, etc. Japanese-American students at U.C.L.A. were the only ethnic minority group favoring this result. It is altogether difficult to understand that so many who had experienced prejudice or discrimination would be for oppression, that is, unless you consider how well the conservative lessons had been learned and that this led to the fiercely enthusiastic adaption of those old attitudes. I am sorry to say that the measure is now law, a step back to the days of legal ghettoes.

In a similar way, the emphasis on tradition and conservatism was better preparation for coping with life in the little Tokyos, the ghettoes of the past, than for adapting to changing opportunities which offer increasing possibilities for advancement along with more frequent exposure to subtle prejudice and discrimination. I will again use myself as an example of this exposure to oppression. Having lived in the middle of America for 15 years, I was unprepared for the extent of the anti-Oriental prejudice in Los Angeles! We looked at the available housing in many areas and we soon realized that as Japanese, we were not welcome in many areas. Because of this we discussed my wish not to expose our children to open rejection because of race. We were fortunate in finding an island of acceptance, a housing area with an insistence that there be no restrictions as to race or religion.

More persuasive is the issue of the positive sense of identity. With the diffusion of the Japanese out of the ghettoes into the larger communities, there has come a need for the development of a Japanese-American identity. Here, the loss of the *Yamato-Dama-shi* can be a real disadvantage. The too eager emulation of the Caucasian counterparts may lead to a *JAP* (Japanese American Protestant) trying to be a *WASP* (White Anglo-Saxon Protestant). Physiognomy precludes this and thus it remains the task of the Japanese-American to remain Japanese and to adapt to American values in a reasonable and reasoning manner.

The Second World War, with the forced relocation of Japanese from the West Coast and the experiences in Relocation Centers, all have changed the people for they were surrounded by barbed wire and guards armed with automatic rifles. This was a rude awakening for many of us. We had difficulty realizing that now we were considered "dangerous." Two vignettes illustrate the depths of this feeling. Many of the Southern California Japanese were initially collected at the Santa Anita Assembly Center, there to await the construction of camps in inland locales. One day a house to house search was ordered. The powers that be were afraid that contraband had been smuggled into Santa Anita. So the military guards were instructed to conduct a house to house search for illegal items such as cameras, short-wave radios, and weapons. Picture for a moment each barrack, each stable (yes, many were housed in the horse stables of Santa Anita) emptied of all the personal belongings. These bags, trunks, and containers held the accumulations, the harvest of two generations of working and striving, little enough to show for 30 or 40 years of effort. This final indignity, the re-inspection of personal effects, resulted in a riot—a milling, angry mob protesting the unjust incarceration, the undignified search, and, most of all, the mass implication of disloyalty and untrustworthiness. All of this because we happened to be Japanese.

My brother had been drafted into the Army in 1941. The Selective Service Act was passed and the national lottery held to choose those to be called. He went and was trained in the Cavalry. Eager and alert, he was promoted to sergeant. World War II began and eventually they shipped his whole group overseas to fight in Europe—all except my brother, because he happened to be Japanese. He was finally sent to the Intelligence Corps to learn Japanese and he subsequently served as an interpreter. I felt it was marvelous that from being a dubiously loyal cavalryman, my brother had gone into intelligence work, less sensitive and demanding of assured loyalty!

Now the Japanese are accepted as loyal, after the consistent experiences in the Army, where the Japanese either functioned in intelligence, translating Japanese, or in the special Regimental Combat Team. This segregated unit fought in the European Theater. This relocation of the Japanese in the mid-West and in the East offered them an opportunity to live outside of established ghettoes and diluted some of their values with less oppression and greater acceptance. I believe there are more frequent conflicts in values. The Japanese in giving up the *Yamato-Damashi* have been unable to say "I am an American" and make it stick.

If someone asks me what I am, they are not asking if I am a psychoanalyst, or a father, or a native Californian, they want to know if I am Oriental, if I am Japanese. This allows me to feel much more like an American who is considered second-rate. It is like the peculiar comment by friends "Why don't you act like a white man?" The answer is clearly because I am not. Then what am I?

I am no longer just *Nisei*, tied to the immigrants from Japan, confined to the little Tokyos of the past, or limited to menial tasks.

Now I am an American of Japanese ancestry with a need to maintain a positive sense of being a Japanese-American. At times it is very difficult to integrate the diverse roles, discrepant values, and different attitudes. This implies not only a range and repertoire of behaviors but also the judgment to alter activities depending on the situation. The world became complex and infinitely more problematical. My home may still be my castle, but my neighbors may not all be friends. How much more complicated for our first-born son Eric growing up in different cities over half this broad land, no longer as proudly Japanese and yet not actually "American." It was simpler to be a *Nisei*, much as the agrarian economy of the past posed fewer problematical situations and permitted an easier establishment of a sense of identity. How much more vivid and descriptive are the words farmer or cowboy than factory worker or assembler. There is a sense of pride, substance in the farmer, and alienation and obscurity in the latter.

Perhaps in an ambiguous way, the *Nisei* with the pride and substance have given way to Americans who are not considered first-class. Here then is a problem which may be unrelated to personal psychodynamics and much more due to conflicts engendered by cultural differences and the illusion of the melting pot. There is no actual fusion of races, only a combination of values among caucasoids. In this context there are very real differences in values, most especially about male-female roles and the tolerance of passivity versus aggressivity. Japanese women have to be much more subservient than American women. Japanese men have to be much less aggressive than American men. With different roles such as these, there are many potential areas of conflict.

There is an advantage in being born and raised in tightly knit families with great emphasis on the care of the neonate, with attention to the needs of the young child. These early life experiences which I believe have positive results are countered by the increasingly rigid demands for conformity, compliance, and concern for the reactions of others (4). "What will the others think? Be careful or they will all laugh at you!" This began earlier in life with threats that are especially frightening to a child raised by an ever present mother, sleeping and living in the same room, perhaps even the same bed. "If you don't behave, I'll ask them to take you away" (cf. 5). "If you aren't good, I won't like you."

Clinical cases may elucidate the psychopathology apparent during adolescent crises. The following cases are not only representative of Japanese-American problems but in many ways are seen in other cultures. The detailed psychopathology is quite Japanese.

## KIMIKO MARJORIE

Kimiko was 18 and had grown up in a middle-class family. Both father and mother spoke Japanese fluently and maintained the Japanese customs. Through very hard work, thousands of 16-hour days, and rare days off, *Otoosan* (Father) had prospered and become a well-to-do business man. In order to continue with the traditional ways, Kimiko was sent to a Japanese school which met Saturdays, and on Sundays she went to the Buddhist Temple. All in all, she was a member of this close-knit family and sufficiently steeped in Japanese reactions to say "Oishyo" upon sitting down. I saw her initially because she had reacted with hysterical crying and depression when threatened with rejection by a boy friend. She was so upset that I was asked urgently to attend her. She came, her bouffant hair-do disheveled. She had been crying and her mascara was running. Sad and distraught she looked like a Japanese Shirley Temple but responded to my comments about the need to "cool it." Marjorie had been unable to become interested in Japanese boys. Her boy friends were all *Hakujin* (Caucasian). She knew that her parents, siblings, aunts, and uncles all preferred that she date Japanese boys. Because of this, she saw Caucasian boys guiltily. She worried about how *Otoosan* would react since he was quite set in his ways. She had been the apple of his eye, being Kimiko, the eldest child, the first and favorite daughter. Which to be? Kimiko? Marjorie? Marjorie Kimiko? She loved her parents and wanted to conform, to be the favorite daughter, and to bask in the warmth of the family. The problem was, "Japanese boys don't turn me on." She had never dated a Japanese boy and explained, "I really don't see any." However, she avoided situations where she might meet boys her father would accept, only Caucasian boys interested her. In every other respect, she was the obedient daughter. She worked in the father's business and earned her spending money. Kimiko was polite with her elders and worked very hard to get good grades and to behave in an exemplary manner. But at night, she was Marjorie.

As this situation continued, many complications arose. She was unable to tell her parents about her *Hakujin* boyfriends and she could not bring them home to meet her parents. This was a dynamic situation where increasingly her two lives became more separate and less related, the only common interest and bond of union being that they occupied the same body.

Initial crisis developed with the appearance of her boyfriend John who in many ways was the American ideal—tall, handsome, Nordic, bright, and intellectual. After many weeks of dating, she was pinned by him. This was indeed a happy event for Marjorie even though she was not absolutely certain she loved John and wanted to establish a permanent relationship. It was a good feeling to be wanted and to go steady. It might just have been an adolescent idyll had John not become suddenly severely ill. His physical condition was at times critical. During a period of relative remission, he proposed marriage. He was quite honest and told her that his prognosis was dark, that the doctors felt he had only 6 months to 1 year. Marjorie was in serious conflict. She realized she did not love him, but she was pinned to him. John, ever proper, offered to release her, telling her that he did not want her to say "yes" out of pity or out of obligatory feelings.

She could not talk to her mother about this problem since she knew nothing of the relationship. Her father was quite unlikely to understand or to be helpful. Marjorie felt all alone and unable to decide. She felt terribly guilty about not wanting to marry John. In describing this guilt feeling she remarked, "I feel like I was a rat, deserting a sinking ship." When John asked again about marriage, she wept. He gave her an out, that she did not have to marry him and he would understand. They could still be friends. She leaped out of the relationship. She really could not avail herself of John's friendship. When she saw his friends, she felt that they criticized her for not staying with John. His parents were also concerned since they wanted him to have the best of everything during his last few months. They bought expensive things for him and he consulted her about her tastes and preferences, at the same time implying that she would receive these later. This did nothing to lessen her guilt feelings. The parents called her too, hoping that she too would exert every effort to comfort and please him during the rest of his life. Marjorie wanted to run away and hide. She found no comfort at school where mutual friends asked about John. At home no one knew John or of John. Thus there was no way to run.

In desperation, she turned to jaunts with girl friends, a frenetic activity-packed schedule to try to make the hours and minutes unthinking times. One day, she met another boy named John. This John was different. Not the all-American boy and scholar, he was already married and was in the process of divorcing his wife. He was quite the opposite of the first John and demanded much of Marjorie in every sphere of life. She became his door mat and continued to give whatever she could. Although they fought and she felt very upset about this, they also made up and she lived only to be with him. Gradually she began to see John every day and at times twice a day.

Their relationship intensified, and it was no longer possible to live as Kimiko during the day and as Marjorie at night. With increasingly frequent meetings, her parents were confronted with the problem of a non-Japanese man. To add to the gravity of the situation, he was a married man. Over and over again her father said "Kimiko *hakujin no otoko to kekkon shitara nigete shimau kara dameh.*" Freely translated this meant it would not be good to marry a non-Japanese man since they have different values and would desert you. The ultimate problem in father's eyes was that this man who intruded into his home was a foreigner, a man without conscience or honor. One could not expect him to know his obligations, the crucial importance of his *on* and *giri* would not be known to this blue-eyed man.

What does a Japanese man do when confronted by such an overwhelming problem? He asks his relatives to advise and help. If they are not sufficient, he consults his ancestors. The Japanese need no current psychotherapists since they have their *Kami-Sama* to tell them what to do. He prayed to his father and his father's father. This was through the mediation of the Shinto Priest. The Priest said that Kimiko would have to straighten her behavior. If she refused, the family would suffer from poor fortunes and the year would be a difficult one, fraught wih danger and disadvantages for each family member. Furthermore, the priest said that Kimiko should continue to see the psychiatrist but that the primary consideration would be that she give up the non-Japanese man and return to her family. If she did not do this, she would surely cause her whole family to be punished for being bad.

Marjorie thought that these oracular pronouncements were unlikely to be fact. Kimiko feared in her very marrow that the *Kami-Sama* would duly note her transgressions and record these for all the ancestors to note and that they, in turn, would mete out punishment to fit the nature and extent of her transgressions. This she had known from early childhood when she observed her mother place water and rice at the Ancestral Altar and pray for the benevolence of her father's father and his father. Rice was not served to the family until after an offering had been made to the ancestors. Any rare or precious tid-bit such as the year's first persimmon was sure to be offered to the *Kami-sama* first, and only later to the father, the sons, mother, and daughters.

Marjorie-Kimiko could not resolve this problem. There was no solution which was acceptable to her Japanese parents and which suited her own American interests. She longed for understanding and acceptance from her father. He seemed to be adamant about any suitor who was not 100% Japanese. How could she get him to see that John was a decent and good human being. With all this, there were problems with John, who came most uncomfortably close to her father's stereotype of the abominable Caucasian suitor. He was not reliable in his work. John was fired from his first job. On the pretext that his wife insisted, he was for a period reconciled with his wife and Kimiko knew not what to do. She felt there was no good solution and was very upset and cried hysterically. Because of all this, her family hoped that her psychiatrist would help her, first, stop seeing John, and, secondly, feel better. They very consistently communicated this message to the psychiatrist. The family's primary criterion of improvement was Kimiko's discontinuing her relationship with John and doing what the *Kami-sama* wanted, that is return to the family and stop making troubles for the family and the ancestors.

During this turmoil with John, in deference to her family, she came to see the psychiatrist. Her confidence in the psychiatrist and his psychiatry were no more than her family's. If only the psychiatrist could persuade her father to accept John. Marjorie was almost sure that she loved John and John loved her.

Intruding on this happy scene, her psychiatrist confronted Kimiko with the fact that John I and John II were substitutes for one another. Further, Kimiko had identified with John I, as she fantasied he felt and experienced the rats deserting the sinking ship. Then, like John I, she became dependent on John II and lived only to please number 2. In slipping into John I's shoes, Marjorie found John II who meted out punishment which Kimiko felt fit the crime. So upset and absorbed was Marjorie in the problems with John II, that the original John faded into the dim and unsure recesses of her mind. So long as she suffered with John II she no longer needed to be concerned about John I. She suffered no pangs of conscience about this relationship.

Kimiko listened to this formulation of the psychodynamic problem respectfully, but Marjorie continued to expand the relationship with John. Her father tried to bribe her with gifts and goodies. Marjorie wanted only to marry John and to remain in the family circle. This was the problem. She wanted to remain Kimiko and to be Marjorie. During one therapy session, she described a fantasy of being a mistress. She would be the mistress of a middle-aged married man. In her relationship with John, she was acting this out symbolically.

Because Marjorie would not stop seeing John, her famly discontinued her therapy. The conflicts were not resolved and despite John's manifestly anti-social behavior, Marjorie hoped that he would change and that they would be able to marry under the shelter of her parent's blessings.

## JAMES

James was referred to me since he had requested a Japanese psychiatrist. Although his famly was of modest means, he was quite sure that he wanted to see me. He described his main problem as being unable to speak. For example, in class he had difficulty in expressing his ideas. Feeling that others noticed he had this problem, he complained, "They look at me with a funny expression on their faces." At age 16, James had had few of the experiences that might have ameliorated his fears. He had few acquaintances and no friends. His daily routine consisted of going to school and staying at home. In his anxiety about how people would view him, he went nowhere and made no attempts to be friendly or to make friends.

He had much difficulty in talking things over with his family. He was totally unable to tell his father about any problems. His father was also shy, not entirely well, and it was all he could do to keep up his work. There were no common interests, no sharing of joy or pride in mutual work. At times James helped his father in his work, but they did not converse and the situation was strained and uncomfortable. There was therefore a mutual avoidance of any situations where father and son might have to relate with each other. In James' view, these problems were colored by guilt feelings engendered by conscious anger and rejection of his father. Despite all this, being an only son, his father hoped that James would go on to college and become a professional person, perhaps in one of the health sciences. This was perhaps one of the few agreed on aspects of family planning.

His mother was very nervous and frequently complained of bodily aches and pains. She helped supplement the family income but there was little joy or joint activities. She would talk to him, but he was afraid to reveal his problems to her. Besides, she was much concerned about herself and her disabilities. She seemed to have little time to assure or comfort him. Thus friendless, with such emotionally distressed parents, he could not be secure even at home. He showed little interest in the world about him and maintained a very impoverished schedule of activities.

He masturbated and felt dirty, ashamed, and unnatural. He had no idea that most adolescent boys masturbate. He confessed that he did with maximum embarrassment. When I told him that boys do, he was relieved. But at intervals, he felt compelled to confess that he had masturbated and continues to do so.

He was glad to see me a Japanese psychiatrist. Since his problem in talking occurred especially with Caucasians, he felt therapy would not work with a Caucasian psychiatrist.

In school although his grades have been average to below average, he unrealistically planned a professional career. After a few therapeutic sessions, he tried to be more social, going out with his classmates. This had a positive effect. He could see that not everyone criticized or looked down on him because of his speech difficulty.

One day he asked me if he would be better off in Japan. There he would not have to speak with Caucasians and he hoped he would feel more adequate and equal with other Japanese. He said he felt one down with Caucasians. I had observed that despite his references to race and feelings of being second-class, he had mainly befriended schoolmates who were not Japanese. For this and other reasons, I advised James that going to Japan would not solve the problem. He has since tried to make new friends but this continued to be a slow, tedious process.

Much of the experienced feeling of inferiority, his anxiety about social rejection, and his inability to speak and respond to others, he attributes to being Japanese. He has observed his experiences much like the man who drank bourbon and soda and suffered a hangover. The next night the man drank scotch and soda. The next morning he woke with an even worse hangover. Then he changed to brandy and soda. Again, another hangover. He concluded, "I knew it. It was the G—— D—— SODA." In the joke, the man ignored the alcohol; in this case, the patient ignored the fact that he was very shy, inexperienced in social interractions and thus at a disadvantage.

James gradually enlarged the radius of his social activities but he remained at a social disadvantage. One day, a girl said "Hello!" to James at school. This was so stressing that he was unable to smile or say "Hello!" Then he castigated himself for being so disabled, so unable to relate to his fellow classmates. It was a mortifying experience.

## DISCUSSION

Kimiko-Marjorie and James are examples of adolescents with negative identities. In the first instance that negative was only in reference to dating behavior, and in the second it was in reference to general social interactions. Both show the disadvantages of being minority group members in their conflict areas. Eric Erikson discussed how Sigmund Freud used the concept of identity in his comments of his "inner identity as a Jew." Freud felt that he had an advantage of being a minority group member and thus able to think unhampered by the prejudiced restrictions characterized by members of the majority.

Erikson has evolved a theory of identity formation as related to psycho-social stages (5). Most recently in discussing identity, he discussed five aspects of identity: 1) individual and communal; 2) positive and negative; 3) past, present and future; 4) conscious and unconscious; and, 5) exclusive and inclusive. As I review these aspects and apply these concepts to our patients, I wish to emphasize the communal identity. It is here that both patients lack the feeling of being a Japanese in the positive sense. What I mean here is a positive prejudice about being Japanese. When the earlier generation was raised in the little Tokyos on the Pacific Coast there was a much more consistent feeling of pride in being Japanese. The spirit of the *Yamato-Damashi* pervaded the values and the attitudes of the Japanese, whether raised in Japan or in America.

This spirit, this ethnic pride, this positive prejudice is like the feeling the Irish have about themselves. They are proud of being Irish and show this in maintaining the traditions of the old sod. Every group needs to have a feeling of pride, of good feeling about one's individual and communal identity. When this does not prevail, one very important basis for the sense of identity is absent and prevents a solid feeling of identity. The Japanese had this feeling, most still have it, but there has been an erosion of the positive feelings for several reasons.

The Second World War was a very important experience. What Japanese-American can forget those years beginning with December 7, 1941? I remember the day. It was Rolfe Larson's birthday and all of us friends who served together in the college service organization were to help him celebrate. I never made it to the birthday party, mainly because I feared that I had changed because of the war and would not be welcome. Only a few months later, I was indeed behind barbed wire fences patrolled by armed soldiers.

How does one explain the war to my 5-year-old son? All he wants to identify are the good guys and the bad guys. As we watched a Japanese movie about men in an army band, our son Andy felt comfortable that these were the good guys. Then the bandsmen encountered American soldiers and Andy asked several times, "Who are the good guys?" Perhaps it was more my dilemma than my son's, but I felt that my response that wars are bad and that it is not clearly good against bad was not adequate. "The Americans were the good guys, huh?" I answered that was right.

An important consequence of the war was the relocation of the Japanese in camps away from Pacific Coast areas. This did several things to the Japanese spirit, it induced conflict about feeling good about being Japanese, diluted the patriarchal authority of father, and exposed many Japanese to a much broader spectrum of Caucasian behavior. The range varied from intense antagonism and total rejection to great acceptance and friendly warmth.

Despite the war and the hatred of the Japanese, there was surprisingly little of this in the mid-western states. Thus the Japanese who left the camps met Caucasians who were friendlier and who had no prejudices toward them. This was a positive experience and changed the situation in this way. With acceptance it was possible to identify with the majority group and to try to be an American. This meant giving up being Japanese in some instances, the more especially since the war continued and served to remind everyone that the Japanese were the enemy. Like the two patients, some developed negative feelings about being Japanese and they tried to substitute being American.

This works only up to a certain point. What should one say when asked, "What are you?" If I say, "American," the response is very often, "Yes, but what are you really?" The question illustrates this conflict in identities. In addition, the dilution of the families with some loosening of family ties has resulted in significant changes in the roles of men and especially women. The father's authority and domination of the family have been decreased. It is not unusual to see Japanese women working outside the home. This has greatly increased since the war and this has also encouraged the women to feel more independent. I do not wish to be misunderstood; this is only relative and I am well aware that the roles in Japanese families remain patterned after the original patriarchal roles.

All of these factors have tended to reduce the positive sense of identity which existed in the Japanese. Currently, there is a conflict due to the fact that there are opportunities in work, social relationships, and even in the reduction of rigid residential segregation. The opportunities have multiplied for one to say "I am an American," but what is now lacking in some instances is the solid sense of good feeling about being Japanese-American. This has been chipped away as a consequence of the war, and the increasing acceptance of Orientals and by changing roles in the families.

To counter these forces, a solution may be to re-emphasize the feeling of pride in being Japanese, the *Yamato-Damashi*. Certainly Japanese schools to maintain the ties with the language, customs, and traditions of Japan are important in maintaining these awarenesses of the past and thus facilitating the sense of being good, acceptable, and first-rate.

Viewing the contemporary scene of busy frenetic Tokyo, one can see the clash and yet again the blending of the modern and traditional.

Prior to World War II, Japan was an example of a rural feudal society hurled into the revolutionary industrial 20th Century. As the nation became industrial, many Western values were partially accepted and even incorporated into the Japanese style of life. Take for example the leading bank of Japan, a modern, rapidly-growing, metropolitan institution which was able to expand with the application of enlightened, progressive banking practices. It even changed its name to present a euphonious and felicitous image. This is an act which would have been unthinkable until recently in tradition-bound Japan.

When the latest building was dedicated, dignitaries were invited to an elegant celebration, an occasion duly noted by the press, radio, and television. A Shinto Priest officiated to assure the pleasure of the gods.

At age 23, college graduate Watanabe-san was able to secure a position with this bank, and very probably he will remain with them the rest of his life. The bank becomes a part of his life fabric. Watanabe-san feels secure and knows well his perquisites. These fringe benefits range from semi-annual bonuses which amount to one-third of his annual salary, to apartments in company owned buildings after his wedding which was also at the company's expense. In the bank, the promotions will come in due course. *Watanabe-san* will often work 60 hours a week (Japanese workers are on a 6-day week) with no expectation of time and one-half for such overtime. He is a "salary man" who is as wedded to his firm much as he is to his bride. In the work situation, he may be adapting to computer methods, but he is also cognizant of the fact that his bank emphasizes service. As the chairman of the board of directors told the story, "My workers are eager to please the customers. Not only do we try to do the most for our customers, but I make sure that we bow lower than anyone else." This emphasis on the new, the modern banking and merchandising techniques, and retaining the old, the emphasis on service, "we bow lower," have been a successful blend.

This need to retain those aspects of the traditional Japanese culture and to add the modern technology and the progressive aspects of Western civilization in Japan is in many ways similar to the problem facing Japanese-Americans—how to adapt to rapidly changing situations and needs in an effective way and at the same time not destroy those aspects of one's past which have been a constructive force.

Traditionally the Japanese family is a close-knit unit, and the children are expected to care for their aging parents. With the adoption of American values and attitudes and with increased governmental aid, e.g. social security, medicare, etc., there has been a radical change in the family constellation and a general loosening of family ties. This is true for all Americans and reflects the societal changes caused by technological changes. Sons and daughters have been relieved of financial responsibility. This has then been generalized by some to sanction a much greater apathy and alienation, even from family members and of course to a much larger extent from all others.

Perhaps this has occurred in present day Japan, for this year, they added a holiday to honor the aging. Such a holiday had not been necessary for the preceding 2000 years, for the aging were honored each day of their lives.

To return to the Japanese-American dilemma, the question appears to be how to preserve and maintain the positive values and attitudes such as working hard, being clean, responsible, conscientious, without being led down a narrow conservative path which says that these values are all it takes. These values pose no problems, but in the successful adaptation to American middle-class values a problem has been generated.

This problem is in the temptation to say, "Well we have been able to do it, we are successful, and we now know how all minorities can also succeed." I do not mean only an over-identification with the values of the middle class in America but also in adopting the conservative views which are too popular. There is an insular quality to these conservative views which fostered the isolation of Japan for 2000 years and also in America the isolationism of the 1930's. How can we be free, responsible humans and yet maintain a human concern for others?

I believe that this is the key to the solution of the Japanese-American problem—that each of us needs to be concerned socially, to do what we can to promote the welfare of others, and to be involved consciously, without the previous automatic system of the family, clan and nation. This is what I hope President John F. Kennedy meant when he said "Ask not what your country can do for you; ask what you can do for your country.

Is it possible to be concerned about others and to express this concern in a realistic way? Some of the very means we have implemented, such as federal legislation for social security, medicare, etc., may have unwittingly caused decreased concern for each other. How can we have government aid and still be interested in one another. How can we promote national programs for social welfare without diminishing concern for all humans without regard to family, clan, or nation? Perhaps the federal measures had nothing to do with the lessening of family ties, but people being human needed to be reminded of the importance of constructive contributions to the common need. Perhaps this is why Japanese-Americans have returned to religion in numbers much more frequent than in Japan. I suppose that religion, whether Christianity or Buddhism, is one means toward increased social feelings. The disadvantage is that neither religion has successfully fostered an involvement with everyman's problems.

As I think about the problem of the Japanese in America, it is apparent that we live not in a melting pot but in a society which, with all its weaknesses, has been able to accept all races of mankind but with varying degrees of tolerance. Can we learn to live without stereotyped hate and with greater tolerance and appropriate acceptance of different races and with enhanced communication without loss of ethnic or individual boundaries? I hope we will be able to see the similarities, adapt to the differences, and consider the diverse values of the others.

An old Basuto proverb says, "If a man does away with his traditional way of living and throws away his good customs, he had better first make certain that he has something of value to replace them."* The verity of such a position is undeniable and highlights the task that must be accomplished, a more general inclusion of all individuals as objects for social feeling. It is like the psychiatrist from Japan who met our Caucasian friend Connie and said "She is like the Japanese." This meant that he accepted her, could empathize with her, and most of all he included Connie in the circle of his family, kin, and nation. We each of us need to include the others in our kinship circles, without reference to race, religion, or national origin, a task much easier said than done. I do have hopes that we can achieve this attitude if everyone will resolve to work toward this goal.

## REFERENCES

1. Benedict, R.: *The Chrysanthemum and the Sword*. Houghton Mifflin Company, Boston, 1946.
2. Bowlby, J.: Separation anxiety. International Journal of Psycho-Analysis, *41*: 89—113, 1960.
3. Caudill, W.: Japanese-American personality and acculturation. Genetic Psychology Monographs, *45*: 3—102, 1952.
4. Caudill, W.: and Weinstein, H.: Maternal care and infant behavior in Japanese and American urban middle class families. In *Yearbook of the International Sociological Association, 1966*, edited by R. Konig and R. Hill. 1966.

* Thanks to Norman L. Paul, M.D.

5. Erikson, E. H.: Lecture "Identity" for the San Francisco Psychoanalytic Institute, Extension Division, January 23, 1966.
6. Yamamoto, J., James, O., Bloombaum, M., and Hattem, J.: Racial Factors in Patient Selection. Presented at the 122nd Annual Meeting of the American Psychiatric Association, May 1966, Atlantic City, N.J.

# Adolescent Crises of the Kiowa-Apache Indian Male*

DANIEL M. A. FREEMAN, M.D.

THE ADOLESCENT CRISES of the American Indian spring not only from minority status but also from the breadth of the cultural gap he has been forced to bridge. Of America's minorities, only the early generations of Negro slaves faced a comparable transition.

The Kiowa-Apache tribe is a small Plains Indian tribe now residing in southwestern Oklahoma. They were among the earliest modern occupants of the southern Plains region, having been present prior to the first contact with white men or the introduction of the horse. They were also among the first to obtain horses from the Spaniards and seem to have played a prominent part in the northward diffusion of horses on the Plains (10).

As a small tribe, probably never numbering more than 400 during any historical period, they retained a loose affiliation with the larger Kiowa tribe. They moved about together and camped together at the time of the annual Sun Dance. However, a distinct identity, language, and culture were retained. Culturally and linguistically they are related to the Apaches of New Mexico and Arizona. Their name springs from their affiliation with the Kiowa. However, since they prefer to be called simply Apaches, the latter designation will be used interchangeably throughout this chapter.

Prior to the introducton of the horse the Plains were only sparsely populated outside of the few river valleys. Despite an abundance of game and vast herds of buffalo, hunters could not subsist in any numbers in most of the area because of the great distances which

*The data for this study were gathered as part of a larger study of Kiowa-Apache emotional patterns during the period of June 1964 to June 1965. The study was supported by the Department of Preventive Medicine and Public Health, University of Oklahoma School of Medicine, Oklahoma City, Oklahoma.

separated the sources of water. With the advent of the horse and a tremendous increase in mobility, new tribes moved in from the periphery to exploit the new possibilities. In a period of great mobility and fluidity, many cultures underwent radical changes as a new equestrian nomadic buffalo-hunting and raiding culture emerged (7).

The Plains Indian cultures were highly adaptable and extremely successful at exploiting their environment. With a stress on supernatural revelation through individual visions and a general stress on individualism, these cultures were extremely flexible and were in a sense "open societies."

All prestige was centered on the adolescent and young adult male, whose main occupations were hunting, raiding, and war. It is the male who has borne the brunt of the stress of change and acculturation to the white world.

The effect of change is not always traumatizing, and it may in fact be growth-promoting whenever challenges are of a type which can be effectively mastered by the potentialities available. This was the case with the rapid change following the introduction of the horse. The outcome is determined by the specific nature and focus of the challenge and by the strengths and weaknesses of the cultural system with which it interacts.

In the traditional Kiowa-Apache way of life, all masculine validation depended on power. Power was obtained in two ways, in warfare and through supernatural vision. The major crisis of Kiowa-Apache adolescence for the past four generations has been the unsuccessful attempt of the male to find validation in a world that has defeated him in war and destroyed the old religious beliefs with their attendant pathways to validation. Despite the adaptability of previous eras, his adaptation today is marginal at best.

Severe alcoholism is today virtually universal among adolescent and young adult males. Although this represents a retreat from reality and is a product of the breakdown of traditional patterns, it will be seen that a total breakdown has not occurred. The pattern of alcoholism characterized by severe binges fits in with traditionally sanctioned patterns of recklessness to provide paths for autonomy and initiative, so that certain progressive functions are served.

The result is a new cultural pattern of integration, so that subsequent progress toward individual maturation is able to occur.

Adolescence has traditionally been prolonged for the Apache male. His teens were a period of intense activity, freedom, and license, as he was primarily engaged in raiding and war. He married only at age 30. Psychological maturation, however, was even further delayed. Initial marriages were often unstable and temporary, and true stability and deepening attachment to one's spouse developed only with an advance in years (11).

It will be seen that today final resolution of the adolescent crisis similarly occurs only once the individual has reached an advanced stage. Final maturation occurs at the time of the advent of the grandparental role.

The process of change from the traditional culture began in 1867 when the Apaches were assigned to a reservation in southwestern Oklahoma by the terms of the Medicine Lodge Treaty. The equestrian nomadic hunting period now came to a close. The buffalo was almost extinct a decade later. Under the stress of change new religions sprang up in the 1880's. The reservation period continued until 1901, when the reservation was broken up and opened for white settlement, with each Apache now being given a separate allotment of 160 acres of land. These allotments were in southern Caddo county, Oklahoma, near the communities of Anadarko, Fort Cobb, and Apache.

To understand the crises of adolescence and of the whole society, and the factors which predispose to them, it is necessary to examine the Kiowa-Apache life cycle in pre-reservation times and the sequence of changes which have occurred since the breakdown of the traditional way of life. Simultaneous anthropological and psychiatric perspectives will be employed in examining the interaction of socio-cultural and intrapsychic processes. The evolution of traditional Kiowa-Apache personality will be considered first and subsequently the process of culture change and its effect on modern adolescent personality.

Knowledge of pre-reservation life is based both upon the work of Gilbert McAllister (11, 12) in 1933, whose oldest informants, had been born in the pre-reservation period, and on data collected from the oldest of present day informants. Although the oldest of modern informants were born in the 1880's and 1890's, a great deal of information about pre-reservation life is still available from them. They remember vividly the precepts and endless storytelling of their grandparents, which constituted the education of the Kiowa-Apache child. These stories were both mythological and biographical and were told and re-told countless times. The preservation of detail is enhanced by the Apaches' marked tendency to concreteness and avoidance of generalization. They limit themselves to re-counting specific episodes of which they have direct knowledge, thus allowing fairly accurate preservation of detail.* From these sources it is possible to re-construct a picture of pre-reservation life.

Despite a century of change, certain aspects of child-rearing and development have persisted relatively intact and continue to operate in ongoing processes within the present period. In the discussion of pre-reservation personality development which follows, present day examples will be utilized occasionally where a traditional aspect has persisted in relatively unchanged form.

## PERSONALITY DEVELOPMENT IN PRE-RESERVATION TIMES
### INFANCY

Infancy and early childhood are magical phases of the individual's development and are characterized by emotions which may flood with overwhelming intensity, shift rapidly, and quickly disappear. Powerful emotions occur at crises and turning points, but, at the same time, adaptive reactions occur. Early intense emotional patterns do not indicate pathology; in fact, they will often be seen to imply strengths. They are molded by the outcomes of subsequent stages and blended into the personality of the adult The ultimate value of a particular characteristic depends on the cultural system in which it occurs.

In following the course of traditional personality development, only those aspects relevant to major themes in Apache personality

* A great deal of data from modern informants has been collected by Dr. William E. Bittle and the University of Oklahoma Field School in Ethnology and Linguistics, which he directs. I am indebted to him for making available to me field notes collected by the field school during the summers of 1961, 1963, and 1964. They have provided a number of illustrations.

will be considered in detail. We will focus chiefly on the maternal relationship, shame, and the development of control, patterns of identification, extra-familial areas of initiative, and the family complex. These will set the background for our consideration of Apache adolescence in pre-reservation times.

Fearful and ambivalent feelings were felt by parents toward the unborn child. Parenthood occurred at a stage when the adolescent crisis had not yet been resolved and when individuals were still trapped between antagonistic fears. The fetus was seen as omniscient and powerful. It would punish a mother who was bad. "A baby knows how it is treated before it is born. If the mother doesn't do things right . . . maybe the mother will die and the baby will live. The baby has more power than the mother because the mother is bad-hearted" (2).

There was a marked fear of closeness felt toward the newborn child. "Me, I don't like to carry my babies too much on my arm. They cried for me but I tried to get away. I tried not to get too close to them. I got up and I tried to get outside. Or I might start doing something else." A similar fear of closeness is illustrated by the comment of a modern informant who was even afraid of a very friendly dog: "There's got to be *distance* between." Similarly, on several occasions when children who craved physical contact tried to cling to me, their families immediately yelled harshly at them, "Get away! . . . Get away!"

Cannibalistic fears concerning the nursing child are evident in myths of snakes or water dog lizards that would bite hold of the nipple of a mother who fell asleep while nursing a child. "Make it respond to your attentions, your cares. If you pay attention to the child then you have that child from then on and have power over it. Then you know that you've got control, that your mind and thoughts are into that little being" (8).

These tendencies were moderated by strong contrary cultural precepts. For example, a mother was advised to try to keep her child close to her body when he was little. When punishing him she should never push him away but rather always pull him toward her (8). One was urged to follow these precepts in order to gain control and in order to "show the people" that one was a good parent. (This need to prove oneself in the eyes of the public will be seen to be a central feature of Apache personality. It was a major motivating factor in positive behavior toward the child.)

Nursing was extremely permissive and was used as a panacea. The child was not only fed on demand but also was put automatically to the breast whenever he showed signs of any discomfort or distress, even if he had just eaten. The degree of permissiveness seems to have been partly due to pressure of cultural precepts, perhaps as part of a compensatory mechanism against fears and desires to get away from the child. Although the mother was supposed to be totally permissive and was never supposed to initiate weaning herself, one gets the feeling that mothers were very uncomfortable about this. The child would be allowed to go on and on nursing regardless of age, until either the mother became pregnant again or community ridicule shamed the child into stopping. The mother would never actively initiate weaning herself. She would rely on the ridicule of others, or, in the case of re-impregnation, would arrange for another person to take the child away from her or to put bitter tasting material on her breast. This pattern of nursing seems to have operated under the strong pressure of cultural precept, operating to counterbalance the mother's fears toward the child.

The extreme permissiveness and use of the breast as a panacea, against a background of markedly ambivalent maternal feelings, served to put great emphasis on the nursing relationship. The irregularities of gratification which resulted from maternal fears sensitized and focused the attention of the child on the nurturant relationship and increased his needs for gratification. At the same time, these increased needs were more than adequately filled. Thus he developed a focus on receiving external sustenance but also a basic optimism that his needs would be fulfilled.

He did not retreat into autoerotic self-gratification as extremely permissive gratification came from without. Rather than turning inward, he was very much engaged in the relationship with his mother, who was accepted and loved in her totality with frustrating aspects accepted as part of love.

The exaggerated need for care and affection emphasized the maternal relationship and caused the dependence on external sources of sustenance to persist. It was not that he feared that sustenance would be cut off, but that he needed to continue to receive it from an external source. (Rather than a fear of starvation, there is evidence if anything of fears being overfed. Also, it will be seen that these developments were vital components of later adolescent trends. The basic optimism that one's needs would be met and that one would come to no harm was fundamental to the daring and recklessness of the adolescent stage. Similarly, the importance of the maternal relationship made separation more difficult and contributed to later separation fears. Finally, just as the child did not retreat into autoerotic self-gratification, the adolescent alcoholic of today does not become an alcoholic addict.)

An additional factor contributing to the importance of this relationship was the uniqueness of the relationship between a parent and a youngest child. Favoritism and rejection of children were present in extreme forms (8). (The conceptual basis for the extremes of favoritism and rejection will be discussed at beginning of next section.) It was the youngest child who held the special position and was favored, pampered, and believed to be the smartest and best. This preference was reflected in many examples in the mythology, and a strong tendency in this direction persists to the present. The special position of the youngest child enhanced the uniqueness of the nursing relationship but led to the severity of the fall when a new younger sibling came along.

Suddenly, the nursling was forcibly weaned and abruptly rejected. After a prolonged period of greatly intensified emphasis on nursing, the child was "poisoned" by pepper or bitter material put on the nipple and fell into a state of rejection, as a younger sibling took his place. The emphasis here should not be simply on weaning or on an "oral" trauma but rather on a total permanent realignment of family relationships which now occurred. Boyer (5) describes a similar pattern in Mescalero Apache culture: "During the first few weeks he cries desperately and tries to cling to his mother whenever she nurses or handles the new rival. It is not unusual to see such a howling child shoved away. . . . He usually turns to his father and older siblings for attention, which is given inconsistently." Alternately, in the less frequent circumstance where the mother did not become pregnant again, the child continued nursing for a longer period of time until he was ridiculed and shamed into ceasing once he had entered the oedipal phase.

Again it was necessary to have cultural precepts to moderate these tendencies and to control the harshness. It was recognized that jealousy concerning a newborn sibling might cause severe emotional reactions or illness in a displaced child. Parents were warned that favoritism might cause other children to get jealous and to get sick and die (8).

## SHAME AND CONTROL

The child was viewed compartmentally as a separate category of being from the adult. He was not thought of developmentally in terms of a linear progression towards adulthood but rather as a static occupant of a separate compartment or as an entity different from an adult. His qualities were conceived of in dualistic black-and-white terms of good and bad and were conceived of as fatalistically pre-determined. Since the child was not thought of as growing from the past into the future and since his qualities were conceived of as innate rather than acquired, the parent had no responsibility for the child having become what he currently was, nor responsibility to shape him toward the future. (Adult concepts and attitudes regarding the child have been discussed in detail by Patricia Freeman (8).)

The parent might simply react to his over-all impression of the child's inherent goodness or badness. This was the basis for the uninhibited favoritism and rejection which have been discussed.

The parent similarly had little obligation to take an active hand in training the child but rather had simply to give it "good advice." This amounted to terse critical pronouncements or general cultural precepts. There was never any attempt to empathize, listen to the child's problems, explain things in terms which the child could understand, nor foresee future difficulties and prepare the child for them. Rather, everything was left "up to the person." The child was left to take the initiative for learning himself. With little guidance or help he would try to copy adult behavior and then be criticized or occasionally ridiculed for his clumsiness (8).

The non-developmental perspective combined with the general cultural avoidance of generalization to prevent organized teaching. Even the grandparent, who played an important role in the education of the child, limited himself to recounting mythology and personal experiences.

The tendency to leave everything up to the individual gave a measure of freedom, but also the responsibility of proving oneself. Although there was no stated explicit timetable for maturation, unless the child lived up to the implicit expectation for performance he would be ridiculed. This led to a constant need to prove oneself and a fear of ridicule and shame, which extends throughout the Apache culture.

Due to the non-developmental concepts and the lack of a tendency to generalize, no organized attempt was made to create an internalized value system. Control was exerted instead mainly through fear and shame. Fears of physical violence and public ridicule were cultivated consciously in the children by the parents (8). Through fear the parent sought to gain control. Ghosts (13) and cannibalistic monsters (12) became universal sources of fear. Children were also frightened by physically cutting them with a sharp object in order to frighten them with their own blood.

Children were early and consistently exposed to the shame of public ridicule. For example, if a child refused to particpate in the dance of the Rabbit Society (to which all children belonged), the other children would jump on him and tear his clothes (11). Throughout life the Apache remained in a chronic state of needing to please, needing to prove himself, and needing to justify himself repeatedly in the eyes of a critical public. (This same need provided the motivation for much of the parent's positive behavior toward the child. He was constantly concerned about what others would say about him and whether others would approve of his behavior as a parent. This concern was evident even in his positive communications to the child. Direct expressions of verbal approval and praise were never given. Positive communication was limited to formalized giving of gifts or a public gesture such as throwing a feast or having the child publicly boasted about by some other person. It is striking that even the public boasting about a child who had accomplished some feat was conceptualized in terms of a parent proving himself to the public: "You show the people that you love the child. It's one way of showing it" (8).)

The cultural tendency to develop a control system based on fear of shame and a need to please interacted with parallel intrapsychic

developments occuring at the same stage. The forerunners of difficulties with impulse control and tendencies toward feelings of
shame go back to the latter portion of the nursing period.

Due to her own adolescent conflicts, the mother was markedly
threatened when autonomous and assertive behavior started to
appear in the child. Her fears of rejection and separation were enhanced, and her frightened and ambivalent reactions at this point
interfered with early processes of individuation in the child. The
child was unable to turn to autonomous and assertive activities,
which lead to mastery and to growing self-esteem. Instead there
was a fear of his impulses, which he somehow needed to control
and suppress. In this setting there also developed hypertrophied
feelings of shame, the feeling of discomfort about oneself when one
meets with disapproval from outside. Thus instead of an early
move toward autonomous activity, feelings of shame and problems
with impulse control emerged.

These tendencies were exacerbated when confusion and rage
impulses erupted at the point of sudden rejection from dependency. This turmoil of primitive rage and intense feelings of shame
determined the type of conscience development which subsequently occurred.

In the first stage of conscience development, shame is felt only
over misbehavior which is discovered and only when the child feels
or anticipates disapproval from outside. At this stage shame is not
connected with the act itself but is merely the sinking feeling when
one feels disapproval. Later, the child starts to adopt the attitude
of the parents and starts to feel that certain types of behavior are
bad.

Although he adopts the critical attitude, the full implications of
accepting blame are very threatening at first. The child can normally only gradually accept that he is the one to blame for impulses
or behavior which are bad. He tries to project the blame for these
impulses onto someone else (9). This transient projection allows a
child to gradually internalize the blame in small doses without
being faced with the full force of self-blame all at once. A rapid
process of internalization severely threatens self-esteem, while a
gradual process allows the child to gradually master the implications.

If a child is already struggling to control overwhelming feelings of primitive rage, he is afraid and unable to have any form of aggressive or accusatory fantasy toward someone else. He is unable to tolerate any form of aggressive impulse for fear that a total disruption might occur. He is therefore unable to blame someone else. Instead, the full force of critical evaluation against himself is immediately internalized. Unable to accuse due to the degree of anger he is already defending against, the child is struck with an overwhelming feeling of self-blame, with permanent effect on his self-esteem.

A critical attitude thus internalized has not been gradually digested and assimilated into values which are the child's own. Rather, the values remain parental. (Although the values are critical and although they originate in the parent, the parent may not in fact be equally "critical." The problem here is the child's inability to cope with even a normal amount of parental criticism and control. The critical attitude, originally of parental origin, is taken out of context and magnified. When, in addition, the parent is in fact harsh and critical, a cumulative effect results.) The child's control mechanisms therefore progress only as far as the development of "anticipatory shame," or the fear of incurring external disapproval.

Without the development of internalized values of one's own, the individual does not develop true "guilt," and therefore does not develop automatic unconscious mechanisms of impulse control. Until this occurs, the struggle to control impulses remains a conscious battle between wish and fear. In the case of the Apaches it will be seen that this struggle continued for some time but that automatic mechanisms of impulse control later did develop, permitting progression from the early adolescent to the mid-adolescent stage.

In the chronic struggle which persisted, impulses could be controlled only by increasingly harsh countermeasures of the conscience. A harsh punitive conscience developed despite increasing external laxity and permissiveness during later childhood and the adolescent stage. This severity of the child's control systems was a reflection of the degrees of the struggle inside.

Thus intraphysic processes of development combined with parallel cultural forces to develop a control system based on the fear of shame. Although later developments brought changes in the

control system and permitted a move toward assertiveness and autonomy, a need to please and a fear of shame remained permanent
imprints on Apache personality.

## IDENTIFICATION

At the time of his abrupt displacement from the favored position
in the family, the Apache child was overcome by feelings of panic
and rage. In the turmoil concerning abandonment, he sought for
ways to regain parental acceptance. The only route open was
through controlling his rage and becoming mother's helper in
caring for the younger sibling. In so doing he not only managed to
retain a degree of acceptance but also underwent a major psychological change.

He was caught between antagonistic fears, on the one hand a
fear of abandonment and on the other a fear of a passive or dependent relationship in which he might be injured or rejected again.
These opposing fears, of separation and of closeness, persisted
throughout childhood and adolescence.

The child needed to retain a degree of closeness with the mother
and yet not fall back into a passive or dependent role. An active
relationship, in the form of an active identification with the
mother, allowed for restoration of a degree of closeness on a new
basis. The child was able to retain contact by becoming like the
mother, in becoming her helper, and yet at the same time retain a
degree of separation by maintaining an active role. A degree of
dependency persisted in his submission to maternal expectations
and in his continuing need to please.

This identification was an important stabilizing factor. Although
dependency cravings and hostile feelings were only lightly papered
over, a new stability and move toward reality and active mastery
resulted. In conceding to the siblings the world of childish pleasures and in identifying with maternal activity and expectations,
the child was now increasingly able to fill an active role.

New possibilities for activity and initiative became available to
him in the extrafamilial sphere. He moved progressively into these
areas, with the strong reinforcement of cultural and parental
expectations. Thus his early identification with the activity and
expectations of the mother led initially to a restoration of equili-

brium by being mother's helper but ultimately led to a progressive move into the extra-familial sphere.

Although this identification permitted a new stability, the child remained acutely hurt by the loss of the mother, and strong submerged dependency needs and angry impulses persisted. These strong submerged feelings were factors in the child's inability to project blame, as was discussed in the section on conscience formation. They recurred later and became important during the adolescent phase.

## INITIATIVE

From mid-childhood onward dependent and passive attitudes were discouraged, while self-expression, independence, and personal achievement were stressed. There was a minimum of organized direct training and a great deal was left up to the individual. Discipline was also erratic, and perfunctory threats were often empty. The child was left with a wide range of freedom for initiative but also the responsibility of proving himself.

He was given social recognition for his accomplishments and public self-expression was encouraged from an early stage. As a member of the Rabbit Society (to which all children belonged), he could boast and be recognized for his achievements. The dance could be interrupted by a boy going up and hitting one of the drums. "Wait now, I'm going to tell you a story. Way down there I kill a rabbit (he hits the drum); over there I kill a bird (he hits the drum); over there I pick up a turtle (drum). There is my witness" (11). A dance or feast might be given in his honor. Alternately, a relative might pay an old man or woman to go through the camp crying out his accomplishments. Thus cultural sanction and a wide range of opportunity reinforced the trend to active initiative.

Surrogate outlets became available for competitive strivings previously frustrated within the family and for attempts to demarcate a sphere of personal privilege. Of particular importance in this regard was the grandparent-grandchild relationship. From mid-childhood onward, this relationship became of equal if not greater importance than relationships within the nuclear family.

"There is a feeling of formality, of conflict, between the parent and child generations not noticed between alternate generations"

(11). The relationship of a child to his parents was one of formality and respect without intimacy. Between grandparent and grandchild generations, however, great intimacy existed. Both referred to each other with the identical kinship term. In fact, in many ways the relationship was one of equality and reciprocity. In many ways they were equals in the social structure, both dependent on the active generation who were the center of Apache life.

The grandparents, who were now past the active stage of life and yet greatly respected for their experience, played the major role in the formal "education" of the child. While skills were learned on the child's initiative by trial and error, tribal values and lore were absorbed from the endless storytelling of grandparents.

The relationship with the grandparent was one of special privilege. Not only was there a feeling of equality and free give-and-take, but the child was in some ways in a position of authority and power. A grandparent could not refuse a grandchild's request. McAllister (11) gives two examples of grandparents being forced against their will to do something because a grandchild requested it. The following example illustrates the persistence of this traditional pattern today.

We were on a short trip, accompanied by two grandparents and their grandchild, who was 8 years old. On the way home the grandson told his grandfather to tell some stories. Although the grandfather was somewhat reluctant, he was forced to oblige. The grandfather explained to me that if I wanted the storytelling to continue I should periodically say, "Haah," as he went along. (This is a characteristic response of the audience to encourage a storyteller.) I did so and punctuated his story with the culturally-expected exclamations and questions. The grandson, however, remained silent.

Periodically the grandfather would interrupt himself: "Are you awake boy?" "Yah." "Well how come you don't say 'Haah'?" "I don't want to." "You better say 'Haah,' boy, or I won't tell the story!" He would continue nevertheless. Alternately, he might interrupt himself periodically with: "You awake boy?" "Yah." "No you're not! You don't say 'Haah.' " Finally, on one occasion when the grandfather interrupted the story, the grandson retorted, "Ah shut up! I don't want to hear your story." The grandfather continued despite his grandson's persisting silence.

The grandfather now became more defensive, trying to see if the boy had been listening and knew what he had been saying, rather than trying to get him to say "Haah." The grandson's main role was to tell his grandfather what to do and which stories to tell. After the grandson had put his grandfather in his place by telling him he was not going to say "Haah," he periodically mocked the grandfather by turning to his grandmother and saying to her, "You asleep?" "No." "Then how come you don't say 'Haah'?" After he had gotten after her twice in this manner, she did say "Haah" once or twice. Although this grandchild is somewhat unusual in the degree to which he is spoiled, the episode illustrates the persistence of a privileged relationship. (The harsh aspects of the boy's manner are not typical of the old pattern, but his position of privilege and prerogative in relationship to grandparents is essentially unchanged.)

This new relationship was in marked contrast to the child's relationships within the nuclear family. It illustrates the new areas for privilege and assertiveness which opened up as the child gave up the world of childish pleasures and turned to extra-familial sources of gratification. Although the feelings of loss and anger could not be left behind, the new channels offered compensatory and restitutive outlets. They allowed the individual to progress to the high level of competent action which characterized the raiding warrior-hunter of the Plains. They also allowed siblings to sufficiently disengage from the nuclear family to permit a new closeness with each other which became essential in adolescence.

The grandparent was important in another way during this period of turning to initiative. He provided, from the mythology, figures with whom the children now identified. The boy moved from identification with the activity of mother to an identification with mythological figures before he moved to an identification with the active father.

In the mythology and the old people's tales of personal exploits of their youth, great stress was laid on ignoring cautions and winning acclaim through daring assaults on the dangerous and impossible. Repeatedly, mythological heroes disregard the cautions of their elders and triumph.

A few examples of the attitude of recklessness and daring in the myths (2) and from the older informants' recollections may be illustrative. "I just went ahead. I do anything." "We're just free. We do what we want." "The sun is the eye of God, and when it's down you can do what you want." "My mother said, 'Don't do this; don't do that.' But I did those things and I learned my own way." Coyote, the mythological hero, cries, "Boy, that's the way I like to live, reckless! . . . . I'm free. I come and go as I like." When warned, he says, "Oh, I don't believe anything bad will happen to me," and he charges forward in the face of danger. (In this last example we see again the theme of optimism, the basic confidence that one's needs will be met and that one will be looked after, springing from the permissive care of the first period of life. This optimism was the basic precondition of the reckless daring which now developed.)

Recklessness and daring were highly valued in the raiding and warfare of the Plains. These qualities were valued in youth, and yet as the man assumed the responsibility of leadership and old age as a grandparent, he was expected to assume the mantle of sober caution. Although he preached the values of caution and sobriety with great emphasis, the grandparent simultaneously gave a double message which offered success to those who ignored his precepts, and he boasted of his own reckless exploits of the past.

Although cautions were offered, and although the myths illustrated and warned of danger for a person who "goes too far," the boys turned with enthusiasm to the path of recklessness. For example, one older informant recalls that when his grandmother warned him about ghosts (a nearly universal source of very great fear in this culture), he went out in the middle of the night to find them. Another grandparent reports that he still has the same problem with his grandchildren today. He always tells the boys not to go down to the creek, because he is not worried if they go there. But he has been careful never to say, "Don't go down by the river"; if he did, they would be on their way.

All of these factors coalesced to produce a trend in latency toward active initiative, daring, and mastery. Increasingly, boys were able to identify with the frightening figure of the active Plains Indian warrior.

An Apache myth tells of children abandoned by their parents who survived, looked after themselves, and later turned against their parents. Their parents had moved away and abandoned them on the order of the chief. Later, when they were reunited with the tribe, they threw a feast for everyone except their parents. "They said, 'They done us wrong; they threw us away!' They told the people that they forgot their folks. They did the same thing to their folks that their folks had done to them. They didn't feed their folks, but they treated the other people nice" (2). The pattern of rebelling against the parents and belittling parental care became marked in adolescence and is particularly prominent in the modern era.

## THE FAMILY COMPLEX

The trends of identification have been followed as they led the child into extra-familial areas of initiative. We must now return to examine certain other features of the relationships within the nuclear family before proceeding to a consideration of adolescence.

The child was never able to cope actively with the situations inside the nuclear family. He was unable to deal with his rage against siblings and against his mother. Not able to take effective steps himself, he submitted to the situation and identified with the mother's activity instead. With simultaneous fears of injury and of separation, he achieved his best resolution by adopting a role which pleased the mother and fulfilled her expectations. Unable to find an active solution to the problems inside the family, he achieved a pseudo-active resolution by turning to substitute forms of activity.

The adolescent activities of hunting, raiding, and warfare served as such substitute outlets. These were "masculine" activities, yet no real progress toward active masculine identification at an intra-familial or emotional level was yet possible. Adolescent warfare activity occurred without a resolution of intra-familial conflicts and prior to the emergence of a true stable identity.

Unable to control his angry impulses against his mother and overcome by overwhelming fears, the child was unable, even in fantasy, to enter into a dominant aggressive role in relation to his mother, which an identification with his active father would have entailed. Furthermore, specific castration fears were enhanced by the practice of cutting children in order to induce fear and gain control. A great-grandmother reports, "When the child is about five years old, you really scare him good and raise him good. You've got to make them afraid of certain things. You might get one old lady, you tell this old lady, 'Come over and bring your knife!' She brings over a chipped piece of glass and cuts the child wherever his clothes are open. She says that next time she's going to do it again" (8).

The female was an object of love but simultaneously an object of fear, and a direct active role in relation to her was impossible. Even less would the child have been able to compete with or confront the fearsome looming figure of his all-powerful warrior father. All of these factors made active oedipal fantasies impossible, and the child turned instead to submitting to the mother rather than identifying with father's active role in relation to her.

Later in life he did move toward an identification with father. The identification with mythological figures served as one intermediate step in this progression. It is only once the progression to full identification with the active masculine role is completed, that the psychological processes of adolescence can reach closure and maturity be attained. Thus the unresolved issues of the family complex are crucial in shaping the subsequent course which adolescence will take.

## ADOLESCENCE

The onset of puberty, with the rising pressure of biological urges, re-awakened all the early emotional conflicts which had become relatively quiescent when the boy first moved into substitute areas of gratification. There was a surge of both the longings and need for love and of the conflicts which were sources of panic and fear. The adaptations of later childhood were not able to cope with this intensified surge of emotion.

In the tumultuous stage of adolescence, the individual attempts to break free from the conflicts of his involvement with his primary family. He tries to achieve an independent identity of his own with new love relationships. Under the best of circumstances this re-alignment is difficult and extends over a period of time.

Full emotional separation from the parents threatens to leave a complete vacuum within the individual. It can therefore only take place by gradual shifts in stepwise fashion, with many fluctuations and backward movements. This process is particularly difficult where the attachment to the parent has become crucial to the individual in maintaining his sense of self.

The abrupt withdrawal from parental ties which started in Apache childhood was only superficial. No real resolution of dependent attachments had occured. An early abrupt withdrawal of this sort does allow the individual to become more tolerant of his impulses and allows him to act upon them outside of the family. Sexual and aggressive wishes can rise to the surface and be acted out. In such a circumstance, however, the move toward true individuation is delayed. Where the conflict between fear of collapse into passivity and fear of separation is too great, the individual is not able to withdraw his emotional ties from his primary family and emotionally re-invest himself in new relationships.

Adolescence is the psychological process of adaptation to the biological condition of pubescence. It makes its appearance at a given state of physical maturation but remains independent in its course, and it is unaffected by the further progression of physical maturation. It is " . . . the sum total of all attempts at adjustment to the stage of puberty, to the new set of inner and outer—endogenous and exogenous—conditions which confront the individual" (4). The process is brought to a conclusion when a sex-appropriate harmonious identity has been established.

An overly sudden attempt at realignment or a premature attempt to jump into an adult role cannot be successful. A gradual process of re-alignment is essential if it is to be complete. On the other hand, one cannot judge a prolongation of adolescence to be necessarily detrimental or pathological. Although the course of the psychological processes of adolescence in Apache culture was more prolonged than in our own, it will be seen that this fits in well with the over-all functioning of the society and with the traditional life cycle.

The psychological processes of "early adolescence" extended approximately to the age of 30 and the processes of "mid-adolescence" to approximately the age of 40 in traditional Apache culture. This should not, however, be considered a retardation. Although there were emotional factors and unresolved issues which prevented a more rapid movement, a more rapid movement would have had no value and in fact would have been disruptive within the context of this culture. Both the early superficial withdrawal from parental ties and the more prolonged gradual emotional re-alignment should be considered in the context of the total culture.

The initial foundations of initiative and daring were laid well in advance of the onset of pubescence. Likewise, the child's prepar-ation for his future hunting and warrior role was begun at an early stage. The roles of the boy and girl diverged, with the girl remain-ing close to female relatives and helping about the teepee, while the boy learned to shoot and hunt and progressively received better treatment. His mother and sisters waited on him and he was accorded much more respect than his sister. He was a potential warrior, hunter, and chief, and they were all 'good' to him (11). As he moved through later childhood and through his teens a clear future role was before him. This role offered the utmost in achievement, power, and respect. The active warrior held the highest status in Apache life and the key to leadership and reli-gious power in later life.

"Usually in his late teens a boy would begin to go on raiding and war parties—activities which seemed to have concerned him primarily during his twentieth to his thirtieth years. This was a period of intense physical activity and, to an extent, great freedom and license. Around thirty most men were married, and the out-standing ones were asked to join one of the societies" (11). Both marriage and membership in one of the warrior societies entailed the beginning of many responsibilities.

Early marriages, in the thirties, were usually unstable and short-lived. Even once a more stable relationship was established, deep-ening feeling and attachment did not develop until after the pas-sage of years. The intimate relationships with one's brothers and formal "friends" or comrades-at-arms (which had been central in the previous period of raiding and warfare) remained much more important than the relationship with one's spouse. "If a wife dies, you can get another woman, but if a brother dies, you won't see him anymore" (11).

Marital stabilization occurred with the passage of years as the children grew up. Both deepening attachment and extensive kinship readjustments now bound the two people together. In addition, emotional maturation had occurred.

The man was now a grandparent and past the active stage of life. He had increasing responsibilities in religious, mediating, and advisory roles and as a bearer of tradition. In some ways he became socially an equal of his grandchildren and entered into a reciprocal relationship with them. At the same time, he remained set apart and valued for his wisdom and experience.

The stages of the life cycle will be further examined as each is considered in detail. We may turn to the psychological processes at each stage.

## EARLY ADOLESCENCE

In early adolescence the individual was threatened by revived and intensified impulses and fears dating back to early childhood. He tried to break free from entanglements with his parents and nuclear family but suddenly discovered a consequent loss of self and loss of the sources of self-esteem.

From early childhood, the Apache child had an intensified need for maternal sustenance. Throughout childhood his sources of identity had been overwhelmingly external. When he moved toward activity, he modeled himself in a way to be pleasing to his mother. Later, as he moved into extra-familial areas, he continued to try to model himself along lines of parental hopes and expectations. In infancy his moves toward autonomy and separation had been cut off, and throughout childhood he had lived in roles built on external expectations. An attempt to break free from parental ties therefore threatened the disruption of his sources of identity and self-esteem.

Furthermore, in view of the degree of his dependency needs, an abrupt separation would have threatened his whole being.

Although progress toward a basic separation and individuation was not yet possible, and although resolution of the deeper issues was postponed, the individual continued to progress along roads of initiative, achievement, and power which remained open to him.

As he broke free of parental authority in extra-familial areas, he grouped together with the other individuals of his own sex. With the collaborative support of the group he gained support in his break with parental values. The group also served an important function in channeling his behavior.

As he started to withdraw from parental ties a concomitant weakening of the control mechanisms of conscience occurred. This was especially the case since the control mechanisms consisted largely of undigested parental forces rather than values which had been adopted as one's own. The weakening of the strength and severity of the conscience permitted the move toward daring initiative and recklessness; at the same time it made the individual more tolerant of sexual and aggressive drives which had previously been suppressed. The individual was now able to act upon these drives in the extra-familial sphere. Such acting out may follow different lines, depending upon the values and orientation of the extra-familial group with which the individual becomes aligned (4). The cultural channellings of his drives and the nature of the adolescent group are crucial at this stage.

Where the process of adolescence is ritualized and formalized by a culture, the individual is offered conventionalized models for his psychic re-structuring and a new self-image which is clear and culturally reinforced. He has a promise of fulfillment and a clear sense of direction. Simultaneously the assimilation of the maturing child into society is promoted. Conversely, where no tradition and custom formalize the adolescent process, the individual has to achieve adaptation by personal resourcefulness. He has the opportunity for a unique, highly original, and personal variant on tradition but has less cultural structure upon which to rely (4). Blos has pointed out that adolescents left to their own devices will spontaneously form competitive organizations with an emphasis on aggressive dominance and competitive superiority. These groups are characterized by a dual-value principle, according to which attitudes applied to the in-group but not to the out-group are not experienced as morally contradictory (4.)

In Apache culture there was a clear-cut model upon which one's new self-image was based and which was strongly reinforced by all aspects of the culture. This was the role of the warrior and hunter. At the same time, however, there was relatively little structuring of the paths toward this goal. Great freedom was left for individual initiative but, as always, the responsibility of achieving and of proving oneself in the critical public eye was left upon the individual. There were no formalized initiation rites nor was there any explicit timetable for progression toward maturity.

The only structure offered to the adolescent was the information that one needed to obtain supernatural power and that there were a variety of ways of obtaining it. Supernatural power was essential to success as a warrior and hunter and led to curative powers in later life. He would need to deprive himself and submit to a test of courage and suffering. Certain cultural institutions also gave a degree of implicit structure for the process of adolescence. Two important social phenomena of early adolescence—the adolescent group and the close friendship—were institutionalized. Recognition was granted to the fantasies, dreams, and visions which play an important role as the adolescent undergoes an emotional re-alignment. Instinctual behavior was idealized and provided sanctioned outlets.

Thus there was a combination of structured and unstructured elements, with only semi-formalized pathways through the adolescent process. Initiative, free choice, and the opportunity for personal resourcefulness co-existed with implicit structure and the requirement for compliance. Cultural patterning was clear-cut enough to channel definitely the adolescent's development yet flexible enough to allow certain innovations. Great stress was laid on individual insights obtained through personal visions, and individuality was stressed throughout. The degree of structuring present allowed for a smooth transition, essential if the adolescent was to become a competent daring warrior; yet the unstructured aspects contributed to the emergence of a competitive organization with emphasis on aggressive dominance and competitive superiority, and operating according to a dual-value principle, as mentioned above. The whole system of Plains Indian warfare may be viewed as the interaction of adolescent groups of this sort.

The grouping together with one's peers is characteristic of the early phase of adolescence. It is the first step in the process of re-alignment of emotional relationships. With the collaborative support of the group, one is able to start the process of separating from dependence on parental figures. The grouping together with members of one's own sex occurs in response to resurgent fears from childhood, particularly fear of females. The group offers an outlet for competitive assertive strivings, offers collaborative support against collective dangers and fears, and institutes a collective code of maleness (4). Shared (extra-tribal) objects for anger and aggression are defined and it becomes possible for ambivalent feelings of love and hate to be separated from one another, with aggressive feelings finding an outlet. This important social pattern of early adolescence becomes dominant through the phase of raiding and warfare.

Another characteristic and important social institution was that of the friend or comrade-at-arms. The relationship with a brother or friend became the most intimate and important one for the Apache at this stage. "Two brothers or two 'friends' are as nearly one social personality as can be obtained" (11). They fought together, shared one another's belongings, and shared one another's privileges and obligations. The importance and intimacy of this relationship have already been illustrated in the fact that a man valued a brother or a friend above his wife, at least for the first decade of marriage.

Not only did these relationships serve a vital role, as friends fought together as comrades-at-arms, but they also served a vital psychological function. The intimate friendship follows the move into the adolescent group, as the next step in adolescent emotional realignment. It will be seen that identification with the close friend served an important stabilizing function at the close of this phase.

The close relationships with a brother and with a friend were regarded as equivalent. Considerable realignment in the relationship between brothers was necessary to permit the degree of intimacy, equality, and interdependency which now developed. This was possible as the conflicts and rivalries of childhood were left behind, as each moved into the extra-familial sphere. Despite strong cultural prescription and the sanction of formalized pattern there is evidence that feelings of conflict between brothers did occasionally break through. Of more importance to psychological development, however, was the relationship with the intimate friend, where this problem did not apply.

The other important cultural institution during this phase was the vision quest. Again both social and psychological functions were served. Sacrifice, submission, and compliance were combined with a maximum sense of initiative and free choice (6). The individual voluntarily sought to submit himself to the test of deprivation, danger, and suffering. Here we see reiterated both the stress on independence and the need to submit and to win approval, which were central themes in Apache personality. Adolescent fantasy, which served a vital role when the individual had started to withdraw from parental ties but not yet substituted new relationships, was institutionalized and granted recognition and importance. In his vision the individual obtained a guardian spirit who would accompany and protect him throughout life. He gained power in warfare, success in hunting, curative powers, and long life.

To obtain power, the adolescent had to go to a terrifying spirit-ridden place and expose himself for 4 days and 4 nights without eating. This incorporated the common adolescent pattern of asceticism. The Apaches did not inflict severe physical tortures upon themselves at this time, as did a number of other Plains tribes, but the element of self-deprivation was present. An additional component was the counter-phobic pattern of denying danger with reckless daring, the roots of which have been seen to extend back to childhood. The Apaches never got over their terror about ghosts (13), to which they were forced to expose themselves recklessly at this time.

In trying to break free from his submissive and dependent tendencies, the adolescent tended to over-compensate and become belligerently affirmative of his male powers and prerogatives. His acting-out was channeled in valued directions, however, and there was little reason to be a rebel without cause. His contribution was immediately desired, valued, and ostentatiously rewarded. The acting-out of impulses not only served as an outlet to permit their discharge but also allowed the individual to identify with the masculine group and a "masculine" ideal.

Paradoxically, at the same time as he was breaking free from submissiveness by his new initiative, he was simultaneously bidding for the affection of his parents and seeking to please them and the whole society by fulfilling the role and expectations which they had for him. This blending of opposite tendencies allowed gradual progression of emotional realignment and allowed the adolescent to progress to effective competence without abrupt disruption or discontinuity.

As the adolescent withdrew from parental ties, it became increasingly important in terms of both his need for external ties and his self-esteem that he be filling a role which others could respect and that he remain acceptable to them. His fear of separation was such that he could only attempt withdrawal if he simultaneously maintained his love-worthiness and his acceptability. It therefore became increasingly important to prove oneself and to exhibit one's worthiness. By living up to exaggerated expectations, he was able to build his self-esteem to the point where he had sufficient security for gradual withdrawal and progression to new interpersonal involvements. While his increasing confidence and security tended to facilitate this process, his difficulty in separating tended to slow the process, with the result that the transition was a gradual one extending over a span of years.

It has been seen that the gradual nature of this evolution fit in well with the structure of Apache society. Throughout the teens and twenties there was ample opportunity for sexual gratification because there was no difficulty with impregnations caused during this phase, as there was little, if any, stigma attached to illegitimacy. In some tribes it was even necessary for a woman to have a pre-marital "love child" to prove her fertility before she would be marriageable. Such children were accepted into the family when the woman married. Therefore the young male's impulses were not frustrated by the postponement of marriage. In the phase of most active raiding, hunting and warfare, the individual was not yet ready for the establishment of a marriage. The fact that the daring competitive social and psychological patterns of early adolescence continued through the twenties contributed to the success of the individual in his primary activities.

## MID-ADOLESCENCE AND THE TRANSITION TO ADULTHOOD

The formation of a close friendship with a member of one's own sex is an essential step in the process of adolescent disengagement from parental ties and movements toward heterosexual love. The friend chosen at this stage is usually one who possesses attributes which the individual admires and which he needs to incorporate into himself to make himself complete. The close interpersonal relationship at this stage not only allows a substitute relationship for those left behind in the family but also establishes a new value and control system by a process of identification. It has been seen that the Apache child only partially internalized parental values in childhood and did not completely assimilate them or make them his own. During childhood no automatic mechanics of impulse control developed but rather simply fear of disapproval and fear of shame. As the tie to the parents weakened at the onset of adolescence, these control mechanisms weakened as well.

In his identification with his idealized friend, however, the individual now obtained a new source of values and ideals. These values became internalized and incorporated as one's own (in the psychic formation known as the "ego ideal"). Thus for the first time a stable set of values appeared, allowing the development of stable mature control mechanisms and ending the struggle between fear of shame and impulsive desire. Whereas in early adolescence impulsivity was difficult to control and required severe sanctions under certain circumstances, caution, wisdom, and sober leadership now started to appear. Older warriors in their thirties and forties became members of warrior societies, one of whose functions was to police raiding and hunting parties in order to prevent the impulsivity of the younger warriors from endangering everybody or scaring off the animals and ruining the hunt. It was at this same stage, in the thirties, that the first moves to heterosexual emotional relationships occurred. Thus the close friendship was important in two ways, as an intermediate emotional relationship enroute to heterosexual love and as a source of ideals and values which became the crucial stabilizing factor leading toward Apache maturity.

Although a "masculine" identity was achieved in the teens, and increasing sobriety and responsibility in the thirties, it was not until somewhat later that a true heterosexual emotional interrelationship was established.

As is characteristic of the psychological phase of mid-adolescence, tender love started to appear in the thirties and led to a series of shifting trial relationships. Even when a permanent marital relationship was established, the man remained close to his mother, closer to his sister's children than his own, and closer to his brother and friend than to his spouse. He had an authoritarian manner in his own family, so that the child was "a little bit afraid of his daddy" (11). There was a feeling of formality and conflict between parent and child generations but friendly intimacy with his sister's children.

Although he became biologically a parent at this stage, he had not yet fully completed the transition to stable heterosexuality and accordingly remained more closely involved with his family of origin. The fact that he was very frequently away from home on hunting and raiding parties further minimized his involvement with the family.

With the passage of years the remnants of defensiveness in relation to females eased and the relationship to his spouse gradually deepened into stable mature love. He became less involved in hunting and warfare and increasingly involved in intra-tribal responsibility. A crucial final turning point seems to have occurred at the point when he became a grandparent. A familial, close, non-ambivalent relationship now became available to him. His previous sphere of activity, even during the parental years, had been extra-familial. No longer active, it was this phase of life which was characterized by close emotional relationships.

All informants report that they felt much closer to their grandchildren than to their children. It was the nature of the grandparental role which was recognized by the Apaches as crucial in the final consolidation. This pattern persists to the present, with grandparenthood remaining a crucial turning point. For example, one great-grandparent criticized a grandparent who was not fully living up to his responsibilities, as follows, "You're a *man* now, not a boy. You've got grandchildren and a good house."

We may summarize by following the course of identifications in the developing male. In childhood he moved from identification with mother to identification with mythological figures. In early adolescence his identification with the close friend led to the formation of the ego ideal. At this stage too he identified with the public role of his father. In his thirties he identified with his father's roles as husband and father, although these were limited. Deeper emotional relationships and a true family role developed only as he finally moved into the grandparental role.

It has been seen that many of the developments of childhood had effects on the course of the adolescent process. Optimism which sprang from the period of permissive nursing became an important factor in daring and recklessness. The early reliance on external sources of identity and the accompanying need to please contributed to the child's and the adolescent's need to mold themselves upon parental expectations. The fear of separation and loss of the parent contributed to the gradual nature of the shift in emotional alignments through the course of adolescence. The converse fear of passivity and collapse into submission helps to explain his turning to extra-familial areas of initiative and contributed an assertive aggressive component to adolescent activity. The nature of the control mechanisms developed during childhood led to the prominence of acting out of agressive behavior in adolescence.

The identification with the active mother was the first in a series of identifications which ultimately led, through effective mastery, to emotional maturity. Throughout life there remained a balance between his fear of submissiveness and bid for independence and mastery on the one hand, and his fear of separation and bid for approval and affection on the other hand.

Cultural patterns of institutionalized self-assertiveness, the stress on accomplishment and self-expression, the vision quest, the adolescent group, institutionalized exhibitionism, and the formal pattern of brotherhood and friendship served to complement the personality of the pre-adolescent child and channel his development during adolescence.

We may now turn to some of the subsequent processes of culture change, their effect on family organization, and the development of the male, and then finally to the adolescent male of today.

## FAMILY STRUCTURE AND CULTURE CHANGE

In pre-reservation times, parents had little direct involvement with their children. The man was usually away hunting or fighting, and when he was at home he did not participate in the duties around the camp but simply relaxed. Upon the adult female fell all the responsibilities of heavy work, preparing hides, drying meat, storing and transporting goods, moving camp, cooking, and caring for infants. As the parental favorite was the youngest, most

parents took little interest in the child when it was past the suckling stage and superceded by a younger suckling. Both parents had
little time for the child in any case. It was the older generation of
adults, too old for the physical demands of active adulthood, who
had time for the children and upon whose shoulders much of the
responsibility for the children fell. Coincidentally the grandparents
themselves entered a stage of life where emotional involvement
with a family was meaningful to them. Thus the close grandparental involvement with the children was based on a combination of economic, social, and emotional factors. Important too was
the fact that, in a sense, grandparent and grandchild were equals on
the social scale. All respect centered on the young active adult.
Even those old people who had medicine power were inferior in
status to the successful warrior; those who did not possess medicine
power were totally dependent on the active generation. They were
subject to the whim of the active generation for support. The
caution was often repeated to parents that they should treat their
children well so that the children would not be mean to them in
their old age. Thus it is perhaps no accident that grandparents and
grandchildren addressed each other by the identical term and
treated each other as equals in pre-reservation times. This reflected
their common dependency and the nature of the family structure.

With the collapse of the pre-reservation hunting and nomadic
way of life, the most severe emotional blow was sustained by the
young adult male. Crushed and humiliated in war, starved into
submission with the inability to find game, deprived of his prestige
and any access to prestige, it was his readjustment which was most
difficult. He had no way to achieve validation or to achieve self-
respect now that culturally prescribed routes were impossible.

Not nearly so difficult a readjustment was that of the young adult
female. In fact, initially the main change seems to have been that
she had less work to do, although she retained her status-defining
responsibilities as a bearer of children and preparer of meals. Much
of her previous difficult work of moving camp, tanning hides, and
making clothes was now gone. For both sexes of young adults, there
was one common effect: both now had fewer outside responsibilities and activities. Both were now around the home and un-
occupied much more than previously, particularly the male. One

wonders to what extent depressed and bitter males, now forced to remain around the camp and deprived of their previous aggressive outlets, took out their anger on their families. Their children spoke of being "afraid" of their fathers. We know that this particular generation of males, when they later reached old age towards the turn of the century, were responsible for an outbreak of witchcraft.

There was a total reversal in the relative prestige of younger and older males. In the traditional Kiowa-Apache way of life, all masculine validation had depended on power obtained in warfare and through supernatural vision. (These were interdependent, in that power obtained in visions helped a man in war, while power obtained in warfare was prerequisite to becoming a medicine man with supernatural powers in later life.) With the collapse of the pre-reservation way of life, the younger generation lost their access to prestige, and no effective substitute has been subsequently devised.

New religions, particularly the peyote religion, seemed to offer a substitute at first. When warfare was no longer available as a path to validation and power, visions became increasingly important. Both peyote and alcohol were valued as adjuncts in this search for supernatural experience. Unlike the disinhibiting effects of alcohol and its potentiation of violence, peyote produced a synesthetic experience of harmony and unity. During a century of acculturation, many of the crises of identity have led to an escape into a fantasy world promoted by these drugs. At the same time, however, the visions they produced had great traditional sanction and importance. Toward the end of the last century, as the authority of the old religion began to crumble and as practitioners of the old religion went increasingly in the direction of malevolent witchcraft (as is frequently seen when a value system is crumbling), new religions began to appear. The peyote religion offered the adolescent an alternate road to validation.

However, the peyote religion, too, soon became a religion of the elderly and of tradition, rather than of youth. While the youth have never found any substitute for the lost prestige of hunting and warfare, the older generation of each subsequent era has held one trump card—they were the purveyors of tradition. This was vital in a system which was failing, in a world which was falling apart. "This is all we have left. We are a poor pitiful people."

Thus a reversal of status occurred. It was now the old man rather than the young man who possessed what everyone valued most. Moreover, this trend was reinforced as economic power shifted out of the hands of the hunter and into those of the older generation who became owners of land.

For a few decades the previously independent and eminently capable period of adolescence was filled with individuals who tried various adaptations—the peyote religion, the Ghost Dance religion, and farming. Men continued to try to take an active role and find a substitute source of pride. The attempts at adaptations were blocked, however; a change in government policy destroyed the last possibility for an adaptation in terms of values to which the Plains Indians adhered. Former hunters of the buffalo showed early signs of adapting well to a new role in raising cattle. White settlers, however, coveted the reservation land and so it was taken away from them. They were given small individual allotments and told to become farmers. As men were now forced into what, for them, was woman's work, the last possibility for masculinity was destroyed. Due to small economically unviable allotments, no experience in farming, unscrupulous credit exploitation, and the introduction of alcohol by the white settlers who now moved in, the attempts at farming failed. After several generations of youths exhausted themselves fruitlessly trying to find a way to adapt, they started to give up. Subsequent generations turned instead to alcohol. Alcohol had been used initially as an adjunct in the quest for supernatural visions. It now became increasingly part of a withdrawal and retreat from reality.

Major changes started to develop in the family. Females moved increasingly into leadership in various phases of life. This is a familiar pattern, seen in many cultures with the collapse of a patriarchy and the gradual emergence of a matriarchy. Of special note was the increasing importance of the grandparental generation. As the parents withdrew and defaulted (as the older patterns which kept female recklessness in check broke down, young females too turned to alcoholism, although to a lesser degree than the males), it was fortunate that an idealized pattern of grandparental participation in child rearing existed from before to fill the gap. Although child care again falls on the grandparental generation, there is now a totally different underlying status structure. The responsibility now falls on the high-status grandparent through default of the low-status parent. In many cases the grandparent came to fill not only a supplementary role which offered affection and interest but also the total parental function. It will be seen that this fusion of parental and grandparental roles led to new problems, as the traditionally sanctioned grandparental hyper-permissiveness led to spoiling of the children, and as the fusion of the two roles made it impossible for the child to move away from his nuclear family into a new and different kind of relationship with his grandparent.

Important changes in the alignment of parent-child relationships also occurrred. In pre-reservation times, fathers were mainly attentive to their sons and mothers to their daughters, particularly once later childhood and adolescent stages were reached. By the 1880's and 1890's this pattern became reserved. As the males became inadequate and dependent, they perhaps found a more comfortable dependency on child females than on threatening adult females. Similarly women perhaps found male children more closely to fill their idealized image of a competent male than could male adults. For example, one informant commented about such changes in the family of a sister and brother who were born in 1884 and 1900, respectively. "When she was sick her mother didn't care too much. My mother said, 'Funny woman! She doesn't care about her children. If my children are sick, I'm sick too.' (The daughter) sure favored her daddy. It's natural, I think, for every girl to be closer to her mother. You can't get your daddy to change your clothes. And it's natural for a father to be close to a boy. I don't know how come her mother never cared for her. Funny, I don't see how a mother doesn't care for her child." On the other hand, the mother favored her son: "She liked him best; left almost all the land for him. He favored his mother. He ought to be a woman; he favors his mother!"

Here the informant has contrasted traditional precepts with the actual family relationships which now had emerged. It is noteworthy that a similar change had taken place in her own family.

(She was born in 1884.) "My daddy done lots for me. Go to the store. Buy me cookies, candy, toy dishes. He liked me so dearly he would do everything for me. He'd let me do anything. Wherever I'd want to go he'd take me. He liked for me to ride horseback all the time, so he gave me a horse, bought me a saddle and bridle. I got so I could even ride a bronc. He taught me how to jump on the horse. I guess I was a tomboy. I made my own bows, arrows. Yah my daddy liked me better, because I was a girl and my brother was a boy. I didn't have much to do with mama. She didn't treat me right. She was always busy: 'Why don't you help me wash the dishes?' But I was lazy. She was scared of my daddy if I told on her. I'd rather have my daddy beside me closer than my mother. I guess you would say I was his boss"(8).

Both girls described here became tomboys, while the boy remained extremely dependent. A reversal of patterns of identification had occurred. The degradation and increasing absence of the male and an increasingly ambivalent relationship to the mother also contributed to the shift in the boy's patterns of identification. This will be further discussed in the next section.

Other important developments include the breakdown of important social mores. Agression now breaks through to the surface and becomes disruptive more easily. This is evident in comments about "teasing" (actually ridicule) and direct verbal agression. "Of course the modern people like us tease and tell jokes. Old Indians didn't like that. They said, 'Don't tease everybody. It's not serious. Don't make fun of people. Don't berate people.' Nowadays we just grind these sayings up, don't listen to advice." "We say the nasty things right back."

The close relationship between brothers has also broken down. "In the old days brothers were pretty good friends. These young generations aren't like that. They don't have good feelings for each other. Some brothers on account of their wives have hard feelings towards each other" (3).

## MODERN CHILD DEVELOPMENT

Many of the traditional patterns of child development persist, although some trends have been emphasized and some new developments have occurred. The changes in the course of child development bring a different individual to the crises of adolescence. Thus the adolescent of today is a product both of a different childhood experience and a new set of adolescent circumstances.

During the nursing period the pattern of over-gratifications persists. Although most newborn infants today are being started on the bottle, most current adolescents were breast fed during infancy, according to the old pattern. Despite the persistence of the use of nursing as a panacea for all types of infantile distress, certain changes in the mother-child relationship have occurred. There is increasing difficulty in parental impulse control, an exacerbation of parental ambivalence and fears, and an increasing difficulty in emotional relationships. These are the products of emotional turbulence at the stage of parenthood. They contribute to irregularity in the relationship between the mother and child and to certain new trends in personality development. The solid core of optimism which was vital to traditional initiative, is now weakened. There is a tendency towards autoerotic self-stimulation where stability in the mother-child relationship is lacking. A basic wound develops in feelings about oneself and the stability of the external world. (These changes are relative, but they have contributed to a shift in emphasis and have a perceptible impact on the course of development.)

Although parental ambivalent feelings and fears of the child were present in pre-reservation times, these are now increased. There is greater fear and intolerance of assertive and agressive behavior in the child. In pre-reservation times this led to difficulties in moves toward autonomy and individuation, difficulties with feelings of agression, and emphasized feelings of shame. These trends are accentuated, wth increasing problems in separation, increasing difficulties with primitive rage, and more overwhelming shame which seriously threatens self-esteem.

These trends tend to increase the dependency on the mother-child relationship and to increase its primacy. The mother remains crucial as an external source of sustenance, gratification, and identity. As has been noted before, the mother is accepted in her totality, with painful aspects of the relationship denied and accepted as part of love. It will be seen that this suffering aspect of love has an importance in certain modern adolescents, although it was not prominent in pre-reservation times.

The reaction to displacement by a younger sibling is sensitized by the same factors which have been discussed for pre-reservation times. It is intensified now by greater separation fears and turbulent feelings of anger as a result of difficulties in the infantile relationship. This increased turbulence accounts for the fact that the same control mechanisms which functioned in pre-reservation times (based on a fear of shame and a need to please) are now less able to control impulses. Even in pre-reservation times this early control system did not function as smoothly as did the later automatic one based on internalized values of one's own. The struggle between impulse and fear of shame is more intense at present, with the result that there is a considerably greater breakthrough of impulsive behavior during adolescence.

When blame is abruptly and prematurely internalized without a gradual transition, and when control is maintained by a continual struggle against impulses, the conscience and control mechanisms become harsh. The severity arises from the premature harsh judgement against oneself and the intensity of the struggle against impulses. In pre-reservation times, the parent-child relationship was one of restraint, and although rejection by parents and society could be severe when one deviated from social norms, the parent-child relationship could not be described as a harsh one in general. At present, however, bottled-up frustration and aggression in the parent has given the parent-child relationship a harsh quality of superordination-subordination. This may reinforce the pre-existing tendencies of the conscience to harshness and severity. The effect, however, is very irregular, as it varies with parental favoritism or rejection of the particular child, the sex of the child, and with the particular adult who is caring for the child. It has already been mentioned that grandparents have moved increasingly into parental roles. Where this is the case the child will be pampered. Accordingly, there is great variability in the attitude and treatment which the particular child encounters from significant adults. Where a considerable degree of harshness is present, it contributes to the formation of a pathological need to suffer.

This need to suffer is based on a need for the love of a person who makes one feel guilty and ashamed. Against the background of the acceptance of suffering as part of love, and the acceptance of exaggerated blame against oneself, the individual identifies with parental harsh judgements of him and aggressive attitudes toward him. Suffering has been accepted as part of love, and he now feels that he must suffer in order to make himself worthy of love (1). In these individuals, the need to suffer contributes to self-debasement in alcoholism during adolescence.

The early identification with the activity of mother, combining submission with activity, continues as in pre-reservation times. While submitting to her expectations, he maintains a form of activity. He thereby maintains a degree of closeness while simultaneously ensuring that he does not fall back into a vulnerable passive role. The modern child comes to this point with more intense fears of both separation and closeness than did the pre-reservation child and clings to this identification more tenaciously than formerly was the case. He persists in role-playing maternal expectations and fails to move out into extra-familiar areas of initiative.

Two external factors tend to reinforce this trend. Insofar as grandparental and parental roles are fused, there is now a single relationship which ambivalently blends permissiveness with punitiveness, in place of the two contrasting relationships which existed before. Whereas the pre-reservation child could move away from the nuclear family into an area of social privilege with the grandparent, this is often no longer possible. Similarly most of the extra-familial spheres of masculine initiative of pre-reservation times no longer exist. A very few do find substitute outlets in the context of the surrounding white culture but the majority do not make this transition. Thus for both intrapsychic and external reasons modern individuals tend to persist in their identification with the active mother and do not move out into extra-familiar areas.

The identification with mother is accentuated by the re-alignment of family relationships. The father is disparaged, inadequate, and not effective as an active model. It has been seen that he no longer has any interest in his sons and takes greater interest in his daughters. Thus no counterbalance exists for the relationship with the mother. It has been seen that just as the father loses interest in his sons and turns toward his daughters, the mother turns toward her sons. The special relationship which exists between mother and son is often an uncontested one, either because the father is absent or defaults, or because the mother can more nearly conceive of her son as fulfilling her conceptualized ideal of the male. While the child continues role-playing maternal expectations, in the background is the realization of his affinity with the inadequate father.

In pre-reservation times the main area of initiative and activity was extra-familial; self-esteem and confidence gained in this area served to counterbalance the frustrations of intra-familial life. Today this relationship is reserved. Extra-familial opportunities are minimal and the main outlets are found in relationship to grandparents (although this may be limited if the grandparents serve as parents) and in superordinate relationships to siblings.

In the child's special relationship with his mother, he develops an exaggerated self-confidence which is divorced from external reality. This self-confidence serves to cope with failures, and with ruptures with society in adolescence. Thus increasingly the reliance on this special role becomes part of a retreat from reality.

The inflation of self-confidence in childhood relationships served a vital role in pre-reservation times, building the warrior-hunter's backbone of daring competence. It has now become uncoupled from accomplishment, however, as unreality replaces coping and mastery. This shift is recognized by the Apaches themselves, who now discourage inflating a child's ego: "If you encourage a child too much, they get to be a failure. You make them feel too proud, as if they are too good. Don't build them up too much. They might never live up to the expectations. If you praise people too much they make a mistake."

## THE ADOLESCENT TODAY

The modern adolescent no longer has access to prestige and has lost the traditional routes to masculine validation. The patriarchal structure of pre-reservation society is now largely gone. There is a wide gulf between the conceptualized ideal male and the weak degraded individuals with whom the child must identify. The one consistent and stable role is that of the female. Alternately, the child may still identify with mythological figures or with his grandparent, but neither of these roles are real. He can never approach the life of the mythological heroes or warriors and cannot for several decades assume the grandparental role.

In childhood, an intensified dependency on the maternal relationship led to his clinging to an imaginary special role. With the reversal of parent-child relationships and the default of his father, the relationship with his mother became more intense. In his special relationship with her his self-esteem is inflated but in a way which is unreal. The exaggerated self-confidence is unrelated to accomplishment, and he is vulnerable when he confronts reality and attempts to adapt.

The crises of identity start prior to the adolescent stage. Exposed to western movies, the child develops a picture of the Indian as being evil and embodying all that is bad. The confusion which develops may be illustrated by an episode reported by a mother concerning her son. He was frightened when he saw Indians in town. She asked, "What are you afraid of? Lots of Indians live in town. Why are you afraid of Indians?" "They kill people!" "Well, what tribe are you?" "No! I'm a nigger."

The problems of masculine identity may be illustrated in the comments of a great-grandmother concerning her 11-year-old great-grandson: "He sure takes care of his sisters. Yesterday he bathed them and washed their clothes as clean as anything. He just learned it from me; I didn't even ask him. Nobody asked him. He just does it by himself. Even washes his own clothes and irons them. If there's sewing to do, he says, 'Great-grandmother, show me how.' He's good about things. Cooking too. I think he'll grow up that way." An increasing tendency for males to assume female roles has been evident for several generations. It is not unusual to see a male take the major role in caring for children or looking after housework, while females have tended increasingly to move into leadership roles.

For the modern adolescent, the traditional channels and cultural structuring of adolescence are gone. Certain features of the traditional masculine ideal remain but are beyond reach. At the same time, the pressure to prove oneself continues. The important traditional relationship with a friend has broken down, and although reliance on the adolescent group continues, its system of values no longer serves as a factor for social integration.

The adolescent today still attempts to find a masculine identity and to assert virility. He attempts to become part of the white world and to model himself along lines he has encountered in school. He is not accepted, however, and is confronted by humiliating rebuffs. In the face of strong conflicts about the masculine role and conflict-ridden feelings of self-hatred concerning his Indian identity, he turns to the few remaining outlets available to him. Most prominent is the armed services, where he may attempt to again fill a traditional masculine role. Great tribal respect is still given to the warrior. But the armed services are unlike anything with which the old Plains warrior was familiar. In place of individualism and a stress on personal initiative, one must now take orders. The stress is on submission. The armed services bring glory and respect, but unfortunately this is only temporary. The soldier experiences an even harder fall when he returns. Other outlets such as athletics and being a ceremonial dancer offer equally impermanent support, and the individual collapses into alcoholism.

Severe alcoholism is virtually universal among adolescent and young adult males. Only one adult male (aged 50) has never been an alcoholic (nor had a single drink). Alcohol promotes a retreat from self-reliance into unreality. The individual seeks to escape from conflictual tension by falling back on one of the earliest modes of tension management. His alcoholism is in the form of drinking characterized by severe binges. It does not serve as an addiction as much as an escape. (It has been mentioned that there is some evidence of autoeroticism in the modern era, where the mother-child relationship is particularly unstable. This is still relatively uncommon, however.) The alcohol allows him to fall back in fantasy onto the inflated image of himself which was created by exaggerated parental expectations. He falls back onto megalomanic defenses and exhibitionism, as he struts and boasts. As he withdraws into compensatory self-inflation, there is often a false sense of power and his judgment is impaired.

The alcoholism serves too as an outlet for agression, now that no idealized outlet for instinctual behavior is available. There is an increased pressure of agressive impulses which overwhelm and break through the controls. Aggressive behavior is no longer confined to socially-sanctioned channels but now occasionally breaks through in socially-destructive directions under the influence of alcohol.

In those individuals where a need to suffer exists, alcoholism may serve this function through self-degradation. In most individuals, however, the degradation and failures are denied by recourse to megalomanic defenses.

Another pattern for managing aggressive feelings may be seen in the relationship to the Federal government. Grievances are accumulated as to mistreatment in the government's hands, yet they are unable to blame Washington directly. Instead, they idealize with Federal government and blame local employees. They thereby split off the harsh aspects from the loving paternalistic image, finding safe targets for anger while preserving an image of a special nurturant relationship. Nevertheless, a great deal of aggression remains unneutralized and suppressed. "We have those things among our people—pent up emotion, pent up anger. It's handed down from way back. It's carried down as long as I can remember." "Just like what my father says: God forgives, but the Indians do not."

Exhibitionism, aggressiveness, and competitiveness, which were valued in pre-reservation culture, are now feared as disruptive and are suppressed. They find outlet, however, in the strutting, boasting, and challenging of the alcoholic.

The general cultural attitude concerning these tendencies has already been illustrated in the quote offering caution against building up a child's pride. Similarly, it is felt that one should not exert oneself or compete: "You can't exert yourself in anything, not even in love." Likewise, modern individuals are inhibited in performing exhibitionistic ritual acts.

In the performance of the Blackfeet Society Dance, if an article of clothing was dropped by one of the dancers, it was traditional for the dance to stop until an outstanding warrior had come forward and recited a deed of valor before picking up the article. Bittle has noted that there is now a self-consciousness and feeling of awkwardness connected with performing this function (3). He quotes one occasion when the person called upon said, in substance: "I'm not a hero, I'm just a plain person trying to get along in this life. I was in both wars, and I thank God that I came out safe. We're supposed to tell our war exploits, but I'm just a plain person, and I thank God that I'm safe."

The alcoholic flies in the face of these and other cultural trends. It will be seen that in so doing he paradoxically undergoes a restitutive process which allows him to gradually progress toward emotional maturation. The prognosis of the alcoholism is very different than is the case in western culture.

Recklessness, daring, and disregard of caution have always been valued in Apache culture. These themes are still very much alive today. From the mythology and from grandparental boasting of the exploits of their youth, the child still learns that success and fame are to be found by disregarding the cautions of elders and by challenging the dangerous and the impossible. As in pre-reservation times, the cultural sanctioning of recklessness fosters a break from familial dependency into initiative and into the collective code of the adolescent group. Today the recklessness finds its outlet in alcoholism.

In pre-reservation times the move to initiative occurred in later childhood and was molded by counterbalancing and integrating mechanisms which allowed a smooth transition through the adolescent process. Today the move toward initiative is belated and the counterbalancing mechanisms are gone. Yet recklessness in binge alcoholism still plays a vital role.

It has been seen that the move to extra-familial initiative fails to occur during childhood. It is only with the rising pressure of biological urges and adolescent turbulence that closeness to the parent becomes intolerable and that separation begins to occur. The turbulence, negativism, and rebellion in this transition is always proportionate to the degree of dependency which has existed before. It is therefore not surprising that, with a lack of cultural channelling and with a great increase in dependency, a tumultuous period of acting-out ensues. The crucial point is that this period allows the first steps of emotional re-alignment to occur. The individual breaks free from the parental relationship and moves out into the adolescent group. A strong, even chaotic, turn to activity is vital to rescue the individual from his now greatly intensified passive fears.

The alcohol serves a second function during the adolescent phase. It not only allows a break to reckless defiance but also fosters fantasy and extra-natural experiences. These are parallel to the pursuit of supranatural experience and search for identity in the vision quest of the past. A retreat into fantasy and the induction of different ego states can serve a pivotal function in adolescent groping and searching and can be crucial to progressive development (4). By trying out new "selves" and new relationships in fantasy experimentation, re-alignment is promoted and maturation can occur.

Finally, the adolescent group, although organized around alcoholism, still plays an important role. It continues to provide collaborative support against common opponents and to define a form of collective "masculine" code.

Despite the elements of unreality, maladaptation, and degradation in the period of alcoholism, maturation does occur.

Although virtually all males are severe alcoholics during the adolescent stage (while the Apaches do not become addicted or continuously intoxicated over relatively long periods of time, their binge drinking is sufficiently severe and sufficiently frequent to totally disrupt family and social relationships and to cause recurrent imprisonments. They are group drinkers rather than solitary drinkers and usually drink themselves into relative insensibility), it is significant that nearly all of them cease drinking entirely or drink only occasionally once an important and responsible role becomes available to them in later life. For a few this time comes during the period of parenthood, if they are able to have steady employment and serve a meaningful role. For the majority, however, it comes when they suddenly discover themselves to be grandparents and to have become the older generation, with familial and social responsibility resting in their hands. This transition is remarkable to observe. "Skid row" bums become pillars of respectability and the cornerstones of society. To permit this progression, essential steps in personality development have occurred, enabling the individual to stabilize dramatically once the meaningful role becomes available.

In pre-reservation times, grandparenthood occurred once the individual had already reached a mature emotional stage. By contrast, grandparenthood today is a precipitant which permits maturation to occur. A stable identification becomes possible and the evolution is relatively swift. With the advent of a stable identity and a continuity of one's meaning both to others and to oneself, resolution of the adolescent phase takes place.

Nearly 100% of males are alcoholics in the later teens and twenties. This drops to 30% in the thirties and forties and tapers to a small minority thereafter. It is interesting to note that those individuals who take to alcoholism acutely and turbulently during adolescence as an act of recklessness initiative stop drinking more easily in later life. A minority who use alcohol to fill a food-like function, as a retreat into oral dependency, are the ones who tend to persist in their drinking.

Post-adolescent Apaches regard adolescent alcoholic irresponsibility in very moralistic negative terms while continuing to sanction the underlying recklessness and to boast about their own youthful exploits. Their moralism is the righteousness of the reformed sinner. They characterize adolescent behavior as "craziness" and feel that adolescents have gone to an extreme. (The degree of their opposition is helpful to the adolescent, as it gives him something to rebel against.) Traditional Apache culture recognizes a continuum between desired recklessness and "going too far." Mythological heroes, whose recklessness brought salvation for their people, all at times went too far, with their impulses breaking through into anti-social or cannibalistic acts.

The old people spoke of the reckless by saying, "He's gone the other way," "He's on the other side," but more significantly, "He'll come back." They compared the alcoholic to a horse who had strayed looking for different ways. "But he'll come back, he'll come back. . . . This is where he belongs."

The expectation is very strong that the alcoholic will return and that when he does he will become active in the peyote religion, which serves as a main stabilizing factor in Apache life. More than anything else, it is the ethic of the peyote religion which gives order to Indian life. Blending Christian elements with traditions from the past, its ethic is one of sobriety, responsibility, and veneration for order and tradition. It complements the grandparental role in converting the reckless into responsible elder adults. In this role as a social integrator, its function is indispensable.

Initially the peyote religion was a religion of younger individuals as they broke from the older ways. Now, however, it speaks as a voice of tradition and waits for the reckless to 'return.' Although it is closed to the adolescent during his reckless stage, it will be a prime factor in helping to consolidate his identity, as his prolonged adolescence comes to a close.

## SUMMARY AND CONCLUSIONS

In pre-reservation times the Apache child developed a continuing need for external sustenance. His control mechanisms were built on a fear of shame and a fear of public ridicule. This resulted in a life-long need to please and need to prove oneself in the eyes of a critical public. During childhood and adolescence, this type of conscience led to a continual struggle between impulsive wish and fear of disapproval.

At the time of the birth of the younger sibling, the infant lost his favored position in the family and an abrupt change in family relationships occurred. At this stage he identified with his mother and became mother's helper, thereby retaining her approval while simultaneously starting to turn to extra-familial areas of gratification. With strong cultural reinforcement he turned now to initiative, daring, and extra-familial activity. He entered a special relationship of prerogative with his grandparents and belittled the importance of parental care.

Cultural patterning supported a smooth move toward competence and the individual moved toward the role of warrior and hunter. The adolescent group, the formalized institution of the friend, institutionalization of impulsive behavior, and special recognition for adolescent fantasy and visions gave support to the individual during the process of adolescence. At the same time there was a stress on self-assertiveness, initiative, and individualism, which gave flexibility and the sense of free choice.

During his twenties the individual was primarily engaged in hunting, raiding, and war. This phase psychologically corresponded to a prolonged period of early adolescence. In his thirties he passed through the phase of mid-adolescence, with the first emergence of heterosexual love and stable control mechanisms based on an in- ternalized set of values derived from identification with the close friend. Although he became biologically a parent, he had relatively little familial role but increasingly had more tribal responsibilities. During this stage he was more closely attached emotionally to his family of origin than to his spouse and offspring. By the stage of grandparenthood a deepened emotional attachment to his spouse had developed and an important intra-familial role in relationship to his grandchildren now became available to him. He was now past the active stage of life, but in a phase of life which was characterized by close emotional relationships.

With the breakdown of the traditional pattern of life, the adolescent lost his status-defining extra-familial role. Changes in family structure occurred, with reversal of the relative prestige of younger and older males, increasing importance of the grandparents in caring for children, a gradual move of females into leadership roles, and a reversal of parent-child alignments. Adolescent males for several generations have unsuccessfully tried to find substitute adaptations and a meaningful role.

Severe binge alcoholism is virtually universal among adolescent and young adult males. In a retreat from reality, they fall back in fantasy on an inflated self-image created in the special relationship which now exists between mother and child. More importantly, however, the move to independent initiative now starts to occur. The alcoholism serves as a path for reckless assertiveness and a break with parental ways. In a period devoid of a valued role, the individual goes through a chaotic break from dependency to initiative. He continues gradually in his progress toward emotional re-alignment, so that when a meaningful role later become available for him maturation can rapidly occur. For a few this occurs with the advent of stable employment but for the majority it awaits the advent of the grandparental role. The alcoholism abruptly ceases and the individual moves from debasement and ostracism to mature responsibility and respectability. He become a bearer of tradition as he moves into the close relationship with his grandchildren and becomes a participant in the peyote religion.

Thus a new cultural integration has emerged, with a new pattern to the life cycle. The alcoholism occurs in a period of few commitments and does not prevent progress toward maturation which will subsequently occur. The degree of social disruption created by his absence is minimized by the nature of the social structure. The disruption is much more severe in cultures where the adult male would normally have an important intra-familial role. (Cirrhosis seems to be remarkably uncommon. A survey of 1600 discharge diagnoses of Kiowa, Comanche, and Apache Indians at Lawton Indian Hospital for the 2 years of 1956 and 1963 revealed only two diagnoses of cirrhosis unassociated with gall bladder disease, and three cases associated with gall bladder disease.)

His move to a negative identity is not really a deviant development but rather a universal and sanctioned stage. Two contradictory value systems of recklessness and sobriety co-exist, each with a function at a specific stage. Each has its own traditional antecedents and sanctions in the past and is integrated into the pattern of life which has now emerged.

## REFERENCES

1. Berliner, B.: The role of object relations in moral masochism. Psychoanalytic Quarterly, 27: 38–56, 1958.
2. Bittle, W.E.: Unpublished field notes, 1956, 1961, 1963, 1964.
3. Bittle, W.E.: The Manatidie: A focus for Kiowa-Apache tribal identity. Plains Anthropologist, 7: 152–163, 1962.
4. Blos, P.: On Adolescence. The Free Press of Glencoe, Inc., Glencoe, Ill., 1962.
5. Boyer, L. B.: Folk psychiatry of the Apaches of the Mescalero Indian Reservation. In Magic, Faith, and Healing, edited by A. Kiev, pp. 384–419. The Free Press of Glencoe, Inc., Glencoe, Ill., 1964.
6. Erikson, E. H.: Identity and the life cycle. Psychological Issues, 1: 1, 1959.
7. Gladwin, T.: Personality structure in the Plains. Anthropological Quarterly, 30: 111-124, 1957.
8. Freeman, P. A.: Kiowa-Apache Concepts and Attitudes Regarding the Child, Unpublished master's thesis, University of Oklahoma, Norman, Okla., 1965.
9. Freud, A.: The Ego and the Mechanisms of Defence. International Universities Press, New York, 1946.
10. Jordan, J. A.: Ethnobotany of the Kiowa-Apache, Unpublished master's thesis, University of Oklahoma, Norman, Okla., 1965.
11. McAllister, J. G.: Kiowa-Apache social organization. In Social Anthropology of North American Tribes, edited by F. Eggan, pp. 96–169. University of Chicago Press, Chicago, 1937.

12. McAllister, J. G.: Kiowa-Apache tales. In *The Sky is My Tipi*, edited by Boatright, No. 22, pp. 1—141. Texas Folklore Society, Dallas, 1949.
13. Opler, M. E. and Bittle, W. E.: The death practices and eschatology of the Kiowa-Apache. Southwestern Journal of Anthropology, *17*: 383—394, 1961.

# American Middle-Class Adolescents as Psychiatric Inpatients

WALTER WEINTRAUB, M.D.

IN RECENT YEARS, the number of American middle-class adolescents referred and accepted for inpatient psychiatric treatment has greatly increased. Many of these young patients are being treated on adult psychiatric units in general hospitals. Since most administrators believe that the percentage of adolescents on a mixed ward should not exceed 25 to 30%, the hospitalized teen-ager is in a very real sense a member of a minority group.

There are several ways in which adolescent patients constitute a minority group with a separate identity when admitted to a voluntary adult psychiatric hospital. In the first place, teen-agers are the only non-voluntary patients in the institution; as minors, they are signed into and out of the hospital by their parents or guardians. They often do not see themselves as ill; to a greater extent than older patients, they tend to project their difficulties onto parents and other adults. Their dependent status and great use of alloplastic defenses lead to frequent elopements from the hospital. Second, due to problems of disposition, adolescent inpatients may be hospitalized for longer periods of time than adults with comparable psychopathology. They, therefore, have a large stake in administrative matters and frequently become responsibly involved in the milieu therapy program. The very dependence which leads to prolonged hospitalization for adolescents may paradoxically result in their exercising considerable power on their units simply on the basis of seniority. Third, because of their youth, charm, and seductiveness, adolescents often become "special patients" and take up a disproportionate share of the doctors' and nurses' time. Fourth, the teen-ager's strong need to group with his peers leads to the establishment of close relationships with other hospitalized adolescents which often continue long after discharge from the institution.

## PSYCHOANALYTIC THEORY OF ADOLESCENCE

Although the present state of analytical knowledge of adolescence leaves much to be desired, we must still turn to psychoanalysis as our best source of psychological data.

There is general agreement among clinicians that puberty ushers in physiological and psychological changes of such magnitude that, in Anna Freud's words, "It is normal for an adolescent to behave, for a considerable length of time, in an inconsistent and unpredictable manner" (6). This turmoil can be attributed to the attempt of the ego to cope with the greatly reinforced sexual and aggressive drives. Since an essential task of adolescence consists in the replacement of parents and siblings as sexual objects by extra-familial figures, extreme dependency conflicts commonly develop. During no other period of life is such a variety of adaptive mechanisms employed in an attempt to achieve psychological homeostasis. Neurotic symptomatology, anti-social behavior, depression, and psychotic regression may manifest themselves almost simultaneously in the behavior of certain adolescents. Erickson has taught us not to attribute to this decompensation the same seriousness we would if we encountered it in adult patients (4). Nevertheless, the second decade of life is the crucible from which one emerges either confidently prepared for adult life or doomed to a lifelong struggle with unresolved infantile conflicts.

The tasks that the adolescent must accomplish have been succinctly summarized by Jacobson: "In adolescence, the sexual maturation process leads to a temporary revival of pre-oedipal and oedipal instinctual strivings, thus reviving the infantile struggle. But now the incestuous sexual and hostile wishes must be finally relinquished. Moreover, the adolescent's affectionate ties to the parents must also be sufficiently loosened to guarantee his future freedom of object choice and to permit him a sound re-orientation toward his own generation and a normal adjustment to adult social reality. This is the cause of his grief reactions, which have no parallel in childhood. What makes this emotional task even harder is the fact that it involves, in addition, a definite and final abandonment of his practical and emotional dependency on the parents" (10).

Erickson has stressed the adolescent's search for identity and the possible pathological consequences of role-confusion.

In attempting to cope with the greatly increased pressure for gratification of sexual and aggressive urges and the need to direct these feelings toward extra-familial persons, the adolescent may react in a number of characteristic ways. When these reactions are extreme, they constitute the spectrum of adolescent psychopathology encountered by the clinician. The following discussion closely follows the outline published by Anna Freud (6).

One of the most common adolescent responses to the re-awakening of genital and pre-genital incestuous phantasies is to displace the feelings from the parents onto parent substitutes or leaders of peer groups. In moderation this is a normal and even healthy phenomenon. In certain instances, however, the teen-ager finds the presence of his parents so disturbing that he may actually run away from home. Another danger is the possibility of identification with anti-social individuals and involvement in criminal activities as in the following example:

Jane, the 14-year-old adopted daughter of middle-class, professional parents, was referred for admission by a juvenile court after she was arrested for defacing neighborhood property. According to her parents, Jane had been a difficult and irritable infant who cried almost constantly. At about the age of 5, she began to develop into a shy, withdrawn, "well-behaved, model" child. Although she was not a good student, she had given her parents little trouble and they were free to pursue their careers with relative freedom. The appearance of pubertal changes at age 13 signaled a dramatic change in Jane's behavior. She was caught stealing in school, tried to run away from home, and became involved with a teen-age delinquent group. Jane neither argued with her parents nor expressed any direct hostility toward them but she found their presence intolerable. Neither she nor her parents could account for the phenomenon. Jane agreed to hospitalization but pleaded with the court social worker that her parents not be allowed to visit her.

An adolescent reaction familiar to most parents is the turning of feelings of love into the opposite feelings of hate. While a certain amount of rebelliousness is within the range of normal teen-age behavior, extreme defiance can seriously disrupt family unity and impair the adolescent's general functioning. At times it can reach near homicidal proportions.

If the adolescent, instead of directing his hostility toward his parents, turns it inward, deep depression may result. In these instances suicide is particularly to be feared.

A certain number of young people react to the threat of ego dissolution by attempting to ward off all impulses. The result is adolescent asceticism which is, fortunately, usually a transient phenomenon.

George, a 16-year-old high school senior, sought private outpatient therapy because of an inability to "feel." He referred to the condition as "emotional anesthesia" and dated its onset to puberty. He described periods of extreme "self-discipline" during which he ate little, exercised strenuously, and refrained from masturbation. These periods alternated with spells of self-indulgence consisting of over-eating, perverse sexual behavior, and neglect of school work. George claimed that although this self-indulgence "relieved tension" he derived no sensual pleasure from it. He described his mother as very domineering and overtly seductive. She walked around the house scantily clad, showered him with kisses, and wrote sentimental "love letters" to him when he was away at camp. George frequently reported frank incestuous dreams in which erotic feelings were experienced.

Not infrequently, adolescents may attempt to resolve incestuous conflicts by seeking homosexual relationships. Some homosexual acting-out is quite common in young adolescent boys and is usually a transient phenomenon. In late adolescence, such behavior cannot be so easily dismissed. Whether or not homosexuality becomes a permanent solution in these cases depends to some extent upon the degree of sexual gratification experienced.

A very serious symptom of adolescent turmoil is an increase in accident proneness. This phenomenon which in its extreme form appears to be related to early disturbances in the mother-child relationship is particularly dangerous in a society where millions of teen-aged children drive automobiles. Certain accident prone youths clamor for freedom and seem deeply to resent any form of limit-setting by their parents. In reality, they are apt to interpret parental permissiveness as "not caring." In certain instances, as in the following example, the adolescent seems to be destroying himself with the unconscious approval of his parents.

Jerry, a 16-year-old son of wealthy parents, was brought for psychiatric treatment after he was arrested for stealing property from a neighbor's home. Both parents worked full-time in a family business and Jerry was looked after by a series of domestics, none of whom stayed very long. The boy's requests for material things were instantly gratified and during the 6 months prior to his difficulty with the law he smashed two new cars. Each time his parents quickly provided a new one. Jerry became involved with a gang of middle-class delinquents, began taking drugs, and made several suicidal gestures. It was only when the parents' reputation was at stake that Jerry was brought for treatment. When inpatient therapy was recommended, Jerry balked and his mother refused to coerce him. Out-patient therapy was arranged and the boy appeared to welcome the opportunity to discuss his feelings with the therapist. His parents, however, seemed to see treatment not as a means of working out Jerry's problems but as a way of controlling him for their convenience. Although they agreed at first to meet periodically with a social worker, they refused to return after a few sessions. Jerry terminated treatment shortly afterwards and soon was in difficulty with the police again.

## AMERICAN SOCIETY AND THE MIDDLE-CLASS ADOLESCENT

It follows from the above discussion, I believe, that an adolescent will thrive best in a society in which his role is clearly defined; his rights and responsibilities are unambiguously outlined; and his sexual and aggressive fantasies are not prematurely and repeatedly aroused beyond the capabilities of his fragile ego to master them.

For a variety of reasons, 20th-century middle-class American society does not seem to provide many adolescents with the support necessary to reach adulthood without serious disorganizing experiences. From pre-adolescence on, children are encouraged to participate in a bewildering variety of poorly-supervised, sexually stimulating activities—experiences which in practically all civilized societies are reserved for adults. I know of no other country in which elementary school children of "good families" learn ballroom dancing, attend pajama parties, and are allowed to watch adult movies and television programs. In no other country are middle-class children permitted to attend mixed parties at age 12, to date at 14, and to drive at 16. One can say that many "sophisticated" American 18-year-olds have been exposed to a range of social stimuli it used to take half a lifetime to experience.

Although few would argue that compared with their European counterparts American children are grossly over-stimulated, there is no general consensus among professionals as to how this affects their personality development. In my judgment, permissive child-rearing practices combined with premature arousal of sexual and aggressive fantasies are two of the major causes of adolescent mal-adjustment in our country.

While certain of the specific "adult" stimuli to which American children are exposed are new, the relative blurring of role-distinctions based upon age is not. In his classic analysis of New World society, de Tocqueville (19) described over a century ago the structure of the American family in words that ring a con-temporary note: "[Americans] have found out that, in a democracy, the independence of individuals cannot fail to be very great, youth premature, tastes ill-restrained, customs fleeting, public opinion often unsettled and powerless, paternal authority weak, and marital authority contested".

De Tocqueville believed that "family democracy" was inextric-ably linked to political democracy. This is also the opinion of those liberal American social scientists who hold that a "democratic" family experience prepares children to function as free, democratic citizens. When de Tocqueville made his observations, the United States was the only stable democracy in existence. It is understand-able, therefore, that he attributed to democratic political insti-tutions certain aspects of American family life which probably developed from our peculiar frontier experience. During the past 100 years, political democracies of great stability have developed in Switzerland, Great Britain, the Netherlands, the Scandinavian monarchies, and other European countries. Although a certain "democratization" of family relationships has slowly occurred in these nations, very marked role-differences based upon sex and age remain.

While living in Switzerland and France for a number of years, I was able to observe that Europeans continue to make a more serious, and—to my mind—a more realistic distinction between children and adults. French middle-class children, for example, are expected to do most of their teen-age socializing within the extended family unit. Their adolescent years are spent learning a trade or preparing for higher education; the rigors of French schooling leave little time for extensive participation in social or "extra-curricular" activities. When his education has been completed, the French youth is expected to make his way in the world with little or no financial aid from his parents. In other words, he is treated like a child—protected and enveloped in an extended family matrix—until he has achieved the necessary maturity and professional skills to live independently. With minor variations this pattern is followed throughout Western Europe.

What appears to have happened in the United States is that rapid industrialization and urbanization have placed intolerable strains on a family structure developed to serve the needs of a democratic, but primitive, frontier civilization. When land was plentiful and the threat of Indian attack great, it was important that youths achieve independence at an early age. Prolonged formal schooling was undesirable and unnecessary. Survival on the frontier required that basic farming and military skills be acquired as quickly as possible. Rapid development of the country would have been impossible without the presence of many young, highly mobile soldier-farmers. It is not surprising, therefore, that de Tocqueville observed that "In America, there is, strictly speaking, no adolescence; at the close of boyhood, the man appears, and begins to trace out his own path" (18).

It is ironic that in little more than a century we have evolved from a nation in which there was "no adolescence" to one in which teen-aged problems seem to exceed those of any other country. If it is true that a "democratic" family cannot by itself provide children with adequate ego supports, how is it that American society has not developed appropriate institutions to deal with the stresses of an urbanized, industrialized society?

I believe that the answer to this question is to be found primarily in the remarkable speed of change of American institutions. As Keniston (12) has pointed out, we differ from almost every other society in offering no resistance to technological change. Almost every scientific innovation is valued, whatever the consequences. Any notion that the rate of technological change be slowed or that specific innovations *not* be made because of possible social turmoil would be regarded suspiciously by most Americans. There is an underlying assumption that unimpeded technological progress will eventually solve the problems it has created. (Recent concern over air pollution is probably the first serious soul-searching we have done concerning the mixed blessings of industrialization.)

One of the most serious examples of the impact of unrestrained technological change upon American family life is the effect of the automobile on courtship habits. The camaraderie enjoyed by young boys and girls has existed since colonial days and could be fairly easily supervised in a small, tightly knit community. Urbanization, permissive child rearing, and the automobile have combined to create patterns of early adolescent dating which can only make the conscientious parent uneasy.

Another consequence of our change from an agrarian to an urban society has been a considerable lengthening of the period of formal education for middle-class adolescents, who are, therefore, often completely dependent upon their parents until well into their twenties. In addition, they are conditioned to a standard of living which tends to prolong dependence even longer than necessary. On the one hand, therefore, American adolescents are provided with many of the external trappings of adulthood yet do not possess the training and experience which make true emancipation from parents possible. There is little doubt that early participation in unsupervised social activities by adolescents destined for a prolonged period of economic dependence favors irresponsible sexual and aggressive acting-out.

Curiously, ancient societies with an authoritarian family structure may be better equipped to neutralize the disrupting effects of technological change. In Switzerland, for example, where political democracy and technological progress have not appreciably affected role-distinctions based upon sex and age, children under

16 years of age are barred from movies, television is considered to be adult entertainment, and formal dating usually begins in the late teens. In the United States, on the other hand, where adult-child differences are much less institutionalized, children are allowed to do pretty much as they please unless their parents specifically intervene. Recent history has amply demonstrated that the average "democratic" family simply cannot intelligently censor movies and television or police adolescent dating.

In many societies the pressure for adolescents to conform to a specific code of behavior is exerted largely by the parents. In America, this influence is exerted by a variety of sources, not least important of which is the adolescent peer group. When society places so much importance on popularity, adjustment, and the ability to function in groups, parental authority is subtly undermined. Adolescents know this and play on their parents' fear of social isolation to achieve their ends. When an American teen-ager makes a questionable demand of his parents, he has won half the battle if he can demonstrate that his friends are enjoying the requested privilege. In Europe this tactic is much less successful, probably because society there is more family- and less community-oriented.

Another source of adolescent disorganization in our society is the extent to which young people are evaluated for accomplishments over which they have little or no control. If a European teen-ager is polite, conscientious, and hard-working, he is considered to be "good" and little else is expected of him. This is not enough for many American middle-class parents. Their children must also be attractive, slim, popular, talented, and well-adjusted. The following example illustrates how unreasonable parental expectations can help lead to a breakdown of an adolescent's defenses.

Linda, an attractive 14-year-old high school freshman, was referred for residential treatment because of a "school phobia." Her symptoms had begun a year previously after Linda's father had left her mother for a younger woman. The young girl reacted with a variety of feelings. Linda felt abandoned by her father and there were strong feelings of hostility directed both toward him and the other woman. At the same time, she thought of mother as inadequate and shared her feelings of humiliation. One of mother's

reactions to her husband's abandoning her was to become preoc-
cupied with the appearance and popularity of her teen-age
daughter. Linda, a shy girl, was urged to lose weight and mix with
the "popular" group of high school girls. Many of these adolescents
were sexually promiscuous and Linda, whose fantasies had already
been stimulated by father's affair with a young woman, was very
threatened by the erotic social activities of her new acquaintances.
She began to complain of "stomach pains" each morning, would
refuse to go to school, and, when forced to attend, had episodes of
dissociative behavior.

## THE HOSPITALIZED ADOLESCENT

Limitations of space do not permit an exhaustive review of the
many complex issues involved in the inpatient psychotherapy of
adolescents. In attempting to create a therapeutic environment for
disturbed teen-agers, consideration must be given both to the age-
specific needs of the adolescent and to the nature of the society
which has produced him and to which he will eventually return.

On the basis of the above discussion of adolescent dynamics and
certain peculiarities of American customs and institutions, I believe
that a psychiatric hospital admitting adolescents should: provide
a stable, predictable human environment, free of duplicity; avoid
excessive stimulation of erotic and aggressive fantasies; clearly de-
lineate the patients' responsibilities and privileges; provide adequate supervision of adolescent self-destructive behavior; and establish open channels of communication among patients and between the patient and staff groups. The remainder of this paper
will be devoted to a review of certain obstacles which block the
implementation of the above principles and to a discussion of
some techniques useful in overcoming these impediments.

### An Honest, Stable Environment

The need for honesty when dealing with teen-age patients goes
far beyond that which is required in an outpatient setting with
adult neurotics. The latter apparently can tolerate a certain amount
of dishonesty and unfairness without completely losing confidence
in their therapists. Adolescents, however, resemble psychotics in
their constant and implacable testing of the integrity of those re-

sponsible for their care. Once a decision has been made to recommend inpatient therapy, the conditions of treatment should be made perfectly clear to the young patient and his family. They should have, from the beginning, a complete understanding of the hospital rules, particularly those relating to restrictions of patients' freedom. Promises should never be made which cannot be kept; expectations should not be raised beyond what reasonably can be anticipated. If, prior to admission, the hospital was misrepresented in any way to the adolescent patient by his family or the referring agency, the hospital psychiatrist should immediately dissociate himself and the institution from such duplicity by clarifying all misconceptions. Thereafter, no representative of the hospital should be party to any attempt, explicit or implicit, to mislead the patient. On the Division of Adult Inpatient Psychiatry of the University of Maryland, we have instituted as part of our routine admission procedure a pre-admisson home visit by one of our social workers. This has proved to be an excellent way of minimizing misconceptions about the hospital in the minds of the patient and his family.

## Avoiding Over-Stimulation

Although this may appear paradoxical, experience has convinced me that with adequate supervision integration of the sexes on the wards is less stimulating than the segregation of boys from girls. Having integrated wards, however, enormously complicates the problem of setting appropriate limits to adolescent sexual behavior. Formulating reasonable guidelines is made difficult by the fact that middle-class Americans differ widely among themselves with respect to the amount of freedom they permit their children. Certain teen-agers come to the hospital with a history of having had intercourse before the age of 13; other adolescent patients have had a much more sheltered life and their parents look suspiciously upon the most innocent heterosexual contacts.

The problem is further complicated by the fact that hospital staff members often disagree among themselves with respect to the amount of sexual liberty adolescents should enjoy. Psychiatric residents and young nurses often consciously promote sexual experimentation whereas the older, more conservative, nurses and aides tend to favor stricter limits. The resulting message to the young patients is a contradictory one and may lead to sexual acting-out within the institution.

The setting of strict limits to adolescent sexual and aggressive behavior, which I favor, is impeded by the pervasive myth that strong prohibitions encourage acting-out. There is absolutely no evidence that firm controls are noxious when based upon the principal that what is pleasurable and appropriate for mature adults is not necessarily so for adolescents. It is true, however, that harsh parental restrictions motivated by repressed sexual urges can be stimulating to children. Clinically, one of the most knotty problems to handle is the acting-out by adolescents of the repressed sexual conflicts of puritanical parents. Typically in these cases, an outwardly stern and rigid couple bring to the hospital a young girl who has become sexually promiscuous; not infrequently the girl is already pregnant. The parents, although loudly demanding that the hospital maintain absolute discipline, indirectly excite the child's erotic fantasies. If sexual acting-out does follow, parental guilt, mobilized in response to the vicariously felt pleasure, may be assuaged by angry incriminations against the institution.

In general, boys do not act out heterosexually in the hospital to the same extent that girls do. As Jacobson (11) has pointed out, teen-age boys are more apt to deal with the threat of incestuous heterosexual relationships by resorting to regressive, perverse behavior. Homosexual experimentation is therefore a common manifestation of male adolescent sexuality. It is usually only when adolescent boys are involved in long-term individual psychotherapy and begin to identify staff members and patients with parents and siblings that heterosexual acting-out within the institution may become a serious problem.

The acting-out of adolescent girls is more apt to be heterosexual and, therefore, more dangerous. Girls transfer erotic feelings from incestuous to extra-familial figures at a relatively early age, and, when their self-esteem is closely tied to receiving narcissistic gratification from men, heterosexual acting-out may begin almost immediately after admission to the hospital.

An effective way of dealing with inappropriate sexual behavior among hospitalized adolescents is to encourage them to help establish and enforce their own guidelines. On the Division of Adult Inpatient Psychiatry of the Universty of Maryland, a Young Adults Club has been organized. This club, to which all adolescents and adults under age 25 may belong, plans social activities for the young patients. An area in the hospital has been turned over to them for use as a clubroom. It has been clear that left to themselves the adolescents will formulate and conform to a far more severe set of rules than the staff would ever establish. They have been encouraged to make and enforce their own rules of conduct within their area; supervision is available and the club members understand that their regulations are subject to staff approval. The adolescents have invested a great amount of time and energy in furnishing their clubroom and in planning and carrying out fund-raising projects.

We have discovered that providing a "hang-out" for the adolescents has eliminated their former tendency to wander around the general hospital and the surrounding neighborhood—a phenomenon which no amount of discipline or restrictions could control. It is my impression that they have developed a much greater sense of responsibility for their sexual behavior and, as a result, have less need to use it as a weapon against their families and the hospital staff. The fact that the Young Adults Club has been able to assist the adolescent patients in channelling sexual urges is an example of how peer group pressure can be constructively used in a hospital setting.

*Clear Lines of Authority*

Parents of disturbed adolescents are often incapable of making decisions in a firm, unambiguous manner. In certain of these families, the children appear informally to take over and act in areas where the parents are indecisive (5). Clinicians generally agree that this confusion as to where the locus of power in the family resides may contribute to adolescent disorganization. It is, therefore, most important that the decision-making power in the hospital be clearly defined and made explicit to all staff members and patients. Investigators who have analyzed hospital administrative practices seem to agree that when genuine confusion exists as to where the decision-making power resides, apathy, frustration, and even de-structive acting-out may result. For example, Cumming and Cum-ming (3) in their study of a backward state hospital concluded that much of the resistance to change was attributable to the gradual usurpation of medical authority by senior ancillary personnel. Recently I was able to observe that many of the difficulties inherent in the hospital treatment of influential people arise from a tempor-ary displacement of power from the clinicians to the top admin-istrators (20).

I believe that the process of decision-making can best be observed and understood when the hospital administration is decentralized to the point where clinical decisions are made only by individuals possessing the requisite information. One way of accomplishing this is to establish autonomous wards directed by experienced medical administrators. These supervisors should be permitted to make all final decisions in matters relating to their units. The medical director of the hospital should not intervene directly in ward ad-ministration. He should be familiar enough with the ward super-visor's work to know if the latter is doing an effective job. If he is, he should be allowed to work without interference. If he is not, he should be replaced.

Providing a stable, predictable human environment for adoles-cents is greatly facilitated by having autonomous wards. Under this system they need never be transferred from one part of the hospital to another.

It has been my experience that the amount of destructive acting-out, of extreme adolescent rebellion, and of regressed, infantile behavior is greatly reduced when patients of both sexes, of all ages (from adolescence on), and of all degrees of disturbance are mixed on the same ward. The better integrated patients serve as models for the more acutely disturbed ones and exert constructive social pressure. The absence of a "maximally disturbed ward" en-courages the staff and patients to set limits through social rather than mechanical techniques. Converting to a unit system results in a decrease of all forms of regressed and immature behavior and lessens the need for massive tranquilization. Once the necessary staff and patient co-operation is achieved, units containing several very disturbed patients need not be continuously locked.

Psychiatric opinion is very much divided on the question of whether adolescent inpatients should be mixed with adults or treated on separate units. This ambivalence is perfectly illustrated by George Gardner (7) who in the same paper has advocated both approaches.

For a number of reasons I favor the residential treatment of adolescents on adult wards providing the ratio of teen-agers to adults does not exceed 1 : 3. In the first place, although American society makes a fairly distinct separation between adolescents and younger children, no clear demarcation sets off teen-agers from young adults; in terms of responsibilities and participation in social activities, there is often very little difference. Second, a considerable part of the problems faced by young adults can be directly traced to an unsatisfactory working out of adolescent conflicts. It is my impression, and some recent work bears this out, that teen-age patients and young adults with unresolved adolescent problems can have a mutually beneficial influence if combined in a group (13). This seems to be particularly true of immature, married adults with children. Third, the presence of older patients provides useful figures upon whom adolescents can displace and work out parental conflicts. (By the same token, middle-aged patients often find that having to live with teen-agers helps them focus on difficulties with their own children). Fourth, there is little doubt that the presence of older patients has a moderating effect on the destructive and sexual acting-out of adolescents within the hospital. Older patients are not seen as authority figures to the same degree as are staff members and there is thus less need to test the limits imposed by the adult patient group.

The adolescent's push for freedom and his strongly ambivalent feelings toward authority figures make it desirable that he be granted a circumscribed area of autonomy. In granting this freedom, however, the hospital administrators must be prepared to live with the consequences and not jump in and take over should things go wrong. In other words, adolescent patients must know where their rights in the hospital begin and end. To allow them too little initiative is to encourage both dependency and rebelliousness; to promise more freedom than can be realistically granted is to deepen their apathy and cynicism.

It is tempting to assert, as others have, that decentralizing hospital authority and encouraging greater staff and patient participation in decision-making leads to a more "democratic" distribution of power. One must not, however, confuse metaphor with reality. The charming Anglo-Saxon illusion that all human imperfections can be cured by extensions of the democratic process has, unfortunately, influenced the thinking of certain hospital psychiatrists. Claims that increased hospital "democracy" is psychotherapeutic cannot be dismissed as harmless rhetorical exercises since they often serve as smoke screens for institutional power struggles.

Although it is most useful for everyone associated with a ward to be delegated whatever responsibilities he can shoulder, no attempt should be made to persuade staff members or patients, particularly adolescents, that the unit is or can ever become truly "democratic." Genuine ward democracy is impossible because the nurses, aides, and patients have only delegated powers. Unless it is clearly understood that the ward administrator and his medical superiors have ultimate responsibility for ward management, many staff members and patients may over-estimate the amount of authority they can legitimately wield. When events lead them to discover the realistic limits of their powers, they may react by shirking responsibilities they have heretofore competently exercised.

The realities of American society require that the notion of adolescent "independence" be interpreted in an extremely flexible manner. The following episode, which occurred in the hospital, illustrates the point.

In order to purchase a stereo phonograph, the Young Adults Club voted to carry out a fund-raising project. The Activities Department offered to help pay for the phonograph but the young patients indignantly refused. They insisted that they wished to solve the problem themselves. After considerable discussion, the Young Adults Club decided on a bake sale as the most suitable money-raising enterprise. A day was chosen for the sale and permission was obtained from the hospital director to hold it in the cafeteria. It soon became apparent, however, that none of the girls knew how to bake. In order to avoid a catastrophe, a number of nurses and secretaries were cajoled into contributing cakes and cookies to the sale; it turned out to be a huge financial success.

At a staff meeting shortly afterwards, I sharply criticized the behavior of the adolescent group. It appeared to me that the young patients were deluding themselves and the staff in pretending that they had acted independently. I felt that if they were willing to accept cakes from staff members there was no logical reason for them not to have taken the handout proffered by the Activities Department. Many of the staff disagreed. They protested that gross manipulation of adults is a valuable skill of normal American adolescents and that the bake sale, therefore, could be considered an acceptable example of patient initiative.

## Open Channels of Communication

Research carried out in small, private hospitals leads one inevitably to the assumption that minimizing distorted communication among staff members and patients is psychotherapeutic. The studies of Caudill (2) at the Yale Psychiatric Institute and of Stanton and Schwartz (17) at Chestnut Lodge have demonstrated that clarifying messages within a hospital can lead to the resolution of collective disturbances.

During the past 10 years, there have appeared in the literature a number of reports (8, 9, 14, 16) which impressively demonstrate the existence of grossly pathological patterns of communication in families with emotionally ill offspring. Although it is not yet clear to what extent these distortions and ambiguities actually contribute to the genesis of disturbed behavior it is only common sense to minimize the possibilities of misunderstanding resulting from poor communication in the conduct of inpatient adolescent psychotherapy.

As part of the program, the ward should provide an open forum in which all unit problems can be discussed. This is best accomplished by scheduling a daily patient-personnel meeting. Attendance by all patients and ward personnel should be mandatory. In these meetings any action of any patient or staff member affecting the well being of others on the ward is a suitable subject for discussion. It is important that no ward behavior be considered secret. It is essential that all attending the meeting be encouraged to reveal as soon as possible any action on the part of any patient or staff member which is upsetting to others on the ward and which may constitute a source of present or future ward disturbance. The patient's therapist must attend these meetings and take an active part in them. The question of how this may affect the "confidential relationship" of doctor and patient will be considered below.

The great value of the daily patient-personnel meetings is that it provides a real life experience rather than a "way of life" for the hospitalized adolescent who ought not to be viewed as in a state of limbo waiting for his intrapsychic conflicts to be resolved in individual psychotherapy. This type of "hotel therapy" mentality is harmful since it encourages regression and unduly prolongs hospitalization. Psychiatric hospitalization should be an extremely meaningful period in the young patient's life. Living in close proximity to others in a setting where maximum verbal expression is encouraged makes it possible for the most fundamental problems of life to be considered. It is an opportunity for patients to reconsider their value systems, to work through a number of painful separation experiences, as other patients and staff members leave, and to be confronted almost daily with ego-syntonic behavioral patterns. In my experience, daily patient-personnel meetings lead to a much more meaningful self-examination in individual psychotherapy.

If all ward personnel, including the patient's "therapist", attend patient-staff meetings, how is it possible to maintain open channels of communication without compromising the confidential relationship between patient and physician?

The therapist's watchword should be "respect all confidences; keep no secrets." It is only by distinguishing between a true confidence and a shared secret that a patient's privacy will not be protected at the expense of his safety.

An examination of the Latin origins of the words "confidence" and "secret" sharpens the distinction. "Confidere" means "to trust altogether"; "secretus" may be translated as "divided off." The implication is clear. To betray a patient's confidence is to risk losing his trust; to share his secret only with the patient is to divide the hospital into factions.

In practice, the distinction between confidence and secret, although a delicate one, is not impossible to make. A wise mother does not necessarily tell her husband about their daughter's sexual problems; if she keeps from him the fact that daughter damaged the family car, a major family problem may result.

It is precisely for adolescents who have been raised in families where secrets are treated as confidences that inpatient psychotherapy has one of its chief indications.

The inpatient psychotherapist should, therefore, indicate at the start of treatment that some of what his young patient tells him during an "hour" may be shared with others in the hospital. In reserving the right to reveal certain information received during an "hour," however, the therapist can no longer logically insist that his patient tell him everything. As Stanton and Schwartz (17) have noted, some inpatients withhold information from their therapists until they are discharged from the hospital. In my judgment, this is a price that must be paid. To be consistent, we cannot have it both ways.

The anti-therapeutic effects of inappropriately shared secrets have received little systematic attention in the literature. T. F. Main (15) has published a beautiful illustration of the staff-splitting potential of secret-sharing among patients and nurses. The problem is an extraordinarily intricate one and deserves intensive investigation. The following clinical illustration indicates what may result from inadequately distinguishing a confidence from a secret.

Miss Kent, an 18-year-old art student, was admitted to the Division of Adult Inpatient Psychiatry following a suicide attempt. During the course of her hospitalization she became pregnant as a result of an extra-mural affair. Miss Kent told her resident-physician, Dr. Alfredo, of her condition and pleaded with him not to divulge the information to the nurses, aides, and other patients. He agreed to her request. On the following day, Miss Kent described to several of the staff physical sensations which they recognized as classical symptoms of the first trimester of pregnancy. When Miss Kent's behavior was discussed at the next staff meeting, Dr. Alfredo refused to clarify the situation, stating that a confidential relationship with his patient was involved. He was unable to give any direction to the nurses as to how they should react to Miss Kent's advances. Dr. Alfredo recognized belatedly that his inability to distinguish a confidence from a secret had placed him on the horns of a dilemma. He had to choose between betraying the trust of his patient and losing the support of his staff.

On a mixed adult-adolescent service, teen-agers should participate in two types of group processes. In addition to the daily ward meetings, which include both adult patients and staff members, they should help plan activities geared to their age level. As indicated above, we have found that a Young Adults Club, open to adolescents and adults under age 25, admirably serves this purpose.

It is not superfluous to add that American middle-class adolescents are superbly equipped to take part in a program of milieu therapy. Many have already participated in the "democratic" resolution of family problems. Although this practice often thinly disguises the abrogation of parental responsibility, the fact remains that teen-agers tend to be familiar with the process of arriving at a decision through group consensus.

### The Defensive Use of Autonomous Peer-Group Activities

The desire to participate in relatively autonomous peer group activities is apparently a basic adolescent need (1). If the hospital administrator does not encourage the constructive expression of this drive, teen-age patients will not lack ingenuity in organizing self-destructive group activities which may be extremely difficult to control.

Fostering autonomous adolescent group activities, however, does present a real danger. In a psychiatric institution dedicated to the exploration and resolution of intrapsychic conflicts, extensive involvement of adolescents in peer-group activities can, in certain cases, dilute the intensity of the individual psychotherapeutic experience. Teen-agers generally appear more mature and "healthy" in the absence of authority figures. Certain of the hospital staff, particularly the activities therapists, may be beguiled into thinking that severely ego-damaged adolescents are not really disturbed at all but are simply being made sick by the doctors and nurses. If all hospital personnel clearly understand that a mature relationship with authority figures is important in an adolescent's general emotional adjustment, the danger of hospital-sanctioned avoidance of self-examination will be minimized.

### CONCLUSION

Throughout this paper I have emphasized the problems hospitalized adolescents create for the medical and nursing personnel. I would be ungrateful, however, if I did not mention their capacity to contribute constructively to the development of the hospital. In progressive institutions utilizing concepts and techniques of milieu therapy, experimenting with new ideas and methods is enormously enhanced by the presence of a nucleus of long-term adolescent patients. Although teen-agers do not generally create new ideology, they can catalyze changes in the hospital social structure.

## SUMMARY

In recent years, the number of American middle-class adolescents admitted to adult psychiatry units in general hospitals has greatly increased. Because of their age-specific needs and problems and the peculiar conditions under which they are hospitalized, they constitute a well-defined minority group within the institution. In this paper, I have tried to show why modern American customs and institutions are particularly stressful for teen-agers, and, specifically, how the impact of unrestrained technological change on "democratic" family life has enormously complicated the transition from adolescence to adulthood. Finally, some of the obstacles to the effective treatment of adolescents on adult services have been considered and a number of remedial suggestions have been offered.

## REFERENCES

1. Buxbaum, E.: Transference and group formation in children and adolescents. *In Psychoanalytic Study of the Child*, ed. by R. S. Eissler, Vol. 1, pp. 351–365. International Universities Press, New York, 1965.
2. Caudill, W. A.: *The Psychiatric Hospital as a Small Society*. Harvard University Press, Cambridge, 1958.
3. Cumming, E. and Cumming, J.: The locus of power in a large mental hospital. Psychiatry, *19:* 361–369, 1956.
4. Erickson, E.: *Childhood and Society*, Ed. 2, p. 262, W. W. Norton & Company Inc., New York, 1963.
5. Ferreira, A.: Decision-making in normal and pathological families. Archives of General Psychiatry, *8:* 68–73, 1963.
6. Freud, A.: Adolescence. *In Psychoanalytic Study of the Child* ed. by R. S. Eissler, Vol. 13, pp. 255–278. International Universities Press, New York, 1958.
7. Gardner, G.: The child and the adolescent. *In The Psychiatric Unit in a General Hospital*, edited by M. R. Kaufman, pp. 228–239. International Universities Press, New York, 1965.

8. Haley, J.: The family of the schizophrenic: A model system. Journal of Nervous and Mental Disease, *129:* 357—374, 1959.
9. Jackson, D. and Weakland, J.: Schizophrenic symptoms and family interaction. Archives of General Psychiatry, *1:* 618—621, 1959.
10. Jacobson, E.: *The Self and the Object World,* pp. 166—168. International Universities Press, New York, 1964.
11. Jacobson, E.: *The Self and the Object World,* pp. 170—171. International Universities Press, New York, 1964.
12. Keniston, K.: Social change and youth in america. Daedalus, *Winter:* 145—171, 1962.
13. Knorr, N.: Mixed adult and adolescent group therapy. American Journal of Psychotherapy, *20:* 323—331, 1966.
14. Lidz, T. Cornelison, A. Terry, D. and Fleck, S.: The intrafamiliar environment of the schizophrenic patient: VI. Transmission of irrationality. Archives of Neurology and Psychiatry, *79:* 305—316, 1958.
15. Main, T. F.: The ailment. British Journal of Medical Psychology, *30:* 129—145, 1957.
16. Morris, G. and Wynne, L.: Schizophrenic offspring and parental styles of communication. A predictive study using excerpts of family therapy recordings. Psychiatry, *28:* 19—44, 1965.
17. Stanton, A. and Schwartz, M.: *The Mental Hospital.* Basic Books, New York, 1954.
18. Tocqueville, A. de: *Democracy in America,* edited by R. D. Heffner, p. 229. Mentor Books, New American Library, New York, 1956.
19. Tocqueville, A. de: *Democracy in America,* edited by R. D. Heffner, pp. 234—235, Mentor Books, New American Library, New York, 1956.
20. Weintraub, W.: The VIP syndrome: A clinical study in hospital psychiatry. Journal of Nervous and Mental Disease, *138:* 181—193, 1964.

# Minority Group Status and Behavioral Disorganization*

EUGENE B. BRODY, M.D.

T HE APPARENT VULNERABILITY of adolescents to emotional disturbance—to disorganization of customary behavior patterns—has often been attributed to problems in their transition from one social status to another. The conflicts associated with lack of role stability and other aspects of the life of adult minority group members may also predispose to vulnerability of this sort. One such aspect concerns the power to regulate one's own life. The majority does not necessarily include more people, but it is always in possession of more power. Thus, one *de facto* synonym for minority status is powerlessness. This broadens the concept to include not only those who can be defined on the basis of ethnic or racial characteristics, but also those who are powerless by virtue of poverty. Recognition of the powerlessness of the poor has led Rieff to conclude that, while self-*realization* is a goal of psychotherapy for the middle class, self-*determination* is the essential first step for the lower class man (25). The person who is helpless in the face of external economic, political, or social circumstances must devote his available energies to the here-and-now struggle for survival. For him the psychotherapeutic voyage of inner exploration and the examination of unresolved childhood conflicts can be maladaptive as well as difficult.

Within the ranks of the poor at large and those whose connections with community institutions are tenuous, unambiguous social structures have not developed. Their early training and adult competition for survival on an individual basis have not equipped

*This chapter is adapted from material presented to the Department of Psychiatry, McGill University, Montreal, Canada, April 19, 1967.

them to engage in collective action for individual gain. As Harrington (15), Banfield (1) and others have pointed out, the idea of collaboration or organization for achievement beyond that benefiting the immediate family seems foreign to those who live in the "economic underworld" (15) of the United States or the depressed rural villages of Europe. This also appears to be true for those massive migrant populations from the famine . . . and drought-stricken northeast of Brazil who have come to squat in the *favelas* of Rio de Janeiro and the slums of Sao Paulo (5). So far, the broadly defined poor peoples of the world, while transitorily susceptible to power-promising ideologies, seem to behave more as aggregates of individuals than as collectivities, i.e., in Talcot Parsons' frame of reference, groups committed to action on the basis of a shared value system (24).

Status and rank order do exist, of course, within subordinate social systems defined on ethnic or racial bases, but even the most powerful members of the minority may have only limited access to sources of general societal power. The power of a wealthy Negro publisher, in the United States, for example, is limited by the fact that 90% of his readers are Negro. The society-wide decision makers, i.e., those in the dominant white power-holding system, perceive him as identified with a specific subculture rather than with the values, goals, and attitudes of the dominant culture. His primary identity in their eyes is based not on financial or occupational status, but upon color and membership in a minority group.

Some United States groups that began as minorities have moved toward assimilation. Their members have become less visible by virtue of changes in appearance or behavior. The institutions, goals, and values of the dominant group have become their own and, as their members acquired the techniques for achieving these goals, they became upwardly mobile in the structure of the dominant system. This was the story of the Irish in the United States. The first chapter included exclusionary newspaper ads: "No Irish need apply." The last culminated in the election of John F. Kennedy to the Presidency.

So far, only a handful of Negroes have moved beyond the minority limits in the United States. As a group they continue to exemplify the key features of minority status. They are "a set of people who, capable of being distinguished on the basis of some physical or cultural characteristic, are treated collectively as inferior" (20). The facts of color and physiognomy permit them to be categorized at a distance and, once this categorization has been made, their individual characteristics tend to be replaced by stereotypes in the eye of the beholder. To this degree the minority group man, the target of prejudice, is behaviorally vulnerable. No matter how well schooled the majority person is in dissimulation, he will transmit the message: you are inferior, dangerous, hated, or otherwise obnoxious. He will tend to behave toward the minority man in a way which elicits responsive aggressive or hostile behavior and, following the "self-fulfilling prophecy," the elicited behavior, confirmatory of the original belief, tends to reinforce it (21).

Another factor impeding the Negro's movement out of minority status was the obliteration of his culture as he was transported to the New World. A slave is not an adequate culture bearer, and "a society emerging from a group of freed slaves is peculiarly vulnerable to the incorporation of fragmented or distorted aspects of the dominant society which surrounds it" (7). Lacking cultural roots of its own it must borrow from the dominant system which constitutes its emulative reference group. That which is borrowed tends to be the readily available, i.e. what is public and advertised. Examples are symbols of conspicuous consumption, such as automobiles and clothing, and status-related prejudicial attitudes toward foreigners and minorities. But because his contact with the emulative group is so limited, the minority man's knowledge of its actual standards and valued behavior patterns is incomplete and inaccurate. Thus what he does acquire and appropriate as his own is often a caricature of what the majority regards as desirable, and tends to reinforce their stereotyped ways of perceiving the outgroup which he represents (6). This historical background has contributed to the Negro's problem in gaining the techniques necessary for achievement and upward social mobility; it has tended to perpetuate his minority status by combining it with a low socio-economic level, so that his exclusion from the mainstream of American cultural life has been determined both by restriction of opportunities on the grounds of color and by limitation of opportunities because of insufficient money.

Contrasting social histories are seen in the United States Jewish and oriental minorities, although these last are, themselves, visible through skin color and physiognomy. The difference lies in the fact of a strong, transplantable, complex culture capable of providing solutions to new problems and a sense of identity in a new milieu. Members of segregated groups with a strong cultural or religious heritage may reveal their insecurities and try to resolve their problems through overachievement. The main point is that they are *able* to do this and that their achievement gains consistent recognition within their own groups of origin because it fits their cultural heritage. Since all complex cultures have much in common, such achievement also has significance for and is rewarded by the dominant system as well. As Erikson has pointed out, "ego identity gains real strength only from the wholehearted and consistent recognition of real accomplishment, i.e., of achievement that has meaning in the culture" (13). Minorities with strong cultural heritages and values may even strengthen their group identities when surrounded by a dominant society possessing enough values congruent with their own to permit them to survive and to play a functional role within it. Minority group members with no intact history or culture of their own, however, who can acquire only distorted fragments of the values and achievement techniques of the majority, have little chance of reward for activities with real cultural meaning. Following Erikson again, they have diminished opportunity for developing the sense of reality which comes from a life way which is an individual variant of a stable group identity (2).

Within the United States Negro groups, a very small, educated, well-to-do elite has for many years been able to reward its children and give them a sense of identity, not just as Negroes, but precisely and in a restricted sense as members of a special elite, a subcultural "pocket" maintaining an almost hidden existence vis-a-vis the dominant society. It is only recently that Negro athletes and entertainers and then doctors, lawyers, judges, and business men, not necessarily from this elite, have begun to live and compete in the white social world. These people are just beginning to feel the impact of marginality. The marginal man is one who, with one foot in his own minority social world and the other in that of the majority, is not completely accepted by and does not feel completely comfortable in either. His "uncertainty of belongingness" has been considered by Kurt Lewin as productive of self-hatred and high sensitivity to anything in his group of origin that does not conform to dominant group values (4). One reflection of this is the adoption of deprecatory stereotypes about his own group of origin. This is a factor in the dislike of dark skin color and some aspects of lower-class Negro life present in upwardly mobile Negro college students (9). Similar phenomena have been described by Isaacs in Indians who were formerly categorized as belonging to the class of untouchables (16).

The need for identity has been deliberately recognized by Negro leaders in recent years. It is involved in Stokeley Carmichael's effort to gain political leverage through the Black Power movement. It is also involved in the concept of "negritude" used by Leopold Senghor, the poet president of Senegal, as a rallying cry for world-wide Negro culture building. Adam Clayton Powell, the controversial congressman from Harlem, appears to recognize this, too, and his identity building seems to have been based in part upon his success in maintaining status in the white world while demonstrating to his followers that he could simultaneously behave with contempt of that world's laws and institutions. His disregard for ordinary white-enforced social conventions must have provided a potent antidote for his constituents' awareness of their own discriminated-against condition. The low self-esteem engendered by discrimination, by dominant group attitudes and restrictions, requires a sense of identity as an antidote. This sense is crucial to the transformation of a minority from an aggregate of individuals bound together only by an awareness of common misery into a collectivity committed to action on the basis of shared values. It is particularly important when the awareness of misery is life-long. The perception of one's black self as devalued has, at least in the past in the United States, begun very early in life. The studies of Clark and Clark in New York and of Goodwin in Boston identify devaluation from at least the age of 4 or 5 (4). For lower-class Negro boys of 7 to 10 in Baltimore, devaluation appears to be perpetuated by transmitted conflictful messages from their mothers as much as by the impact of direct contact with the white world. On one hand the maternal message urges achievement and stresses the values of human equality. On the other it indicates the absence of true interracial equality and mutual acceptance and the impossibility of significant achievement in the face of white restrictions (3).

Adams wrote earlier of the social emasculation suffered by the Negro man at the hands of the white world, and he, as well as Kardiner and Oversey, suggested the problems of sexual identity formation, especially in the Negro boy, which might stem from this circumstance (17). These factors, plus the matricentric character of the lower-class Negro family and of a majority of the most poverty-stricken families elsewhere, with absent or intermittently present fathers, appear to be important to the low self-esteem of culturally deprived and excluded men.

These are two elements which seem to be of theoretical significance for gauging the relation between minority group status and vulnerability to disorganized behavior. First, the early failure of the father as an adequate gender and instrumental role model might of itself be regarded as predisposing to later problems in sexual identity. These might include a defensive turning to homosexuality in the face of the dominant and seductive power of the mother or, conceivably as the next step, the development of paranoid sensitivity to the possibly derogatory thoughts or dangerous attacks of others, originating in the sexual identity problem but reinforced by the social concomitants of minority status, which require suspicious vigilance in the presence of those who are different. There is some evidence that young adult or late adolescent Negro men, more than comparable whites, tend to be occupied with sexual identity problems when psychotic and to become ill after the severance of significant same sex peer group relationships (4).

Second, the situation is complicated by the developing minority group child's need to resolve anxiety-laden conflicting identifications with figures of opposing symbolic significance, such as the black parent on one hand and the representatives of white value-enforcing institutions on the other. These last include the white God as well as the white Christ, and the white Santa Claus as well as the white president, judge, and policeman. It seems plausible that the problem of reconciling these identifications may become particularly intense at the time when adult responsibility must be assumed.

A third factor has to do with the effects of exclusion from the main cultural stream of the power-holding society. Low self-esteem and hopelessness as a concomitant of distance from social power may perhaps be most easily studied in groups whose lack of self-determination is magnified by their lack of the verbal symbols necessary for the exchange of culturally important information. The migrants who accumulate on the rims and in isolated pockets of the great South American cities constitute such a group. As Willems has pointed out, in Brazil they do not as yet form a true urban proletariat, but rather a poorly assimilated agglomerate of individuals who have transplanted rural ways of living into the metropolitan area (5). Our own studies of a group of these people presenting themselves or brought by others to an emergency psychiatric facility showed a remarkably uniform picture upon thematic apperception test examination. The salient features were absence of any success themes, self-abasement, and failure to see human beings as active, achieving, or, often, sexually different-iated (11). It may be relevant that within a larger but relatively homogeneous group, some of whom presented feelings of sadness and inadequacy, the totally illiterate, recently migrant, unskilled, uneducated, and black showed the most anxiety, showed impeded verbal communication, and revealed delusional beliefs of being superior or having special communication with ghosts, spirits, or mythical religious figures. These data probably reflect both the disorganizing impact of exclusion or alienation from the cultural stream of the dominant system and restitutitive attempts utilizing any available source of culturally sanctioned support, as, in this instance, contact with spirits (9).

Similarly the Andean Indian serfs studied by Klein revealed through interviews and projective testing a self-concept dominated by despair and a perception of themselves as impotent and in-effectual in the face of a powerful and malevolent world. Their defensive preferences were those which might be characterized in an adult North American as indicating pathological regression or incipient behavioral disorganization. These included a defensive avoidance of sensation, defensive immobility, limited communication because of danger of exposure, and a pervasive perception of others as power-oriented and hostile. Yet these people functioned as members of their oppressed village society, and the culture of their group, including the attitudes and values passed on from generation to generation, tended to perpetuate their reality situation by limiting their aspirations and conscious desires (18). In short, their perceptions and attitudes seem more logically interpreted as adaptive than as indicating vulnerability to disorganization.

This seems to be at the heart of the matter. Without question, deprivation, discrimination, contempt, and exclusion from full participation in the dominant culture—all of these have an impact on character and behavior. But to what degree may these concomitants of minority group status be regarded as adaptive, and to what degree as regressive or disorganized? And to what degree is it justifiable to generalize from one minority group to another? For example, the data of unsystematic observation and of mental hospital statistics suggest that both lower-class Negro men and women, are prone to develop more dramatically psychotic states with interpersonal stress associated with alcoholic intoxication or with the stress of jail incarceration than are whites of similar age and sex. Derbyshire and Schleifer have demonstrated that lower class Negroes of both sexes show more florid symptomatology and, particularly, more temporal disorientation, on being identified as psychotic by virtue of public disturbance than is the case in comparable white disturbers of the peace (12). The phenomena are not seen, however, among the Jewish or Oriental minorities. In other words, minority status cannot be treated as a unitary concept any more than social class. The key may not be access to total societal power after all, but rather the quality and range of alternative solutions to problems associated with the lack of such access which are available to the minority group person. This requires an adaptive or functional view of minority behavior, as well as scrutiny of what features of the life of a particular group have protective significance. The two interrelated protective and problem-solving assets of any individual or group are education and membership in a viable ongoing cultural process. These assist in the provision of a broad repertory of interpersonal and intrapsychic problem-solving techniques with a sufficient number of alternatives to meet a variety of circumstances.

In this regard the status-giving importance of historical roots and a stable culture have been noted. The man who suffers a split socialization experience, living in two culturally different worlds—that of family on one hand, and of school and peers on the other—may well suffer from lack of belongingness, hypersensitivity to the feelings of others, depressive or obsessive introspection, and the development of sometimes painful ambition. These features, however, if his culture is sufficiently complex to have transfer value, allow him to function effectively in the *occupations* of the majority world. In fact, the history of European Jewish immigrants into North America and particularly of their children suggests strongly that, while they suffered from certain problems in regard to their *social and religious identities*, they made up for their uncertainties in these regards by the development of a primary *occupational identity*. Psychiatry, and psychoanalysis in particular, may provide especially suitable identity niches for intellectual, able, and ambitious people who are at the same time marginal, tied by tenuous or ambivalent connections to their historical past, and introspective. Even more than psychiatry, psychoanalysis as a career provides simultaneously a philosophy of life, a partial answer to the quest for certainty, an opportunity for intellectual achievement, a social circle of like-minded people, and an adequate income. Perhaps it is no accident that while people in psychiatry band together in professional associations, and do have the capacity to engage in collective action, these abilities are flawed. The flaws are suggested by the ease with which organizational splits can occur on doctrinaire grounds and by the intensity with which belief may be required and outmoded scientific concepts may be defended. Also the flaws are suggested by the fact that the situation of greatest comfort and satisfaction is the one-to-one relationship between doctor and patient where there is no question about who is the seeker and who is the fountain of help and where there is no threat to the helper's status or self-esteem.

This picture is, to be sure, a caricature, but it contains a kernel of truth. It indicates one type of solution for the uncertainty about who one is and where one is going, and for the precarious self-esteem of a minority group man. It is not, however, a solution via regression or disorganization. It represents rather the opposite, a solution based on defensive and adaptive maneuvers which contain anxiety, keep disturbing impulses under control, harness drives in the direction of socially acceptable activity, maintain a tense but rational scrutiny of self and others, and impose a long-time cost on their owners which may be measured after a passage of years in terms of depression, fatigue, or psychosomatic illness.

In psychiatric shorthand, the educated, culture-bearing, minority men may be called internalizers. In this respect they resemble the power-connected members of the upper classes of any highly developed society, who themselves—in spite of their access to official decision making—feel encroached upon and hold on to their institutions, special life styles, and private signals of recognition, one with the other.

At the other end of the pole are those who, historically, constitute an aggregate of individuals rather than a true collectivity, or whose cultures are insufficiently developed to compete with or have transfer value into that of the majority. The shorthand descriptions of these people are similar to those used for aboriginal or primitive groups, the poor, the uneducated, and the culturally excluded. They may be called externalizers, acter-outers, regressors, or disorganizers. A prototypical acutely disorganized or regressed behavioral product is the "Beale Street psychosis" of lower-class Negroes described informally by psychiatrists in Memphis, Tennessee, and the United States border South. As an example of a well-documented comparable phenomenon in a primitive group, one may cite the remnants of the aboriginal Mapuche Indians of Chile, who constitute a well-defined lowest class minority in that country's capital city of Santiago. Marconi and associates have demonstrated a marked and clear-cut predominance of short-term reactive psychoses in this group, with emotional excitement, illusions and hallucinations, fragmented unfixed delusional ideas, and impaired judgment, in comparsion with psychotic episodes observed in the rest of the Chilean population (22). This is compatible with the results of other studies indicating that the bulk of psychotic cases among primitive or aboriginal groups have an abrupt onset, dramatic symptomatology, short duration, and little in the way of subsequent social deterioration. It seems plausible to suspect in these instances a type of acute behavioral disorganization or regression which may not have the same significance as a chronic schizophrenia occurring in a member of a more highly differentiated culture.

The chronic behavioral product of the lowest class minority man may also be labeled as regressed in the sense of being withdrawn from environmental contact, being massively self-protective, and employing simple and relatively undifferentiated means of defending and coping. This outcome is seen in the chronic defensive restrictions of perceiving, interacting, and feeling of the illiterate, hopeless Andean Indian serf. His defensive avoidance of sensation, defensive immobility, and limited communications because of the danger of exposure appear in general to have resulted in an impoverishment of inner experience.

Similar phenomena are seen, although to a less intense degree, in Brazilian slum dwellers who—in spite of their interest in *carnaval* and samba—are sad and passive, occupied with the possibility of death, and unable to see achievement or success themes in projective testing.

In a somewhat different form and in a different context we have described the deprived Negro in the southern United States as suffering from semantic impoverishment, a reduction in the connotative richness of the symbols which he uses. This is regarded as a concomitant of the constant need to deny the harsh realities of his external world and to repress his retaliative hostile impulses against the dominant whites. Such impoverishment, perpetuating his excluded condition by making it impossible for him to participate in the main stream of the dominant culture, has given rise to behavior labeled "pseudomental deficiency." It also, by the same token, may facilitate the development of regressed or disorganized behavior (2).

Again, comparable phenomena have been observed elsewhere. For example, Carothers has reported infrequent delusional systematization in nonliterate Africans whose psychotic response were mainly pictures of mental confusion or dullness, with added excitement, panic, or externally directed violence. Opler considered the high activity level characteristic of psychotic behavior in nonliterate peoples as in part a consequence of the "lack of systematic fantasy . . . acting as ego-defenses." Marconi and his group similarly noted the high incidence of diagnoses of "psychotic episodes in the feebleminded" among their urban Mapuche population (22). Another congruent finding was that, as the level of education rose within this population, so did the proportion of psychoses with primarily cognitive disturbances. The proportion of oneiroform psychoses with primary disturbances in reality awareness diminished.

Up to this point the main emphasis has been on the significance of educational attainment—or, in other words, complex, culturally supported symbolic programming—for the vulnerability of minority group men to behavioral disorganization. The status- and security-giving importance for a minority man of being a member of a historically rooted cultural stream has also been noted, especially with regard to its survival and achievement potential within the surrounding dominant society.

This leads to two issues related to minority status. One is migration, which involves disrupting individual connections not only with a friendship and family network, but with sources of historical and cultural support. There is increasing evidence that this may be an important concomitant of behavioral disorganization diagnosed as psychotic illness. In the inner city of Baltimore, for example, there are higher rates of mental hospital admission for groups who are living out of context, such as whites living in predominately Negro neighbourhoods and vice versa. Hagnell found correlations between schizophrenia and migration in a number of small Swedish towns where correlation with low socioeconomic status was not evident (14). The Stirling County data obtained by Leighton's group did not focus on migration as such, but their observed relationship between membership in a disintegrated community—i.e., one with poor communications, ineffective institutions, etc.—and mental illness seems relevant (19).

On the other hand, whether migration is a cause or a consequence appears debatable. Support for the latter theory appears in the work of Whitely in London, Odegard in Norway, and Turner and Wagenfeld in Monroe County, New York (23, 26, 27).

Their data all strongly suggest that high concentrations of schizophrenic persons within the lower socio-economic group are due to processes of adverse selection—a mixture of failure to achieve in terms congruent with initial advantages, and a tendency to move into areas where relatively anonymous survival with minimal social participation and responsibility is possible (8).

The second issue is that of adaptive cultural changes, or of cultural evolution in relation to the behavior of minorities. The culture of the Andean serfs who have already been described provides an example. They have all of the properties already noted as characteristic of minority status. That is, they are a set of people distinguishable on the basis of physical and cultural characteristics and treated collectively as inferior by their masters. Interview and projective test material already described produced data which, if encountered in white North Americans, would be considered psychotic. Yet the behavior of the subjects was normative for their villages. They worked, supported their families, restrained their hate of the *latifundia* managers and landlords, participated in religious rituals, and only occasionally reported an encounter with a spirit on a lonely mountain path at dusk. As noted before, their attitudes and values, transmitted from generation to generation, tended to perpetuate their reality situation by limiting their aspirations and conscious desires. We must assume that for them the *institutionalization of passivity* constituted a protection against behavioral disorganization. This is quite different from the protective patterns used by European migrants to North America. For them the ultimate goals were *involvement* in the dominant culture, *assimilation*, at least on occupational terms, and the *acquisition* of economic power. For the Andean Indian, in contrast, not even possessing the verbal symbols necessary for adequate information exchange with the dominant group, and faced with an absolute block in upward mobility, the situation was quite different. He confronted an overwhelming threat with no inner resources except his repertory of spirits and mythical figures, and his half-starved affective ties with his own group. One may speculate that with such a limited source of affectional bonds and such a circumscribed group of others who might reflect confirmations of his own identity back to him, his fear of change might outweigh his desire for it. Moreover, in the absence of resources the only response to threat, the only alternative to disintegration, is passivity. This means group withdrawal into parallel personal cocoons which shut out the disturbing stimuli of the hostile environment and help avoid the potential flooding of their inner worlds with phantoms of their own making. I think of this as *cultural regression*, or even as hibernation, permitting the slow affectless motions of work, punctuated by an occasional acute experience of rage, love, or spirit communion, but never with full awakening.

In contrast to this picture of adaptive or adjustive cultural regression may be posed a type of cultural evolution which can be described as *coping* rather than adjusting, or as actively rather than passively adapting. One of the most striking examples now in an early phase of evolutionary change is that of the Negro in America. The civil rights movement and its offshoots, such as the black power idea, are beginning to unite Negroes into a true collectivity with a commitment to common socially significant goals and values. The striving for identity has also produced such groups as the Black Muslims. Another manifestation is the turning to Africa for cultural roots, a phenomenon which has been dramatically facilitated by the emerging black African states which constitute entirely new emulative reference groups for American Negroes. At another level, the self-conscious labeling of aspects of post-slavery culture has led to the coinage of terms heavily freighted with connotations of group identity and unique interpersonal meaning, such as "soul" and "brother." These are common currency up and down the Negro class structure, and even the recently elected Senator Edward Brooke of Massachusetts, the first Negro senator since Reconstruction, has publicly announced that he is a "soul brother."

Motherlands other than African have had changing images in the United States. One striking instance of an effect on the minority group "image" in this country is that of the Italians. Prominent United States Italian stereotypes in the early 1920's were those of the swarthy workman, the garlic-mustached spaghetti cook, and the suave, side-burned gangster, epitomized in real life by Al Capone and on the screen by George Raft. It is true that the Cosa Nostra still holds the headlines, but the shifting identity and the renewed source of cultural roots for this group, insofar as it is not fully assimilated, lie in the revival of the creative image. Leonardo has not been reincarnated, but the connotations of "Italian" now include stereotypes much different from those just noted: art treasures in Florence, wonderfully crafted gloves, shoes, and racing cars, prize-winning films, and svelte actresses. These changes do not, of course, reflect adaptive change in the culture of the United States Italians, who by and large have achieved a thorough integration in the economic, political, and social life of the country. They do suggest, however, the ways in which a variety of shifting historical circumstances may provide unexpected points of reference and status for minority groups.

Similarly, the historical transformation of Israel is imposing a change on the western world's percepton of the Jew. The prejudiced stereotype of fat money-lender, passive bookworm, Eastern European tailor, or frail, bearded rabbi is changing to include figures publicized as the activists of modern Israel. These include the blonde, tractor-driving, and rifle-carrying Sabra; the parachute-jumping archeologist general; and the muscular, sunburned scientist; and, as in the case of the Italians, the chicken soup-bearing Yiddish "momma" is replaced by the slim, sexy airline stewardess, actress, or even girl sergeant in the armed forces. The impact of this new reference group on United States Jews is hard to estimate. It seems probable that their intense investment in the Israeli cause, reflected in massive bond and other support efforts, has been due less to realistic perceptions of the new breed than to the emotional significance of the revitalized concept of a homeland. On the other hand, one hears, from time to time, of concrete manifestations of the changed image in the eyes of others —for example, the admission of Israeli Jews to previously excluding fraternities in Midwestern universities.

In summary, then, there are many varieties of minority status, and the behavioral consequences of such status are determined by a multitude of social, historical, political, and economic, as well as individual psychological, factors. Among these factors are the concomitant occurrence of minority status with low socio-economic level and cultural exclusion; the presence of a complex transplantable minority culture with transfer value for the dominant society; opportunities for meaningful reciprocal contact with emulative reference groups; the presence or absence of effective social power and self-determination; and the opportunity to grow up as a member of an intact family with a father who fills the instrumental leadership role. Furthermore, an evolving culture may protect its members from acute disintegration but restrict their psychological lives as it institutionalizes passivity; or it may temporarily increase the likelihood of acute disturbance while moving toward individual enrichment, as it becomes more of an actively coping force in conflict with the dominant society. All of these factors contribute to the absence or presence of a stable sense of identity, the capacity to collaborate with others in the achievement of meaningful goals, and the vulnerability or resistance of the minority group man to behavioral disorganization.

## REFERENCES

1. Banfield, E. C.: *The Moral Basis of a Backward Society.* The Macmillan Company, N.Y., 1958.
2. Brody, E. B.: Social conflict and schizophrenic behavior in young adult Negro males. Psychiatry, *24:* 4, 1961.
3. Brody, E. B.: Color and identity conflict in young boys: Observations of Negro mothers and sons in urban Baltimore. Psychiatry, *26:* 188–201, 1963.
4. Brody, E. B.: Cultural exclusion, character and illness. American Journal of Psychiatry, *122:* 852–858, 1966.
5. Brody, E. B.: The psychiatry of Latin America (Editorial). American Journal of Psychiatry, *123:* 475–477, 1966.
6. Brody, E. B.: Psychiatry and prejudice. In *American Handbook of Psychiatry*, Vol. 111, edited by S. Arieti, pp. 629–642. Basic Books, Inc., Publishers, New York, 1966.
7. Brody, E. B.: Culture, symbol and value in the social etiology of behavioral deviance. Presented in condensed form to the annual meeting of the American Psychopathological Association, February 17 to 18, 1967, New York.
8. Brody, E. B.: Socio-cultural influences on vulnerability to schizophrenic behavior. In "Origins of Schizophrenia." Romano, J. Ed. Excerpta Medica. In Press.
9. Brody, E. B.: Recording cross-culturally useful interview data: Experience from Brazil. American Journal of Psychiatry, *123:* 446–456, 1966.
10. Brody, E. B., and Derbyshire, R.: Prejudice in American Negro college students. Archives of General Psychiatry, *9:* 619–628, 1963.
11. Cunha, J. and Brody, E. B. Unpublished data.
12. Derbyshire, R. L., and Schleifer, C.: Clinical change in jail-referred mental patients. Presented at the annual meeting of the American Orthopsychiatric Association, April 16, 1966, San Francisco.

13. Erikson, E. H.: *Childhood & Society*, pp. 426–442. W. W. Norton & Company Inc., New York, 1950.
14. Hagnell, O.: *A Prospective Study of the Incidence of Mental Disorder*, p. 175. Svenska Bokförlaget, Stockholm, 1966.
15. Harrington, Michael.: *The Other America*. The Macmillan Company, New York, 1962.
16. Isaacs, H. R.: *India's Ex-Untouchables*, The John Day Company, Inc., New York, 1965.
17. Kardiner, A. S., Ovesey, L.: *The Mark of Oppression: A Psychological Study of the American Negro*. W. W. Norton & Co. Inc., New York, 1951.
18. Klein, R.: The self-image of adult males in an Andean culture: A clinical exploration of a dynamic personality construct. University Microfilms, Ann Arbor, Mich., 1963.
19. Leighton, D. C., Harding, T. S., Macklin, D. B., Hughes, C. C., and Leighton, A. H.: Psychiatric findings of the Stirling County study. American Journal of Psychiatry, *119:* 1021–1037, 1963.
20. Mack, R. W.: *Race, Class and Power*, p. 1. American Book Company, New York, 1963.
21. Merton, R. K.: The self-fulfilling prophecy. The Antioch Review, *8:* 193-210, 1948.
22. Munoz, L., Marconi, J., Horwitz, J., and Naveillan, P.: Crosscultural definitions applied to the study of functional psychoses in Chilean Mapuches. British Journal of Psychiatry, *112:* 1205–1215, 1966.
23. Odegard, O.: Emigration & insanity: A study of mental disease among Norwegian born population of Minnesota. *Acta Psychiatrica et Neurologia*, Supplement 4, 1932.
24. Parsons, T. and Shils, E. A. (Editors): *Toward a General Theory of Action*. Harvard University Press, Cambridge, Mass, 1951.
25. Rieff, R.: Remarks at the Annual Meeting of the National Association of Mental Health, November 17, 1966, New Orleans, La.
26. Turner, R. J. and Wagenfeld, M. O.: Occupational mobility & schizophrenia: An assessment of the social causation & social selection hypotheses. American Sociol Review, *32:* 104–113, 1967.
27. Whitely, T. S.: Sociological aspects of schizophrenia. Mental Hygiene, *42:* 447–503, 1958.